STRANGE OBJECTS

NEW SOLIDS

AND

MASSIVE THINGS

ARCHI-TECTONICS

STRANGE

OBJECTS

NEW

SOLIDS

AND

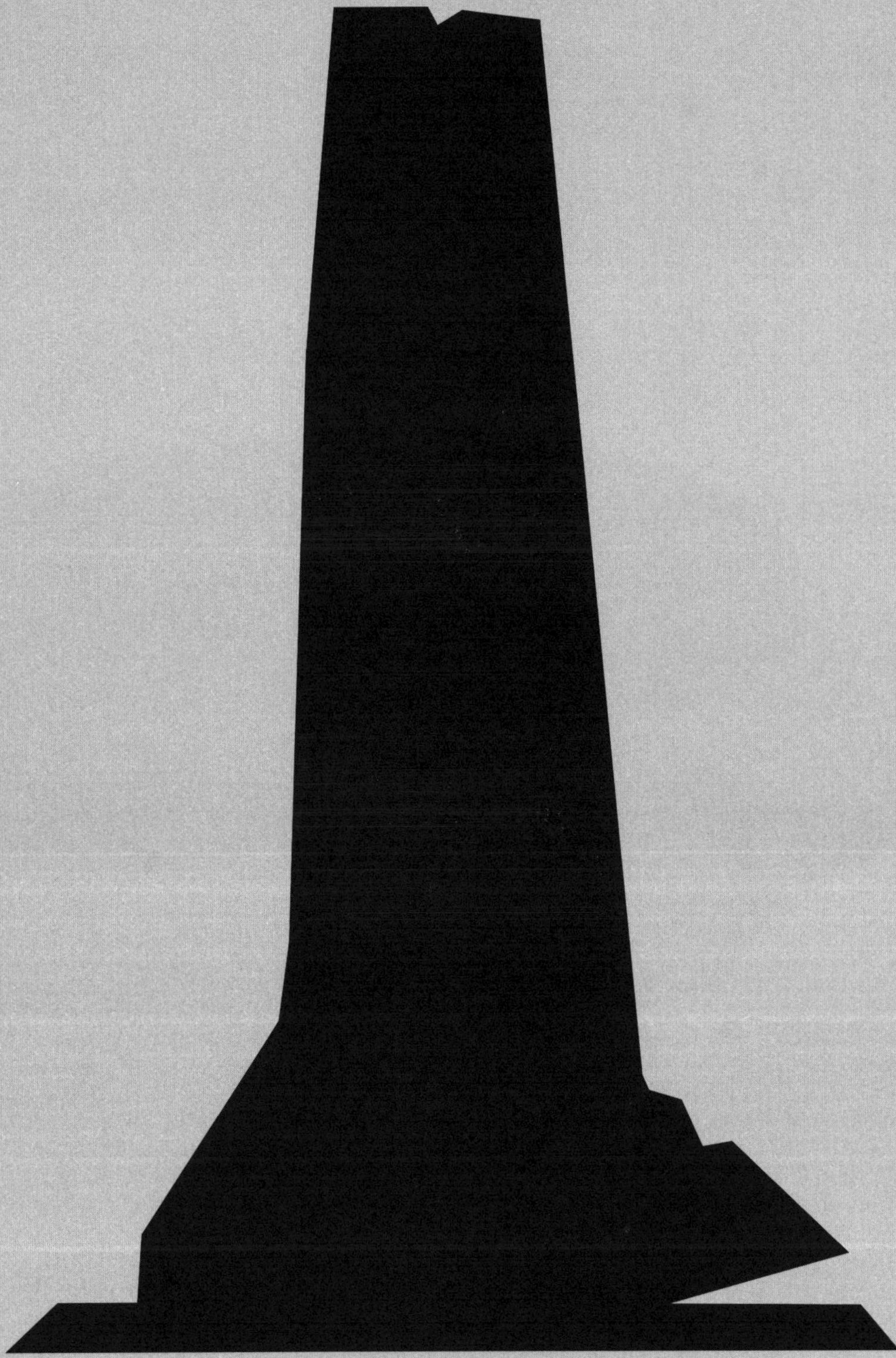

MASSIVE

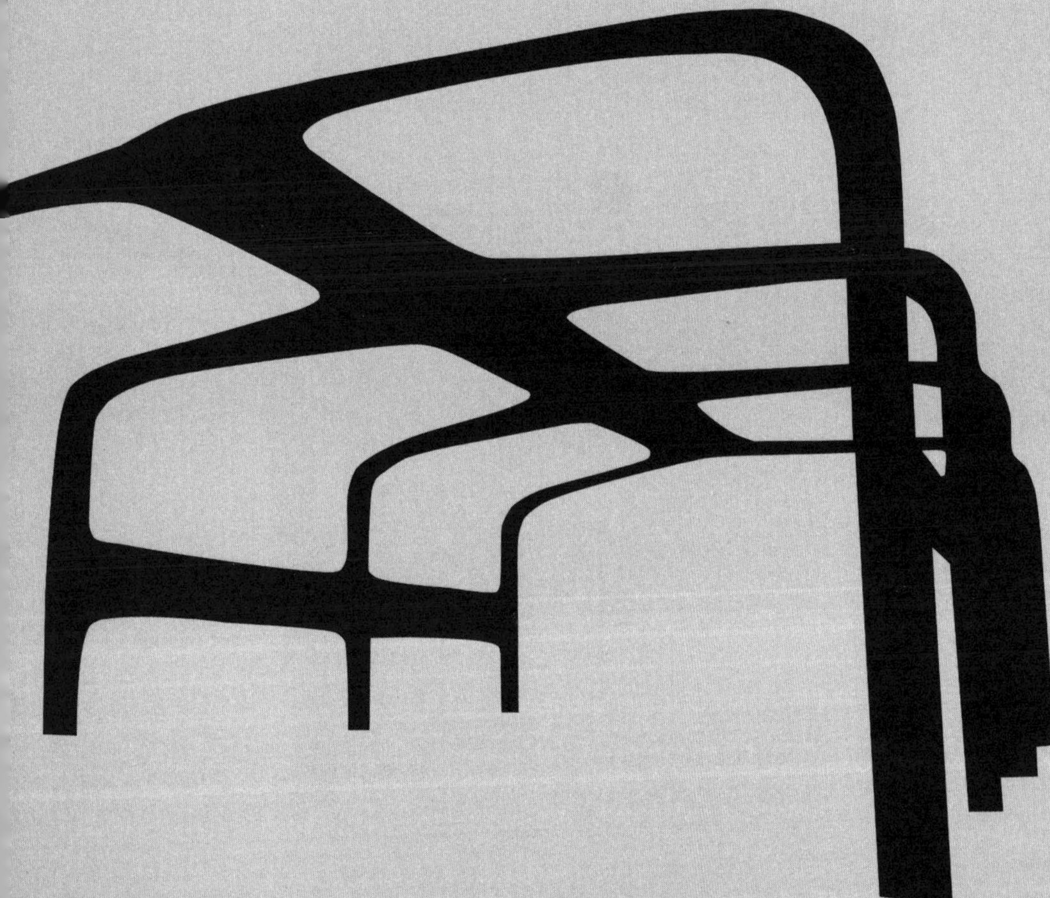

THINGS

A System of Order-Disordered Manual

Jonathan Jackson

When Archi-Tectonics asked our studio, WeShould-DoItAll, to design this volume, we were excited about the book's potential and possibilities. Through years of collaboration with Winka Dubbeldam—with both her practice and through her current position as Chair of the University of Pennsylvania's Weitzman School of Architecture—we knew focus and value would be on experimentation and a non-traditional approach.

We believe that designing books is a primary discovery to work out an individual solution for the individual book based on its individual content, purpose, and audience. This thinking holds true for the various types of design projects that reach our studio. The elements of the equation or context always push our work to distinct places, regardless of the fact that the processes are similar. Yes, in broad terms successful design captures harmony and balances layers of content, it's thorough and consistent, but there is also a need to find a conceptual tension. Embedded within our design process is the search for a tension of two or more given understandings. When our ideas have survived a strenuous filtering process that consist of testing, reworking, critique, and finalization, we hope to have reached new understandings born from that tension. I believe the architecture processes of Archi-Tectonics live in the same vein; in a constant flux of experimentation and questioning of what we understand.

Our approach to presenting this body of work by Archi-Tectonics is to embrace the strange, pinpoint distinction in the processes, and reframe the representation of architecture out of context, pushing it into a framework normally applied to the 'how-to' manual. Taking the works out of the familiar is how the strangeness is revealed. The archetype for an architectural monograph gets framed as a finished product. Instantly dated. Often a required decoration for a coffee table. The essence of this book—both in content and design—speaks to a thoughtful rigor expressed through words and imagery in dialogue with one another. It is well crafted but not pristine. We conclude projects with a cyclical open-endedness, where the reader can piece together how one intervention influences another. A running thread moves through each project, connecting a broader story where the punched holes reflect the idea of a workbook in which the series of projects are tethered together, leaving an imprint and impression that this volume is a part of a grander series of manuals to come.

Strange Objects
Winka Dubbeldam

KERNEL / SEED / SEEDLING

Kernel: The central or most important part of something, a source of development or growth. The emergence of the primary root, known as the radicle, from the *seed*, although in some species the shoot, or plumule, emerges first. Early growth is called a *seedling*.

The notion of Architecture as Object is re-emerging. While modernity considered the building form primarily as an aesthetic composition of planar and linear geometries, there is now a growing consensus to view the building as object, an architectural body that is no longer planar and rational, but solid and opaque. The object as solid—having three dimensions—is not just a different formal trend, but a paradigm shift; a reconceiving of how the architectural object is produced and experienced, changing the very notion of objectivity.

STRANGE BEAUTY

Our design process is aimed at developing an object (as building) not with a focus on a particular aesthetic or style, but on its "coming into being." Edmund Husserl described this as the linguistic translation from the mental, spiritual space of the inventor, where the *originaliter*[1] resides, to a formation of the "ideal object." The design as "growth" origi-

1 Edmund Husserl, "Origin of Geometry," in Jacques Derrida. *Edmund Husserl's Origin of Geometry: An Introduction*, trans. John P. Leavy, Jr. (Lincoln: University of Nebraska Press, 1989), 160.

nating from the seed's "inner logic," often results in another aesthetic, approximating what others might consider unusual, or ugly, by conventional standards. This newly formed original, with its almost ugly or uncanny nature, is in fact an indicator of the autonomous nature of the "building as object," an object with character and identity.

Strange Objects, New Solids and Massive Things investigates an architecture conceived from seed intelligence and growth, rather than a formal design methodology. Although the initial seed or idea might seem of a technological or material nature, the real emergence of the architectural object occurs in the middle of the design process, where the seed or idea is in its "proto" phase. Its true nature reveals itself not in an a-priori form nor in the final outcome, but the proto-body emerges while being tested. The development process is driven by internal seed parameters, instigating the "growth" of the design rather than the composition or the master plan. Our goal is not focused on universal beauty but achieving character, identity, and optimized form.

In his 1757 treatise[2] on aesthetics, Edmund Burke describes this notion as the difference between beauty and the sublime. Beautiful objects, Burke observed, tend to be small, smooth, delicate, and attractive, and produce pleasurable feelings.

2 Edmund Burke, "A Philosophical Enquiry into the Origin of our Ideas of the Sublime and Beautiful," 1757, https://wordsworth.org.uk/blog/2015/03/02/edmund-burke-and-the-sublime/.

The sublime, on the other hand, moves us more profoundly: it often overwhelms and terrifies us, affecting us viscerally, but it also delights us, paradoxically. According to Burke, huge waterfalls, vast mountain ranges, cliff faces, or thunderstorms evoke a sense of awe precisely due to their danger. Their sheer overwhelming power is exhilarating and connects us to the vitality of the material world on an intuitive, sensory level.

Burke states: "The passion caused by the great and the sublime in nature [...] is Astonishment; [...] that state of the soul, in which all its motions are suspended, with some degree of horror. In this case the mind is so entirely filled with its object, that it cannot entertain any other."[3]

3 Burke "A Philosophical Inquiry into the Origin of our Ideas of the Sublime and Beautiful."

Although Burke describes ugliness as the exact opposite of beauty, he also recognizes an affinity between the sublime and the ugly: "But, though ugliness be the opposite to beauty, it is not the opposite to proportion and fitness. For it is possible that a thing may be very ugly with any proportions, and with a perfect fitness to any uses. Ugliness I imagine likewise to be consistent enough with an idea of the sublime; but I would by no means insinuate that ugliness, of itself, is a sublime idea, unless united with such qualities as excite a strong terror."[4]

4 Burke "A Philosophical Inquiry into the Origin of our Ideas of the Sublime and Beautiful."

By merging natural phenomena with human aesthetic judgment, the sublime allows the irrational into aesthetic theory. The sublime describes phenomena that transcend, violate or bypass reason (e.g. the overwhelmingly large or powerful, the dark, inexplicable, indistinct, violent, and destructive). The protobody, as found in the prototyping phase, presents the yet unfinished, the unrefined, where performance is valued over form and design intelligence outweighs style. The particular and complex are preferred over the ideal and universal. Seed originality informs and drives the design process, and, vice versa. The ultimate result strengthens the innate qualities of the seedling.

MATERIAL QUALITIES

The fragility of the kernel or seed requires study and patience. Its capacity as a driver of the design process depends on process-oriented design methods such as advanced digital form-generation and prototyping tools, allowing for new solids and massive forms that are at once self-referential, human, and non-human. The "object" as a solid that is tested, informed, and perfected was already discussed by Husserl, who singled out surfaces as specific qualities from *Thing-Shapes*: "surfaces that are more or less smooth, more or less perfect surfaces: edges more or less rough or fairly 'even.'"[5] These pure bodies have spatio-temporal character and material qualities ("color, warmth, weight, hardness").[6] Husserl conceded that this undetermined character is not accepted in praxis, where things are smooth, straight, pragmatic, and measurable. The protobody, however, accepts this condition of approaching perfection rather than being perfect, and celebrates the rough and more or less smooth, the more or less perfect. This is synonymous with Burke's notion of the oddly proportioned and almost ugly (and, ultimately, a *Strange Beauty*) that can be sublime while evoking a greater emotional, visceral impact than the perfect or the ideal.

5 Husserl, *Origin of Geometry*, 178.

6 Husserl, *Origin of Geometry*, 160.

STRANGE OBJECTS, NEW SOLIDS AND MASSIVE THINGS

The work shown in this book explores the solid as object; deep and complex, with character, expression, and identity. No longer minimal or anonymous, light or thin, but full-bodied, soft, glowing, and transformative, these solids are self-referential and independent Things, composed of matter, and generative in nature. The solid here is not to be understood as impenetrable and inert ("solid as a rock") but as a more complex reading of a variated tridimensional "solid surface." *Thing-shapes* in the process of becoming and generative in nature are the antidote to the singular, the planar, the transparent, and the flat.

Jane Bennett advocates for the vitality of matter, giving agency to Things, "that produce [helpful harmful] effects in human and other bodies. Organic and inorganic bodies, natural cultural objects.... all are affective."[7] This generative character of things and objects echoes what Husserl has described as *Phoronomic Shapes*: "formations developed out of praxis, and thought of in terms of [gradual] perfection, clearly serve only as bases for a new sort of praxis out of which similarly-named new constructions grow."[8] *Praxis*, therefore, describes a process of approximation, an inherently non-linear process of form finding, merging intuition and tool precision towards increasingly abstract, pure geometries. While Husserl's speculations were concerned with the origins of geometry, our digital tools have radically altered the very notion of form and object generation. After two decades of digital design, we have reached a new plateau; a New Normal. While intuition and skill remain at the core of the design process, digital design and robotic production are now the norm, and consequently, digital craft and integral design are the future. Design

7 Jane Bennett, *Vibrant Matter: A Political Ecology of Things*, (Durham, N.C.: Duke University Press, 2010), xii.

8 Husserl, *Origin of Geometry*, 178.

is no longer only represented through drawings, blueprints, and scale models. Non-linear, process-based design emerges here through 1:1 prototyping, allowing for discovery through testing and iteration, to IN-form the design, not to RE-present the idea. Technology, aesthetics, and performance merge into an integrated whole, expressed in Strange Objects Surface Solids, and Massive Things.

"Strange," "Solid," and "Massive," in the Burkean sense, go beyond the merely aesthetic, rational understanding of beauty. What are here described as Proto-bodies and Thing-Shapes touch on the idea of becoming, approximating, and, therefore, occupying a territory between idea and space: exactly where the Proto-body is not yet sharply differentiated or defined. It is where shapes and forms are still in the same "searching" state, with form and identity slowly emerging together. This Thing-shape is not yet "inhabited" nor "inhibited," decipherable by habit, or felt "at-home" with; this is what causes the sense of the uncanny, the appreciation of the "almost ugly." It is not the shock of the avant-garde, or the otherness for otherness' sake, but a seed for a new formation, a new vastness built on an authentic, singular nature and character. The fact that the new Proto form, still strange and obscure, must be read un-inhibited, outside the established framework of signification, is proof of its very capacity to generate new habits and meanings.

SO.01

S.01 SMOOTH OBJECTS

The reexamination of the Object in architecture is not a new formal trend, but a reconceiving of how the architectural object is produced and experienced, changing its objectivity, agency, and meaning. The concept of the *Smooth Object* further expands on the Object's capacity as active matter, its power to evoke a sense of the unknown or indeterminate, but also its capability to reveal, through its strangeness, a kernel of its own formation. Like Edmund Husserl's "Thing Shapes,"[1] or Jane Bennett's "Things,"[2] Smooth Objects are inherently generative, capable of forming new aggregates, networks, and meanings.

PROTOBODY

Where does this Smooth Object originate? We have come to understand the becoming of the architectural body or object as a process of rigorous analysis and gradual solidification, with prototyping and feedback loops as essential tools in the generation and evaluation of emerging forms and efficiencies. The proto-body finds its place in this space of object-becoming. It originates in proto-space, the moment between the emergence of an original idea and the ultimate shape it takes; the state of the still obscure and uninhibited object outside the established framework of signification. These

1
Edmund Husserl, "Origin of Geometry," in Jacques Derrida. *Edmund Husserl's Origin of Geometry: An Introduction*, trans. John P. Leavy, Jr. (Lincoln: University of Nebraska Press, 1989).

2
Jane Bennett, *Vibrant Matter: A Political Ecology of Things*, (Durham, N.C.: Duke University Press, 2010), 30-31.

proto-bodies, material assemblages, and networks yet to be optimized and fully understood in their efficacy and agency, form the core of material and concept innovation.

UNIBODY

The Smooth Object rethinks its structure and state. It takes inspiration from the unibody's fusing of structural and spatial characteristics, which is the norm in car design but seldomly introduced in architecture, where structures are assembled from parts. The notion of the single entity or a single molded unit as a structural three-dimensional whole finds perhaps its earliest example in the architecture of the igloo, a perfect unibody, where its interior parts melt and freeze into a structural whole. The igloo is not a hemisphere as typically understood, but a catanoid (chain) system of revolution in perfect proportions, thus eliminating ring tension and shell moments in this paraboloid and thereby preventing collapse. The intelligence of the unibody as a structural three-dimensional object in architecture allows for the creation of a smooth space with continuous surfaces, textured surfaces, and imbedded technologies.

MASSIVE THINGS

The Smooth Object is uncomfortable; it presents scalar tensions. It is often massive, a notion implying size, scale, and physical presence measured relative to its container or to its "other." Things may seem massive in a relative sense, "out-of-scale," awe-inspiring or even frightening, a phenomenon thoroughly analyzed in the aesthetic theories of Romanticism. As described by Edmund Burke, the sublime is our strongest passion. While it is grounded in terror, it is not necessarily an unpleasant emotion as danger can, in certain circumstances, bring us "delight."[3] The "uncanny" directly relates to Manuel DeLanda's notion of affiliation and contagion, as described in his book *Assemblage Theory*.[4] The Smooth Object celebrates the uncanny and the almost ugly, as it grows out of the proto-space into the proto-body, with its resultant affective quality of the Strange, the Massive, and the Smooth.

3
Edmund Burke, "A Philosophical Enquiry into the Origin of our Ideas of the Sublime and Beautiful," 1757, https://wordsworth.org.uk/blog/2015/03/02/edmund-burke-and-the-sublime/.

4
Manuel DeLanda, *Assemblage Theory* (Edinburgh: Edinburgh University Press, 2016).

SO.02

SO.03

THE BUND, SHAN

PORTS 1961 Shanghai

THE LINER

Ports Design Ltd. was created in 1994 by Canadian entrepreneur Alfred K.T. Chan with his wife Fiona Cibani in Xiamen, China. In 2004, Chan re-launched the company in North America as the New York City-based Ports 1961 with designer Tia Cibani, Fiona's younger sister. As of 2011, Ports 1961 operates stores in Montreal, Toronto, Vancouver, West Hollywood, Manhattan, Paris, London, and Shanghai. Ports 1961 asked Archi-Tectonics to develop the

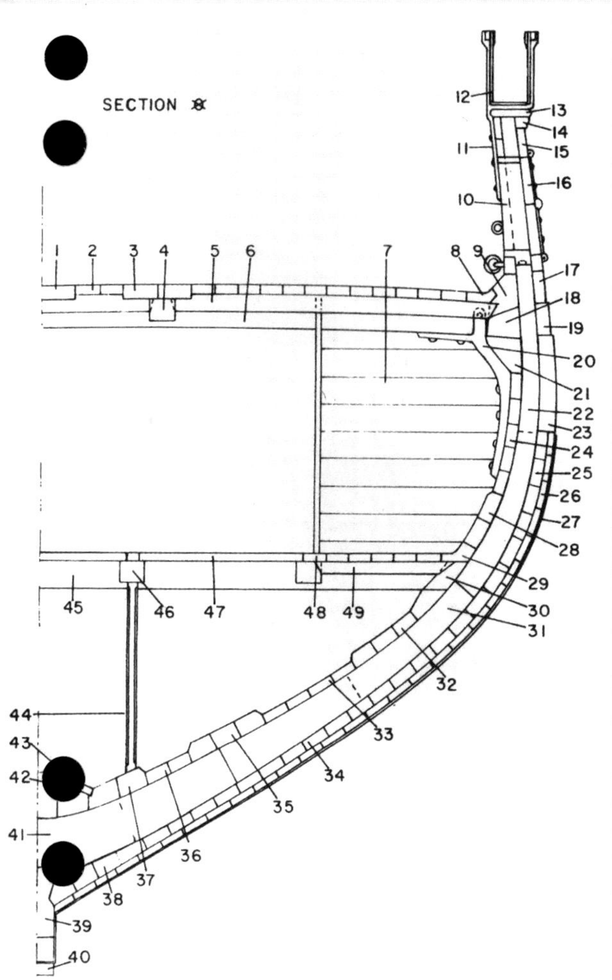

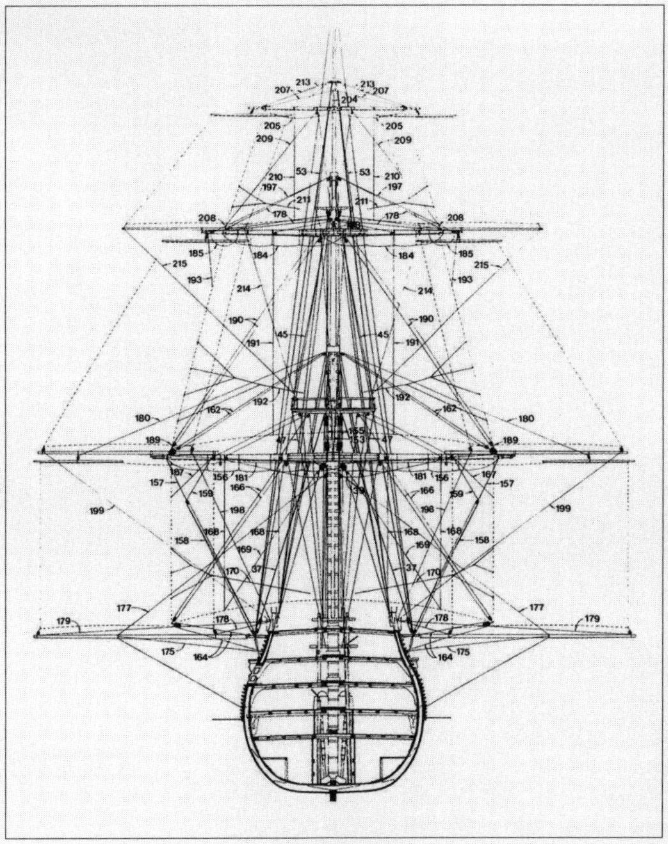

branding for their flagship stores worldwide, with as its first the store in Shanghai, located on the Bund, the city's famous waterfront boulevard.

We were inspired by Shanghai's two main characteristics: its history as a port and its Art Deco-style structures. Ancient ship building techniques, in particular the great bent ribs of the boat frame, translated into developing a fluid "liner" for the space. Borrowed from fashion, the liner forms an inner layer to a garment to conceal interfacing, padding, the raw edges of seams, and other construction details. The lining reduces the wear and tear of the outer layer. For the Ports 1961 space, the liner houses the collection, but also integrates climate and sound systems, recessed lighting, and hanging fixtures.

SHIPLAP PATTERN

RULED SURFACE / UPCYCLED

The upcycling of wood from a demolished house gave not only character to the wood surface but added to the "branding" of the flagship store. Here, branding can be understood as more than the promotion of the particular company by means of a distinctive design but goes back to its original meaning—the Old English brand or "burning." The action of marking an object with a hot iron as a claim of ownership dates from late Middle English. In Ports 1961, this was taken quite literally by CNC-ing the wood surface in its complex convex and concave shapes to create an identity for the store.

The contrast of the archaic nature of the wood texture of shiplap with the robotically CNC-ed surface with its curved hyperbolic surfaces gives the strange effect of familiarity while also appearing alien. The digital imprint of the milling lines that appeared in the prototype's surface were kept and simply rubbed with silver powder-infused oil as a finish.

The liner surface was developed following the complex ruled curved surfaces of hyperbola found in mathematics, created in 3D software. The 3D model was then given to the manufacturer to work

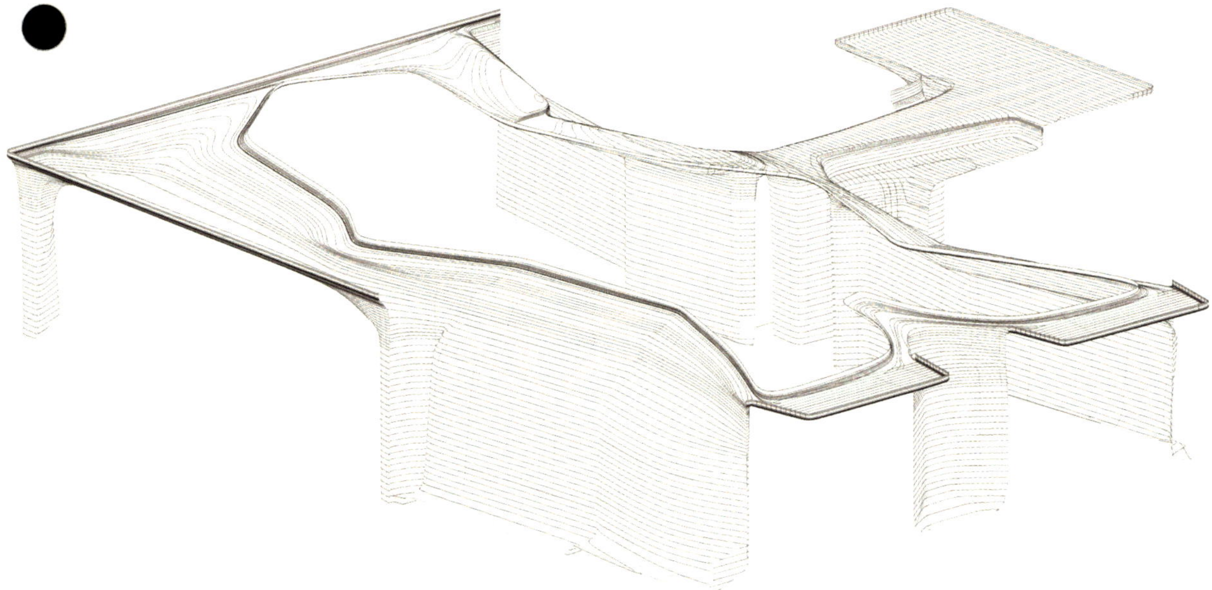

THE LINER

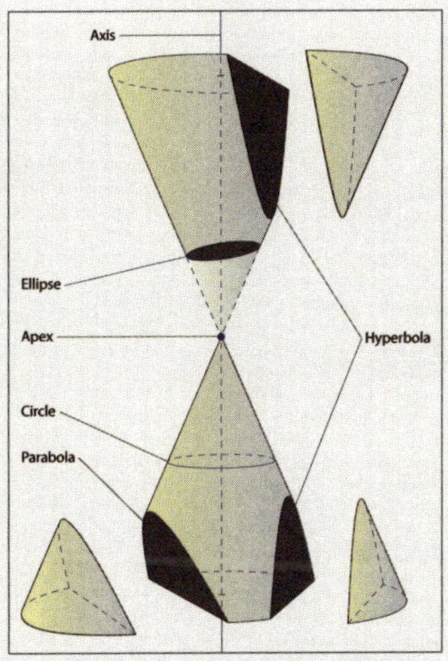

HYPERBOLA

from "file to factory." As the project manager for the space turned out to be a mathematician and expert in hyperbolas, he was excited to be working on this complex surface, and further developed it with fabricators. He did not exaggerate—his execution was flawless, innovative, and fast. The prototype he created in his workshop helped us to understand the best means of construction, which facilitated a seamless installation in the space. He thus prefabricated and facilitated the strange beauty of the curved planes and their installation in a significant manner.

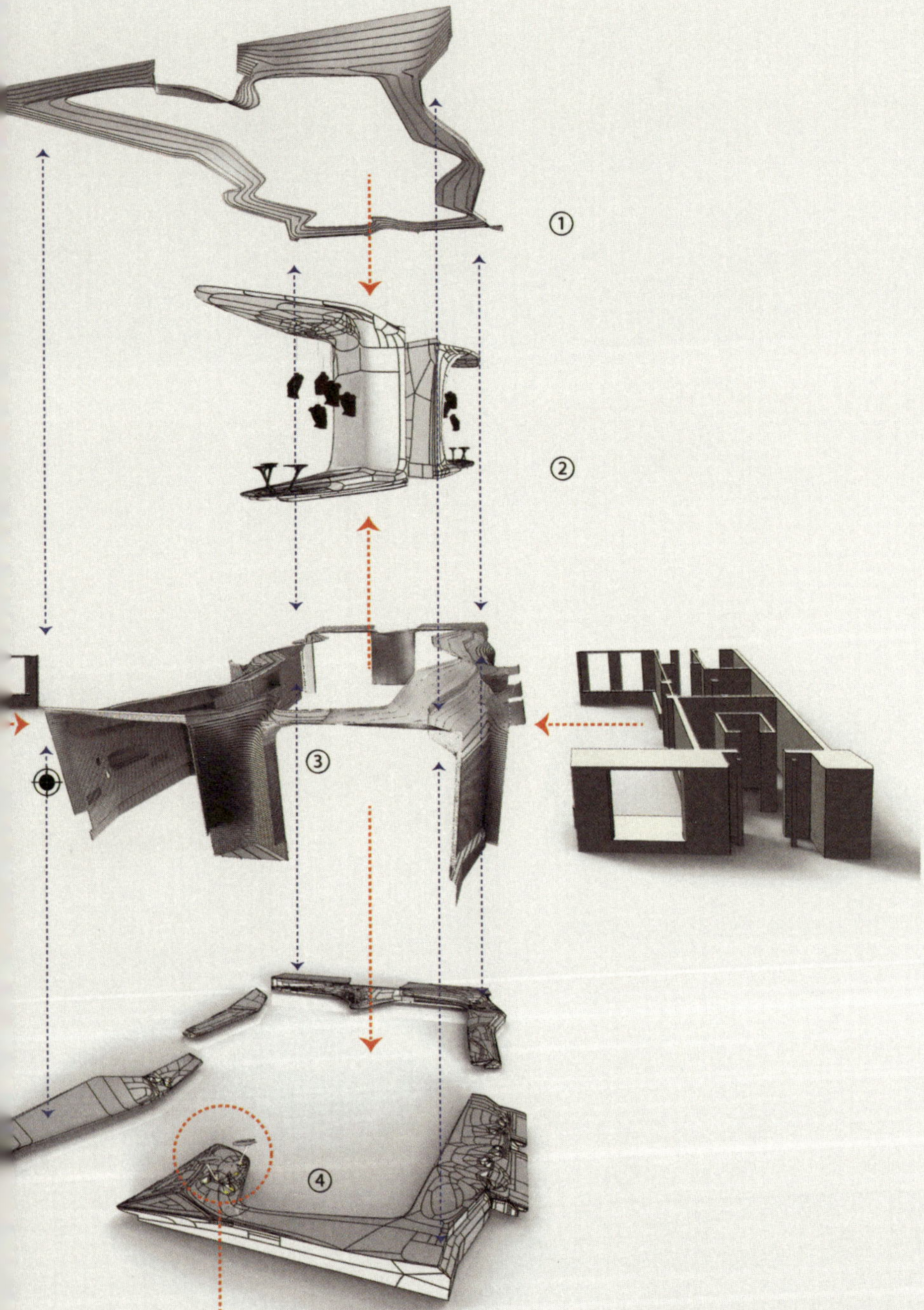

1. GRFC Ceiling + Lighting Elements
2. Highlight Collection in GRFC 3D Elements
3. Recycled Wood Skin Wood Liner
4. Exhibition Platforms+ Integrated Lighting

MOCK

SO.13

SO.14

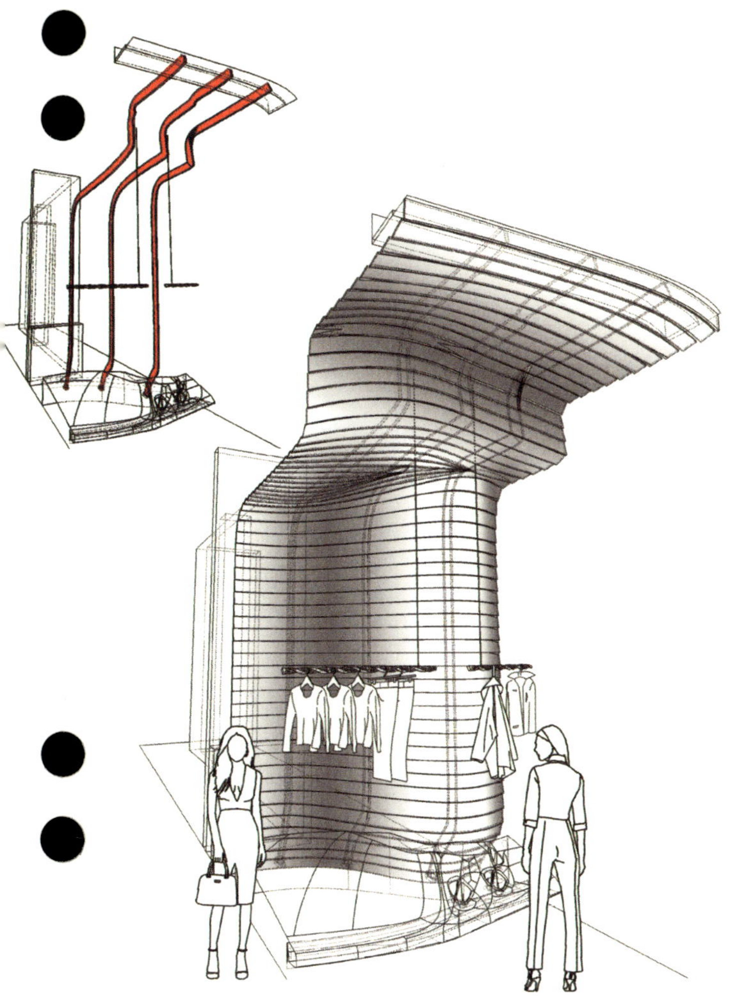

DRAWING FOR MOCK-UP

PREFABRICATED SOLIDS

Why prefabricate? A lot of precious time was gained in the process. As the contractor was demolishing the interior and cleaning up the large space on the Bund, the new components were prefabricated in the workshop. Prefab construction makes for fast and clean production, shorter construction time on site, high efficiency, and precise quality control. It reduces waste and noise pollution on site, as well as off-gassing of the materials. The prefabricated components were assembled on-site in a precise fit, making for continuous folded walls and large seamless ceiling and column elements.

These strange massive objects add a scalelessness to the space, and reinterpret "normal" spatial qualities, allowing for the fashion pieces to float in between the folds and to occupy the wood liner. Utilizing renewable or upcycled materials creates a different aesthetic and smart, clean manufacturing techniques create a highly customized, and comfortable space.

SO.15

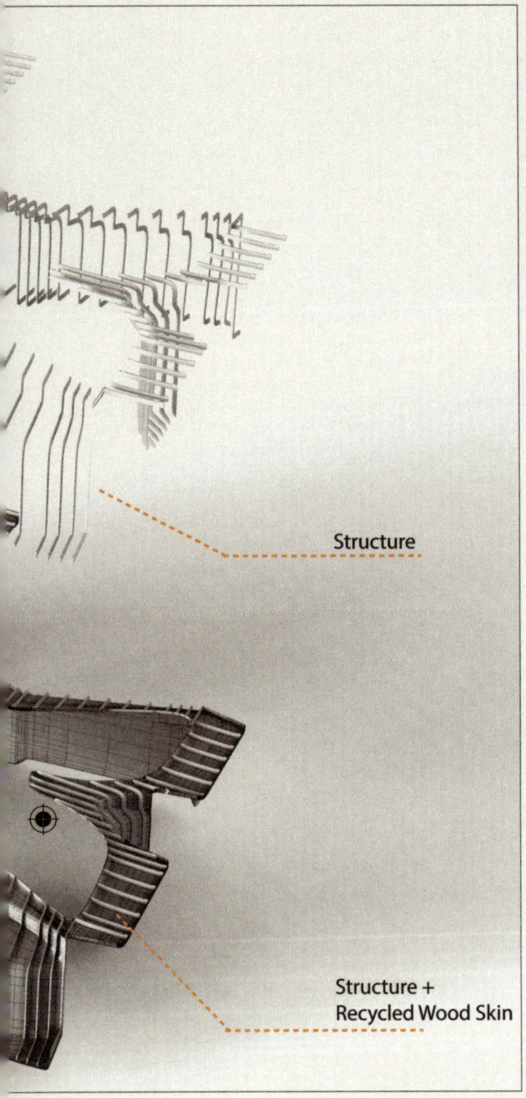

DRAWING FOR MOCK-UP

SO.16

PROTOTYPE / STRANGE OBJECTS

As in most of our projects, the design is very much developed in the prototyping phase. The "Strange Object" quality often appears in this phase, as we study resulting effects and allow found accidents to create the character we are looking for. For the wood liner, we used 1:1 mock-ups to test and refine the formal design concept, and to integrate climate and sound systems. The upcycled wood was CNC-milled and its newly found texture, most

SO.17

SO.18-20

CNC-ED RECYCLED WOOD LINER CONTAINS ALL SYSTEMS: AC, LIGHTING, SOUND SYSTEM ETC.

PREFABRICATION

often sanded down to a smooth surface, purposely was left unsanded. Instead, the somewhat rough robotically-milled textured elements were merely dusted with silvery powder and impregnated with oil. Several high-end technologies were incorporated in the liner—slots for air cooling, small round perforation clouds transmit music, and CNC-ed low wood platforms fold out to carry felt seats, nickel bronze tables, and recessed lighting.

GRFC PREFABRICATION

GFRC

Made of cementitious glass fiber-reinforced concrete (GFRC), the columns and ceiling shapes were prefabricated and installed seamlessly on site. The engineered cement mix is incredibly lightweight yet has increased durability and load-bearing capacity. The GFRC ceilings also function as thermal regulators and fire protection for the space. Ceiling installation of the prefabricated elements was quick and simple due to the ceiling's lightweight qualities, and the seamless finish creates a massive scale in this open retail environment.

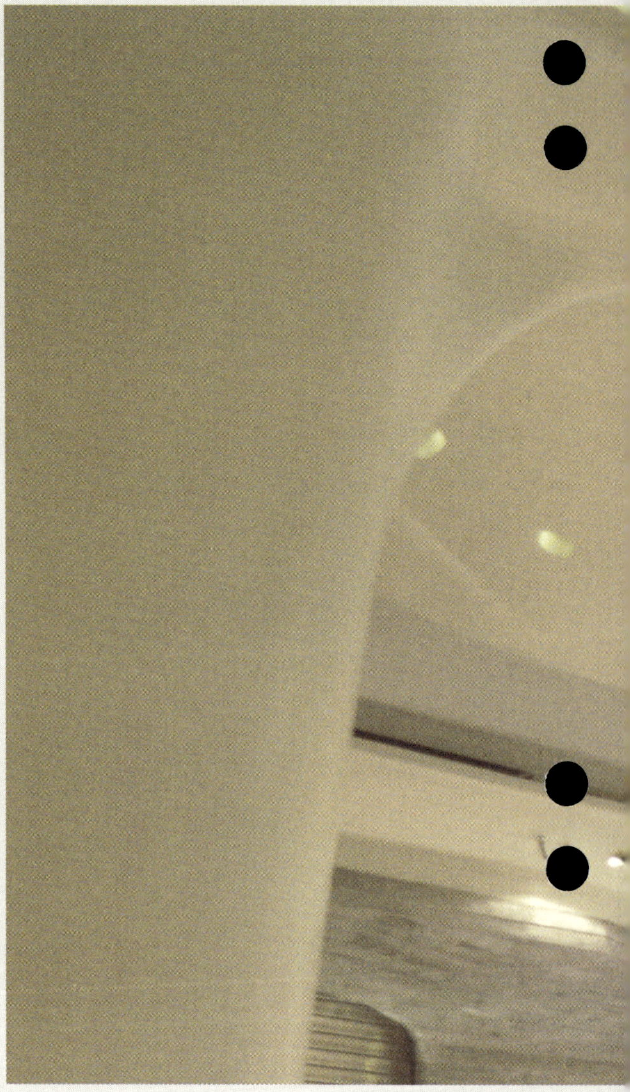

SO.28

PREFABRICATION

The rough wood liner reveals soft, glowing, silvery volumes inside. Two large columns transformed into center displays extend into platforms and suspended ceilings that carry custom-designed suspended mannequins. Where the wood liner showcases the current collection, the inner displays reveals the fashion highlights. These large prefabricated GRFC columns radiate out into the ceiling; long flowing ceiling elements integrate LED lighting in their reveals. Below, custom woven silk carpets follow the shape of the objects in the space, accentuated by LED lighting and creating comfort in an easy manner.

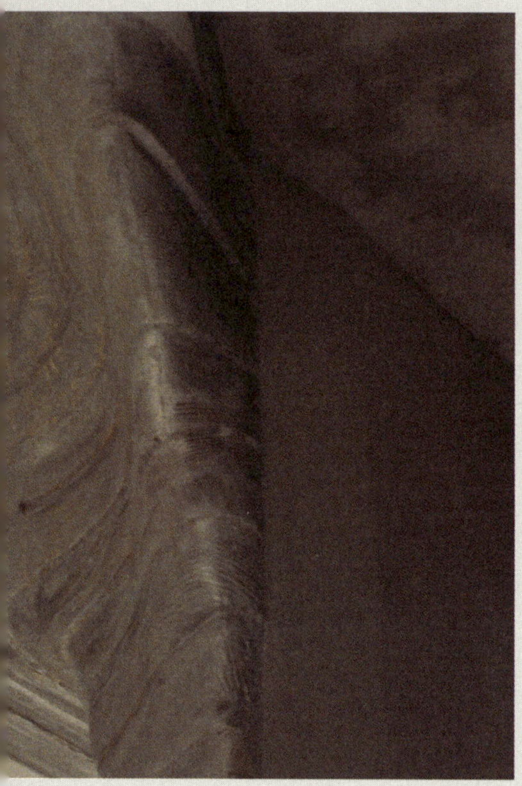

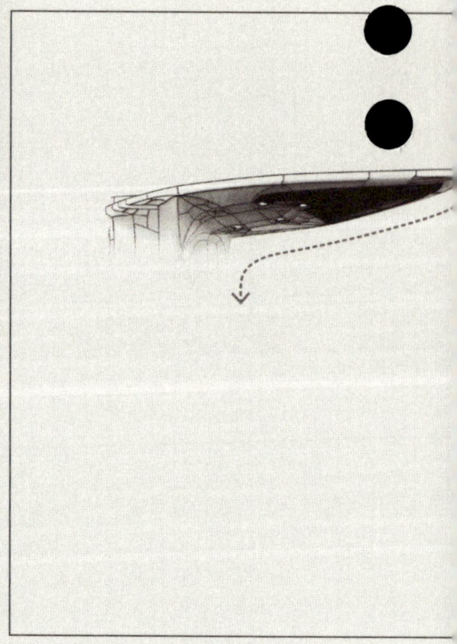

INTEGRAL LIGHTING

Indirect recessed LED lighting enhances the fluid geometry of the space, with lighting concealed in the platform and ceiling surfaces, thus creating a contrasting glow. All surfaces, the clothing, and accessories are indirectly lit. Direct spotlights highlight specific displays from above and below, literally lifting them out of the glowing surfaces they are placed within. The final effect is a sensuous, rich, textured environment that delivers maximum dramatic impact to this new flagship store on the Bund.

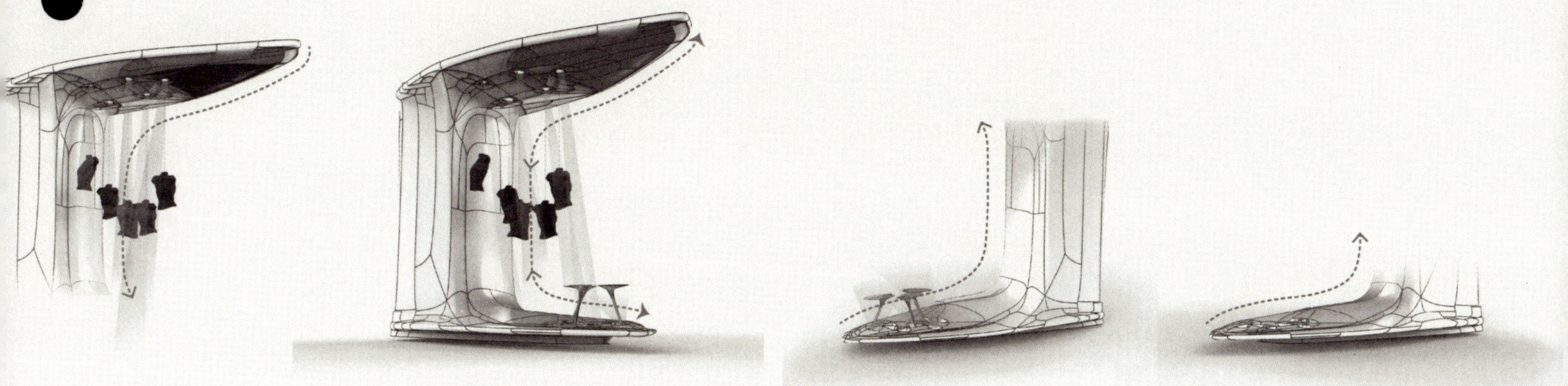

GFRC PREFABRICATED ELEMENTS

SO.32

SO.33

SUSPENDED MANNEQUINS

BRANDING / COMPONENTS

For the protodesign of future Ports 1961 stores worldwide, a series of key retail elements were designed. The word *mannequin* is French but is originally derived from the Dutch word *mannekijn* meaning "little man," with its first known use in 1730. For Ports 1961 the mannequin was revisited and custom-designed as a sculpted, suspended body. Bottom and top integrated lighting create a glowing effect on the mannequins. In the low CNC-milled wood platforms below custom felt seating and custom solid poured nickel bronze display tables were installed. Television-mirrors, recessed in the curvy column surfaces, showcase the latest fashion shows in Paris, Milan, and New York.

SO.34

SO.35

NICKEL BRONZE CUSTOM-DESIGNED TABLES

SO.36

SO.37

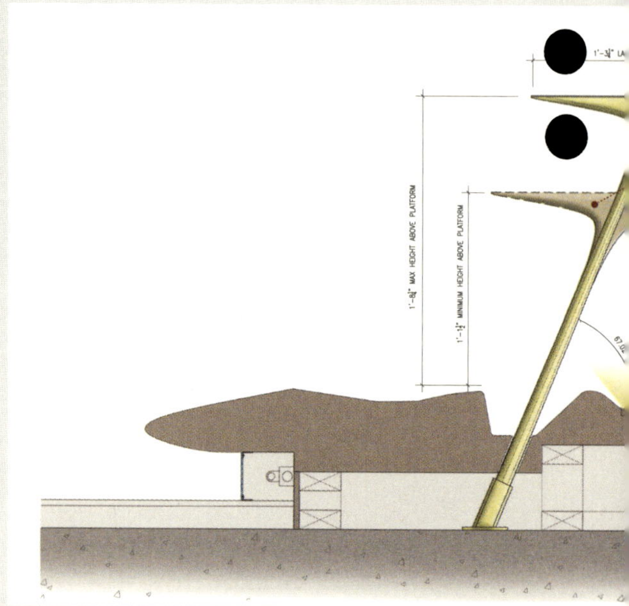

COMPONENTS

The suspended mannequins feature the collection's main fashion pieces in the center of the store. As clients move through the space, their movement causes the delicately suspended mannequins to slowly turn and reveal the clothing gradually from all angles. Low lights reinforce this almost hypnotic movement and very large chandeliers by Barlas Baylar, composed of chrome mesh veils, add to the mystery.

SO.38

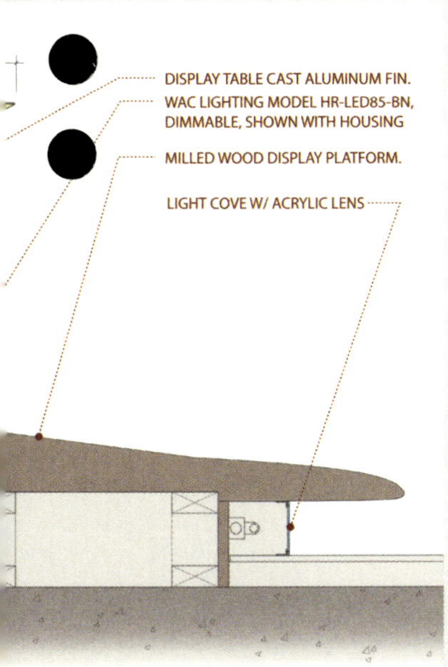

DRAWING SECTION

CUSTOM-DESIGNED MANNEQUINS

SO.02

SO.03

The Port of Shanghai dates back to the 6th century. It opened for international trade in 1842 and is now the largest port in the world. (https://en.wikipedia.org/wiki/Port_of_Shanghai)

SO.04

The *Beagle*, a survey ship, has become synonymous with Charles Darwin and his groundbreaking work, *On the Origin of Species*. Darwin traveled onboard the Beagle Fitzroy's survey ship for his expedition from 1831-35. (https://en.wikipedia.org/wiki/Second_voyage_of_HMS_Beagle; https://www.scientificamerican.com/article/charles-darwins-travel-beagle/)

SO.05

SO.06

SO.07

Shiplap refers to a special type of interlocking board, similar to tongue-and-groove but with a tighter, overlapping fit. Here we simulated it in a CNC-routed surface.

SO.08

SO.09

A hyperbola is formed by the intersection of a double cone with an oblique plane. The cut consists of two separate curves—also called branches. Points on the separate branches, where the distance is at a minimum, are called vertices. (https://en.wikipedia.org/wiki/Hyperbola)

SO.10

SO.11

SO.12-13

SO.14

SO.15

SO.16

SO.17

Smart object: the rough texture of the CNC-ed recycled wood liner reveals at points its "smart" character, as it is holding and distributing sound, lighting, and central air through specific patterned openings.

SO.18

SO.19

SO.20

SO.21

SO.22

SO.23

SO.24-26

GFRC is glass fiber reinforced concrete, an engineered hybrid material that contains cement, polymers, and glass fibers that are ingrained in the cementious matrix. GFRC was first created in the 1940s in Russia, but it wasn't until the 1970s that it became a commonly used building material. It produces an extremely lightweight yet durable material, that can be prefabricated and installed seamlessly onsite. (https://www.architecturalfiberglass.org/history-gfrc/)

SO.27

SO.28

SO.29

SO.30

SO.31

SO.32

BRANDING

1. the action of marking with a branding iron as often done with cattle.
2. the promotion of a particular product or company by means of advertising and distinctive design.

The word has a Germanic origin, related to "brand" which means to burn. The use of "branding as a verb, to describe the act of marking something with a hot iron as a means of indicating ownership, dates from late Middle English and eventually developed into a marketing term. (https://www.lexico.com/en/definition/branding; https://www.etymonline.com/word/brand)

SO.33

SO.34

SO.35

SO.36

SO.37

SO.38

SO.39-45

INSCAPE WELLNESS

PROTOBODY

The INSCAPE meditation space opened in New York City in 2018. This first protospace in Chelsea occupies a large 6,000-square-foot storefront with extensive retail, lounges for guests, meditation domes, and the headquarters below. Meditation requires a different state of mind, a transition into another space to transform one's mood and state of being. This transformation from our hectic lives does not happen instantaneously; a strong concept was needed. It is upon entering the INSCAPE space from the bustling streets of Manhattan that the relaxation process starts. As one walks into a casual

lounge with natural linen seating, cardboard hanging lights, and bamboo shelving, the senses are relaxed through soft music and filtered air with aromatic oils. The visitor's tension slowly fades, and the transformation has started. It is only then that one encounters massive hanging domes, suspended from the ceiling with their curved bamboo bottom barely touching the floor. These strange shapes, or protobodies, don't reveal immediately their interiority; it is only upon entering the Dome, that the radiating gridshell structure appears, creating an intricate space that is at once immersive, deeply meditative, and calming.

Seemingly simple and clean, the space is also intricately engineered; an expansive system of speakers creates surround sound, automated LED lighting and filtered air are all integrated in the large ellipsoid meditation spaces. These ellipsoids, a "Dome Room" and an "Alcove Room," are huge bulbous shapes, whose size challenges the space; they immediately create another atmosphere, a different experience and character to the space they occupy.

SOUNDPROOFING FOAM
Lenght: 128 ft / height: 8ft
Controling internal sound and absorbing external noises

BENDABLE PANELS
Length: 128 ft / height: 8ft
Finition: White satin

LED LIGHT RING
Length: 128 ft
Color: Warm white

TRANSLUCENT STRETCHED FABRIC
Mesh surface: 1796 SqFt
Ellipsoid length: 53'
Ellipsoid width: 33'
Ellipsoid height: 8'
Finish: White translucent

BAMBOO GRID
Variety: Phai Sang Mon
Mesh surface: 1796 SqFt
60 Poles
Max length: 30'
Min length: 21'

PREFAB SHELL
17 elements of which 10 with bench
Primary Structure: plywood
Finish: Pre-veneered Bamboo
Top: Hardwood + bamboo joint
Max length: 8'

PREFAB DOOR FRAME
Primary Structure: plywood
Finition: Pre veneer Bamboo

WOOD & PLEXIGLASS DOOR
Butterfly opening
2 X 36' gates
Min height: 7'
Max height: 9'

BAMBOO FLOORING
1500 SqFt

INSCAPE STUDIO 1
50 people
1500 SqFt

UNIBODY

The structural component and characteristic of the unibody, as is the norm in car design, is crucial for the INSCAPE meditation space concept, where modes of object generation were understood as an integral part of a holistic design strategy. The Dome, the main meditation room, is a seemingly simple space, devoid of technology, but it is actually a highly engineered structure with an immersive light, sound, and air environment. The spiraling bamboo Dome frame was developed parametrically and tested in a 1:1 prototype, robotically CNC-ed by collaborator and car designer, the Aria Group in Los Angeles. The prototype allowed

the team to test the strength of the Dome structure and its effect as a spatial construct as it meets the rounded ellipse bench shape. It also helped to develop the design logic for prefabrication of the Dome, decreasing construction time, increasing ease of assembly, and ensuring the perfect fit. Material effects and ecologies were studied, and bamboo was introduced as a strong, flexible and renewable material. INSCAPE not only redefines the architectural experience of the meditation concept, but also incorporates holistic design and fabrication innovations.

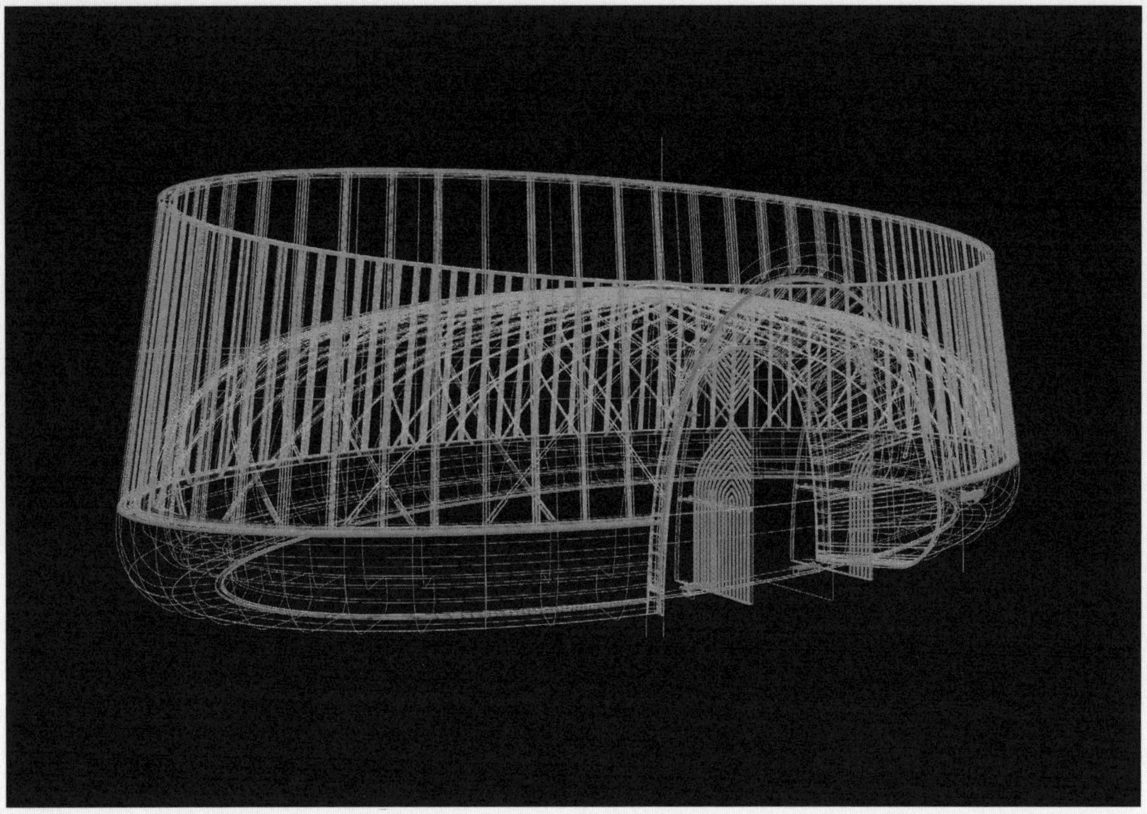

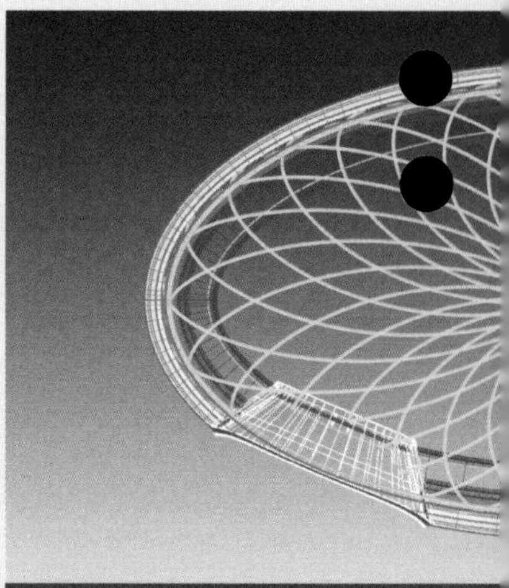

IMMERSIVE ENVIRONMENT

The large ellipsoid volume changes traditional two-dimensional elements (walls and ceilings) into three-dimensional holistic objects—ellipsoids transformed into a dome. The Dome's base is designed to be an ellipsoid bamboo bench from which a spiraling bamboo dome emerges, ending in an open oval oculus. The spiraling grid dome is covered by a linen sail, behind which a fully immersive light and sound environment is created. The Dome, which looks like a simple space devoid of all technology, is in fact a highly engineered environment. A grid of concealed micro speakers creates a soothing ambient soundscape, in tandem with carefully orchestrated LED lighting that adjusts in intensity and color depending on the selected meditation. Lighting has powerful healing aspects; scientific research in the 1960s demonstrated the remarkable effects specific wavelengths of light have on all living things. Research has concluded that light containing the entire spectrum of wavelengths, from infrared to ultraviolet, is best for overall health and wellbeing. Interestingly, in the absence of natural sunlight, an artificial light source containing a fuller, more complete spectrum of visible light, particularly the blue wavelengths, would have the same effect on plants as natural sunlight. Narrow-band blue light is as effective as bright white light for the treatment of SAD [seasonal affective disorder]. This research and the use of state-of-the-art computer modeling, digital fabrication tools, and advanced building materials, allowed for the creation of an immersive experience that effectively blurs the boundaries between the physical and experiential.

SO.55-57

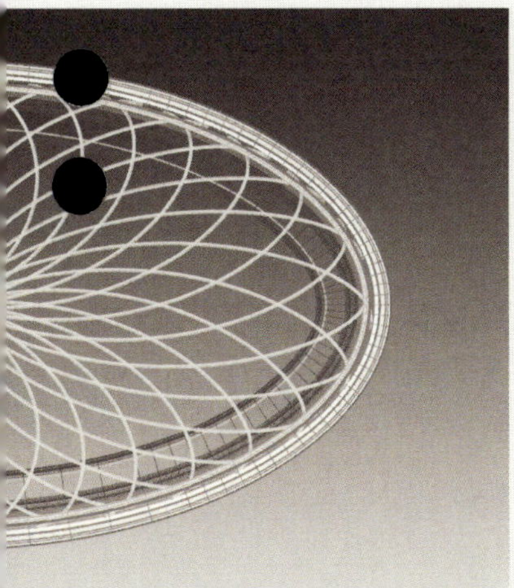

RADIAL GRIDSHELL DOME

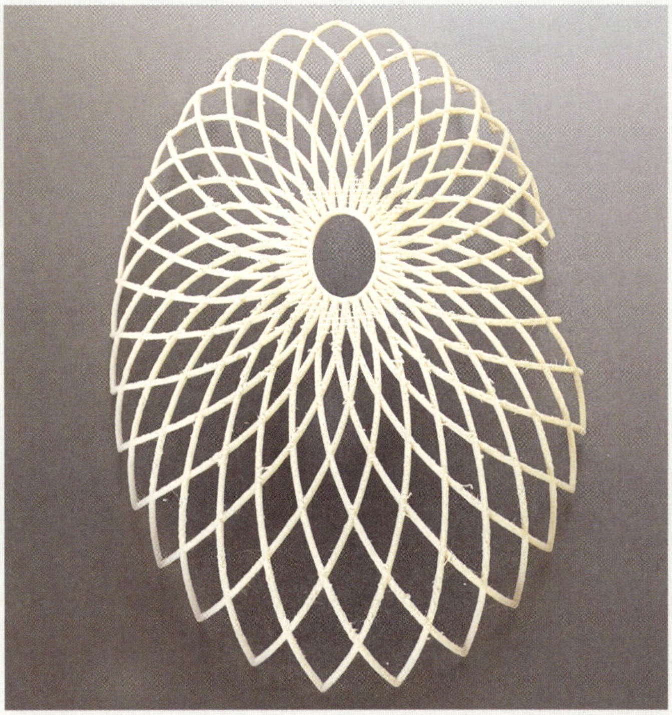

SO.58

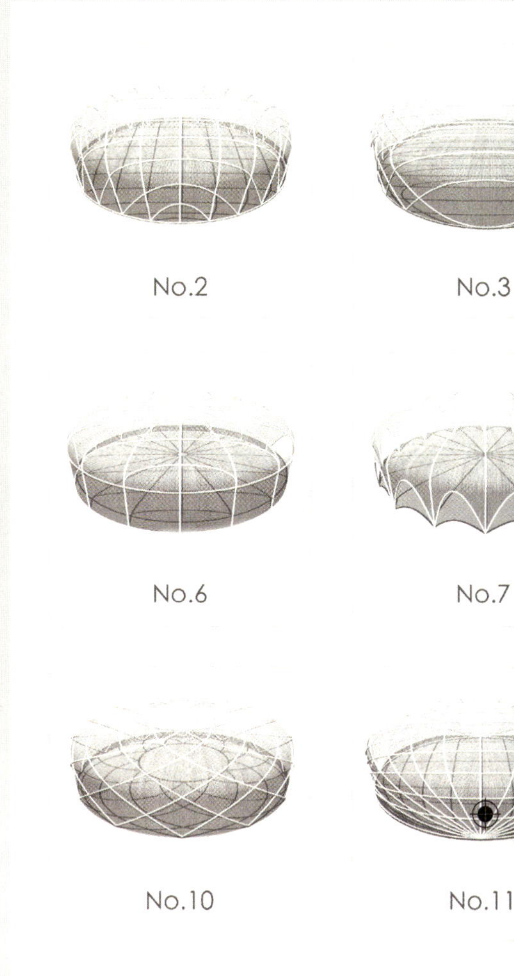

GRIDSHELL STUDIES

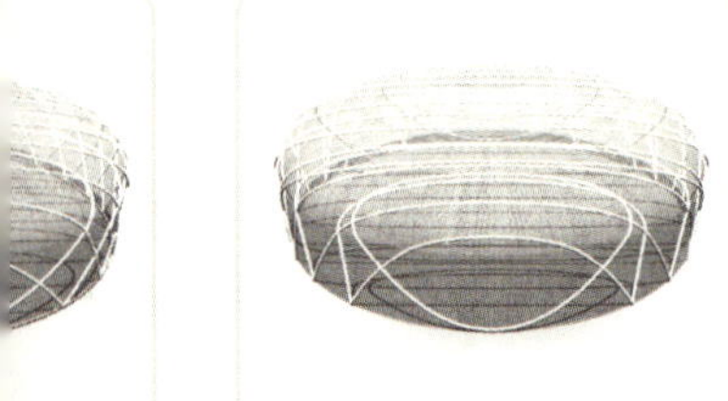

No.4

No.8

No.12

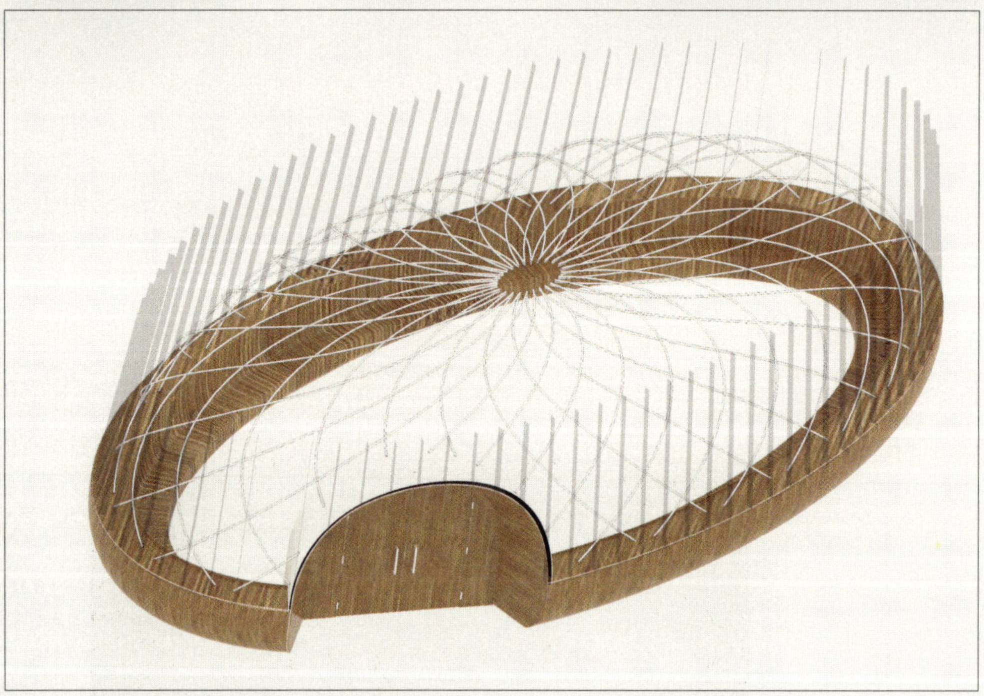

PROTOTYPING

SYNCLASTIC DOME (ELLIPTIC PARABOLOID)

INSCAPE, like many of Archi-Tectonics's projects, was tested in a rigorous 1:1 prototype. The dome is conceived as a gridshell, a radial structure, that derives its strength from its double curvature, and constructed of a lattice. This free-form and free span dome allows the space to be free of any columns and the minimal appearance was facilitated by thorough testing of the strength and size of the individual bamboo members. This synclastic dome or elliptic paraboloid has identical curves and both dimensions are curving in the same direction. In this orientation, the dome is also under compression everywhere. Huge pressure was on the bottom frame holding the dome in place: the real-scale mock-up was needed after extensive parametric modeling and computational strength testing. In collaboration with the Aria Group, the gridshell prototype was further detailed, and the necessary fastening methods developed, as

ARIA GROUP, CAR DESIGN

well as a pattern that allowed for 3D bending of the bamboo veneer on the three-dimensional surfaces. More importantly, the mock-up assisted the client in understanding the spatial effects and qualities of the space. At the client insistence the whole team meditated in the factory's prototype, including the manufacturers—quite the experience.

ARIA GROUP PROTOTYPE

PERFORMANCE TEST IN THE PROTOTYPE

Performance testing as defined in science is in general a testing practice performed to determine how something performs in terms of responsiveness and stability under a particular load. It also serves to investigate, measure, validate or verify the quality and attributes such as scale, reliability of structure and usage.

Here the performance test was exercised to test the performance of the structural span of the proto dome as built by the Aria Group in a 1:1 scale, but also to set the standards of use. The most interesting part was that the client performed an actual meditation session right there in the prototype in the factory with the whole design- and fabrication team attending.

SO.70 SO.71 SO.72-73

SPIRALING GRIDSHELL

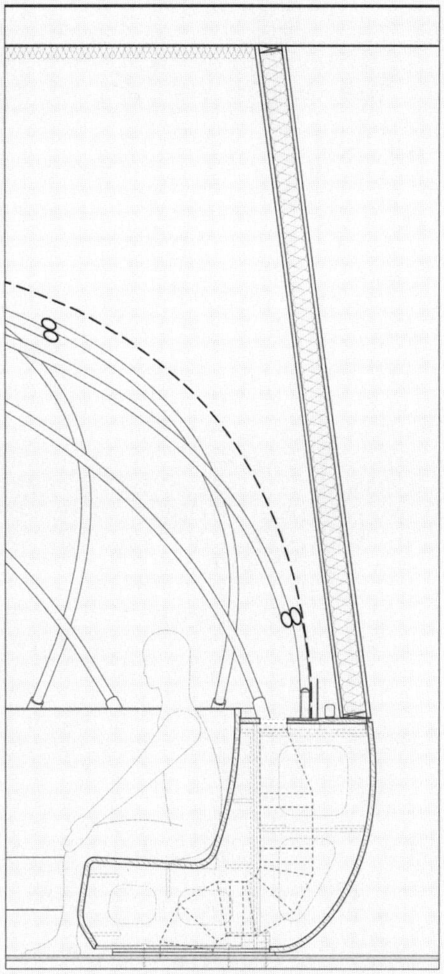

PREFABRICATION MOCK-UPS

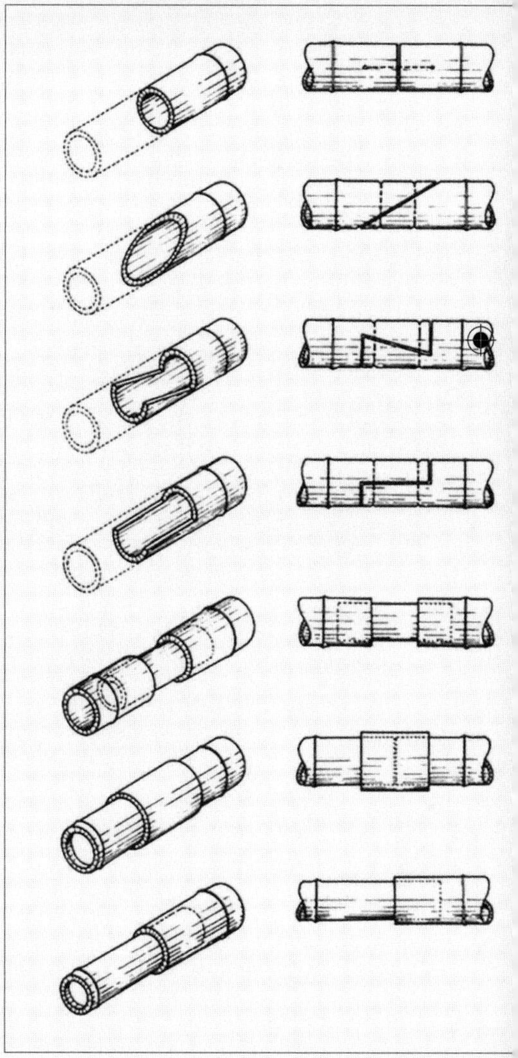

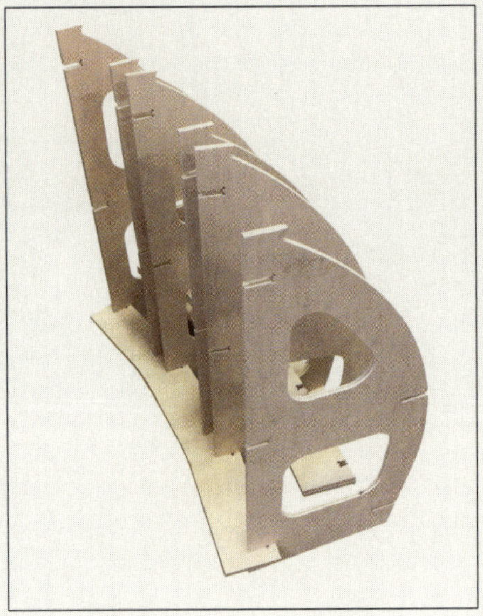

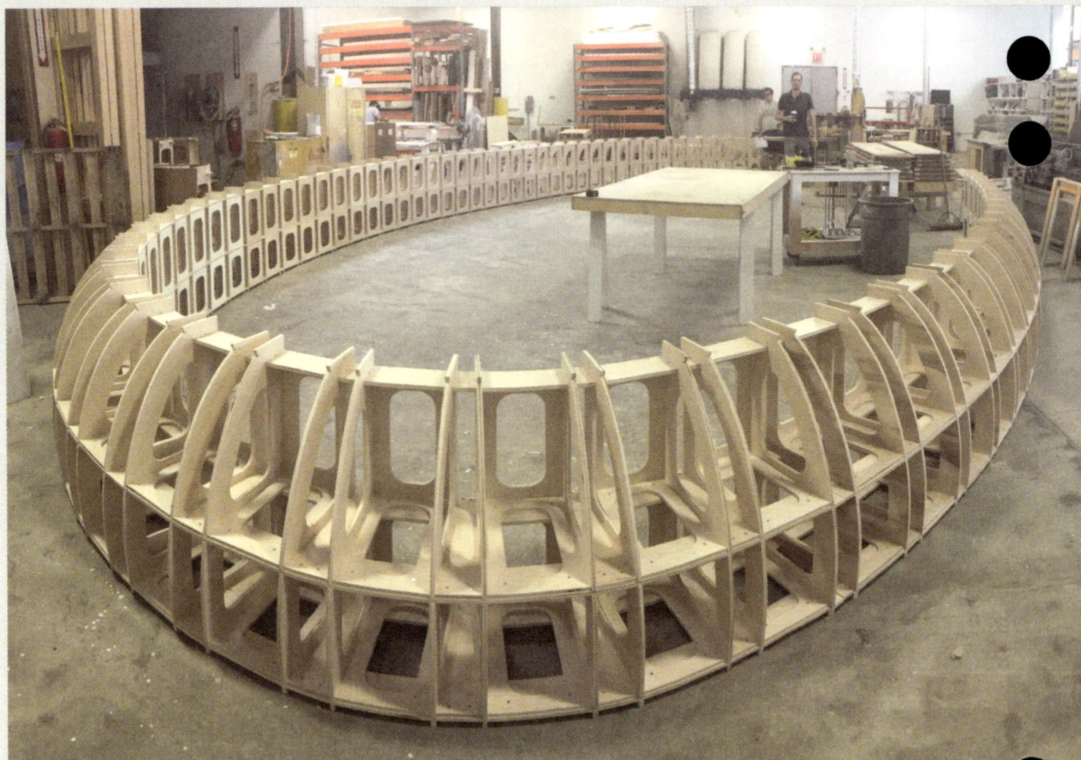

TIETZ-BACCON STUDIO

PREFABRICATION

As the goal of INSCAPE's owner was to roll out more meditation spaces, the next step was to find a local prefabrication facility. Digital design fabricators Tietz-Baccon were hired. Their 8,000-square-foot manufacturing studio includes CNC milling, CNC routing, laser cutting, and water jets. Further detail engineering ensued, and precise attachment details

SO.77

SO.78-79

SO.80

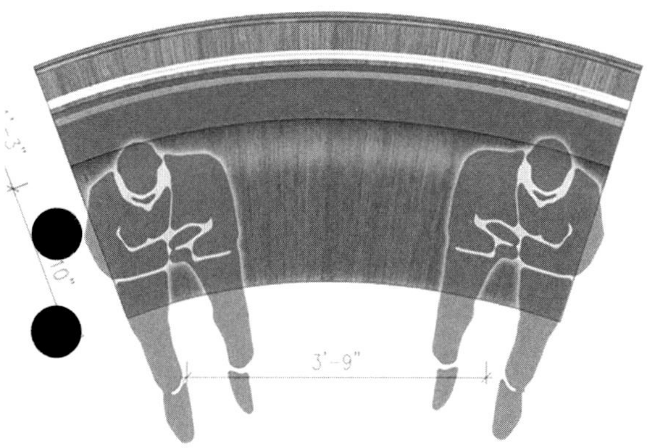

PREFABRICATION MOCK-UPS

were tested and studied. The fabricators developed a unibody wood frame with an integrated air system, and a detailed top plate that holds the oval spiraling dome in place. A template was created for on-site installation, after which the massive shapes were erected in the very short time span of three weeks. Our direct collaboration with advanced manufacturing companies enhances speed to market, lowers building costs, increases productivity and, most of all, quality. Of course, prefab construction and the use of sustainable, recycled materials also result in minimal waste and transportation costs, and it affords a high level of customization and precision.

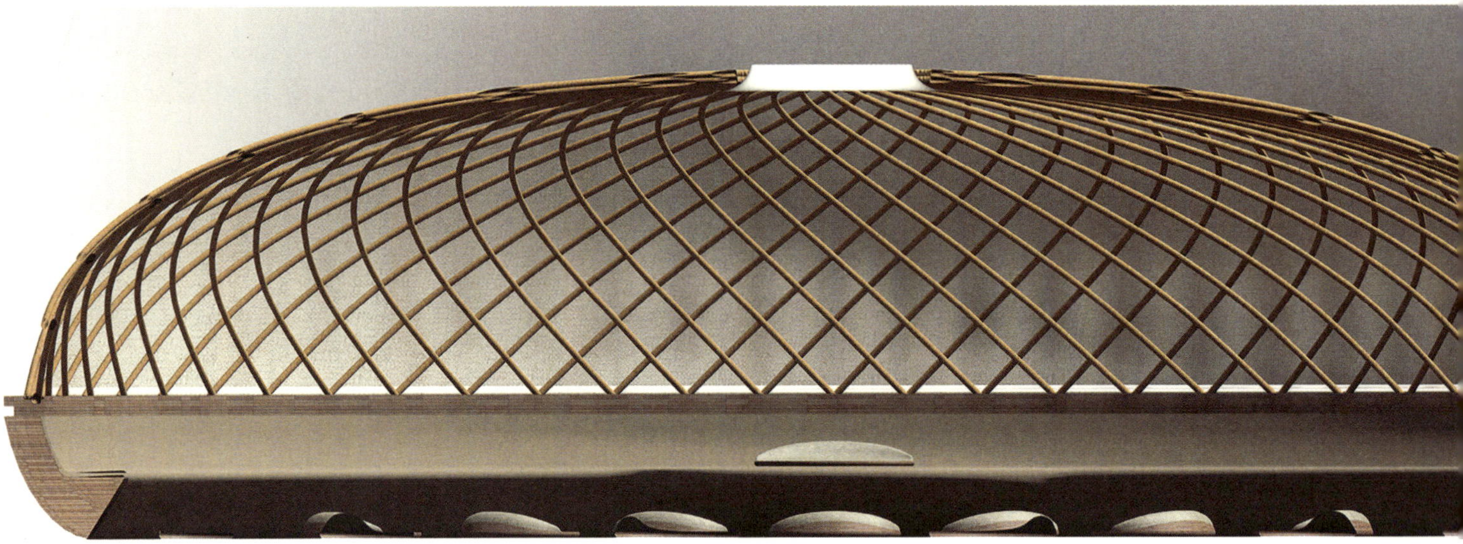

SITE INSTALL

MASSIVE SHAPE

Archi-Tectonics developed the massive ellipsoids, starting from a "no judgement" concept. As a meditator is not necessarily a yogi, different seating methods are provided. A low bamboo seating oval was developed from which a bamboo spiraling dome frame emerges, to be met at the top by an oval oculus. This low seating allows for "normal" seating, while one can also sit leaning against the ring or in lotus pose on the custom-designed seating pads (Ligne Roset) in the middle. Tranquility descends.

The spiraling dome was enveloped in a canvas cover, hiding the indirect LED lighting and a complex grid of micro speakers. The Dome is kept as a private, intimate space, and is not immediately revealed on

the outside. A deep bamboo portal guides one inside this large lazy shape that seems suspended from the ceiling.

SO.85-86

SO.87

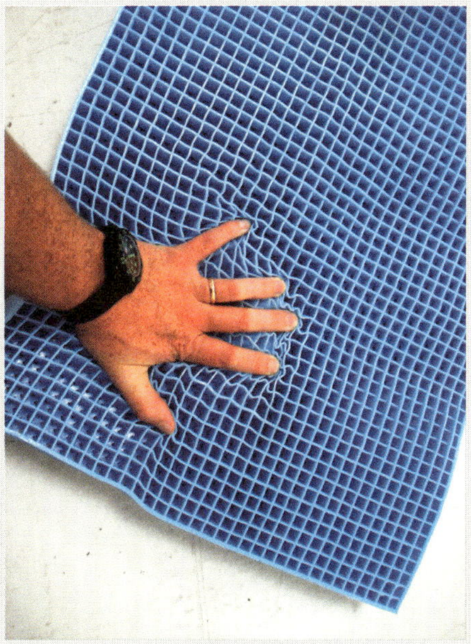

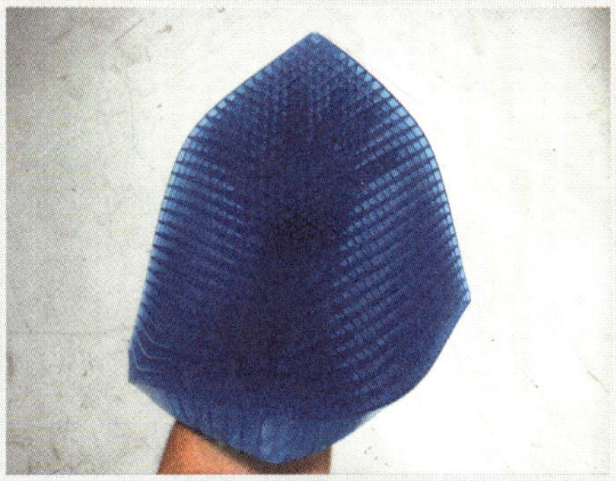

CUSTOM MEDITATION PAD

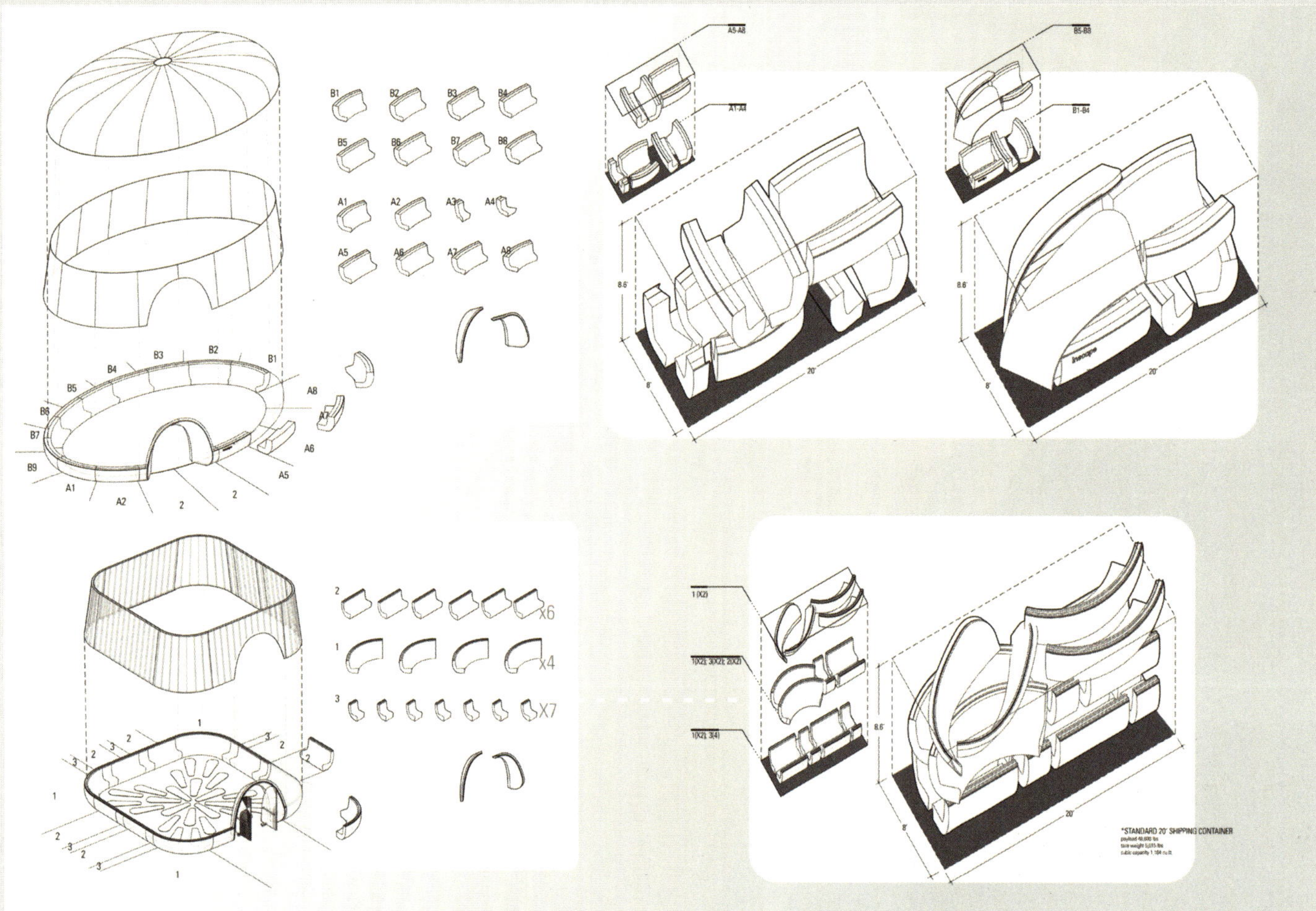

MANUAL FOR LOCAL FABRICATION AND PACKING DIAGRAM

MANUAL / PACKING DIAGRAM

As INSCAPE's unique, brand-defining space was intended as a prototype for future expansion of INSCAPE worldwide, a Fabrication & Assembly manual—rather than construction drawings—was created. This manual, or reference book, provides instructions and guidelines on how to prefabricate and assemble the dome spaces, promoting local fabrication and reducing transport costs. In case local fabrication was not available, a packing diagram was generated to facilitate a tight fit and reduce space needed in a standard shipping container. This allows for intermodal shipping, ensuring that all elements fit in one container, reducing costs and speeding up the shipping process.

THE DOME

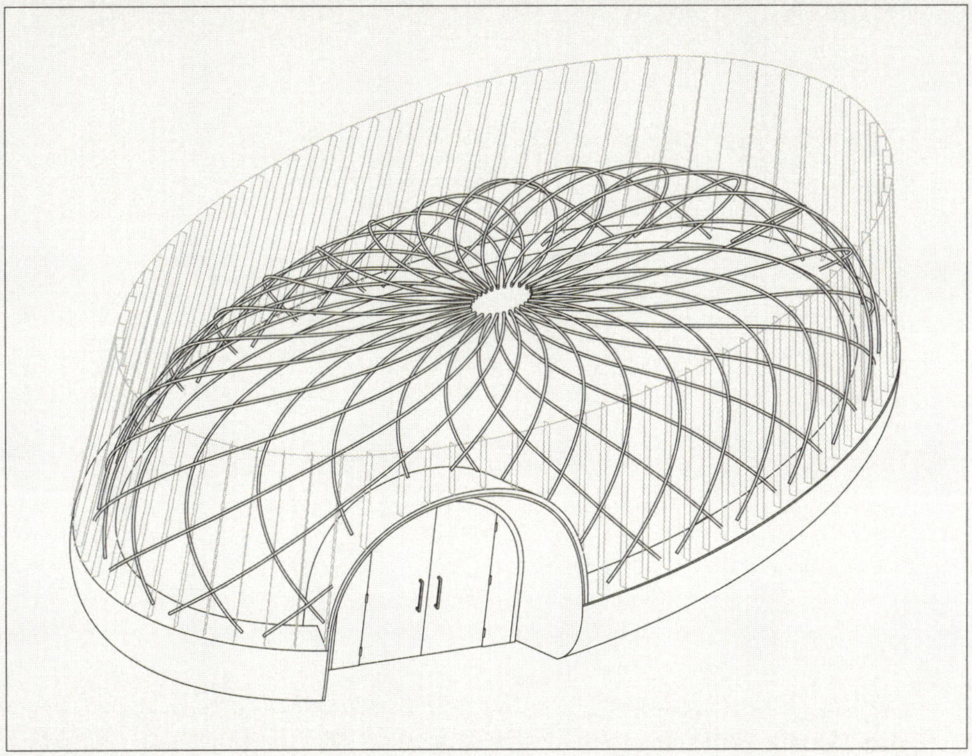

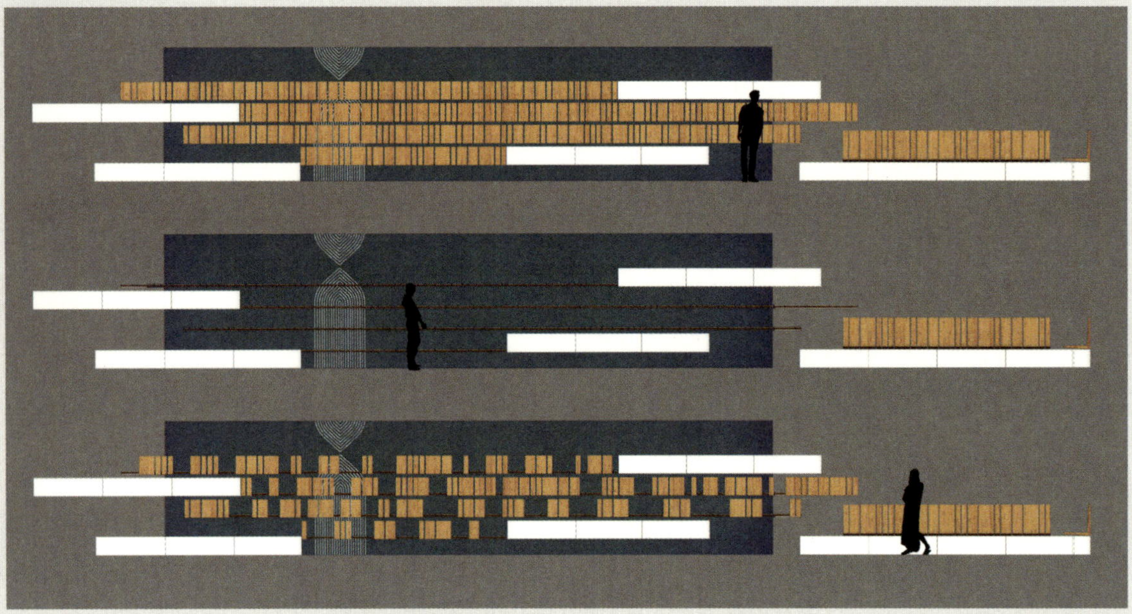

PROTOTYPING PHASE

RETAIL CONCEPT

As a startup, INSCAPE was initially not sure whether retail would be integrated. Providing a bamboo folding system as a multi-functional object was the solution. Randomly sized foldable bamboo plates can function at once an acoustical "art" wall or a retail concept. The beauty of the foldable system is that it is fully adaptable: the shelves can be all up, all down, or alternating randomly. The shelves are self-supporting; they are developed as a three-dimensional wedges that carry themselves when folded down. Extensive prototyping helped test the folding system to fine-tune its self-supporting aspect and easy movement. However, retail turned out to be a great success in the wellness branch, and the shelving system was soon expanded to integrate storage units and matching bamboo seating in the windows.

THE ALCOV

THE DOME

SO.46

SO.47

SO.48-49

SO.50

A spheroid, or ellipsoid of revolution, is a quadric surface formed by rotating an ellipse about one of its principal axes: in other worlds, an ellipsoid with two equal semi-diameters. (https://en.wikipedia.org/wiki/spheroid)

SO.51

SO.52

SO.53-54

SO.55-57

SO.58

SO.59-60

1:1 PROTOTYPE MADE BY ARIA

Aria Group is the premier leader of full-range design, engineering, and manufacturing solutions for the transportation, aerospace, entertainment, and production Industries. Aria Group has over 20 years of expertise combining the latest advances in rapid manufacturing technology with innovative design and creative engineering and is located in Irvine, California.

SO.61

SO.62

A gridshell is a structure that derives its strength from its double curvature (in a similar way that a fabric structure derives strength from double curvature), but is constructed of a grid or lattice. (https://en.wikipedia.org/wiki/Gridshell)

SO.63

Robotic CNC allows automatic machining of complex 3D shapes. First introduced by John T. Parsons in the 1950s, the defining feature of CNC machines is their accuracy. (https://www.scmgroup.com/en/cmsadvancedmaterials/news-events/news/the-history-of-computer-numerical-control-cnc.n68699.html)

SO.64

SO.65-66

SO.67-68

SO.69

SO.70

SO.71

Section showing connection of ellipse bench to the radial dome with recessed LED lighting. Lighting changes to positively inflect on the circadian rhythm.

SO.72-73

SO.74-75

SO.76

SO.77

SO.78-79

SO.80

The oval bench as hollow structure incorporates air cooling, aroma therapy, and recessed LED lighting.

SO.81-82

SO.83

SO.84

SO.85-86

The meditation seating pads are made with wondergel, which provides support while relieving pressure points.

SO.87

SO.88

A packing diagram for intermodal shipping, in an intermodal container, that is a standardized unit of transporting cargo, which requires more than one transportation mode.

SO.89

SO.90-91

SO.92

SO.93-95

Our circadian rhythm is the 24-hour cycle of the body's internal clock, which among others regulates our sleep-wake cycle. Our internal clock is directly influenced by environmental cues, such as daylight, which is why our circadian rhythm aligns to notions of day and night.

SO.96

SO.97-103

ASIAN GAMES PARK 2022

APRIL 2021

NO WHITE ELEPHANT

With two iconic stadiums and an innovative mile-long ecological park landscape, this winning proposal for the 116-acre Asian Games 2022 park sets a new paradigm for the design of sustainable athletic facilities and ecological sports parks, as well as their post-game legacy. The 2022 Asian Games, also known as XIX Asiad, is a multi-sport event celebrated in Hangzhou, China in September 2022. Hangzhou will be the third Chinese city to host the Asian Games—

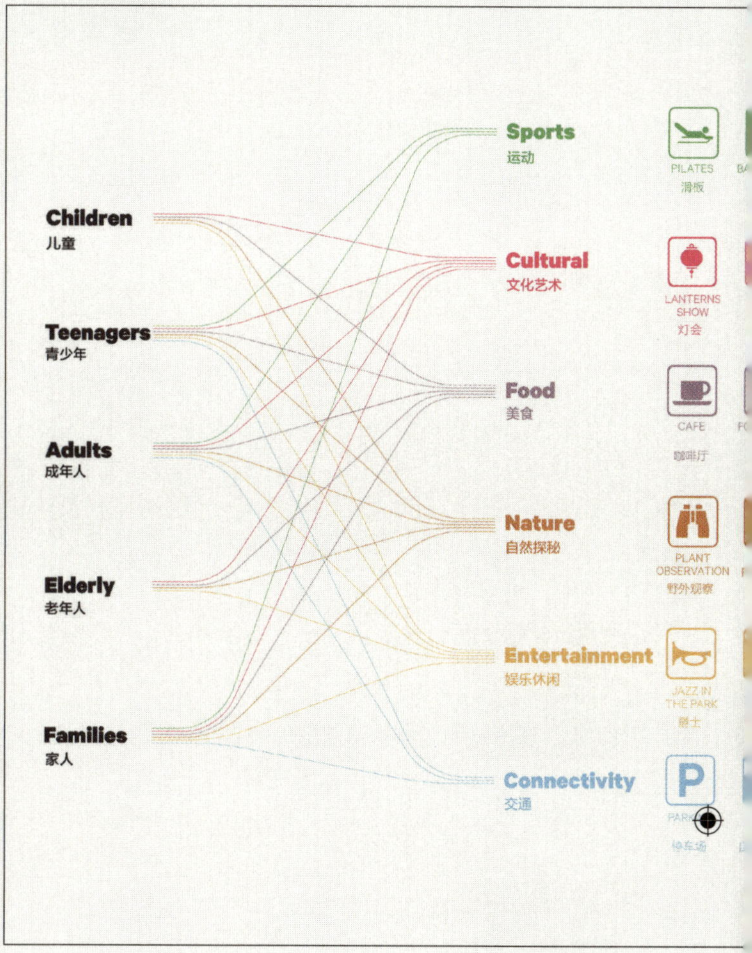

following Beijing as host city in 1990 and Guangzhou in 2010.

While sports stadiums and parks created for seminal events such as the Olympics or the Asian Games are typically highly representative structures created at great expense, their short use during the event itself hardly justifies the impact on resources and the urban environment. More often than not, these projects remain "white elephants" within their context once the games are over. Our design approaches the task with a much wider frame of reference and time, reflecting both the heritage of the existing context, the sustainability of all new structures and their long-term impact, as well as future contribution to the urban environment. As such, the project is not solely an answer to the immediate task at hand—the need to accommodate the Asian Games—but represents a future investment in the city and the culture of Hangzhou.

SO.108

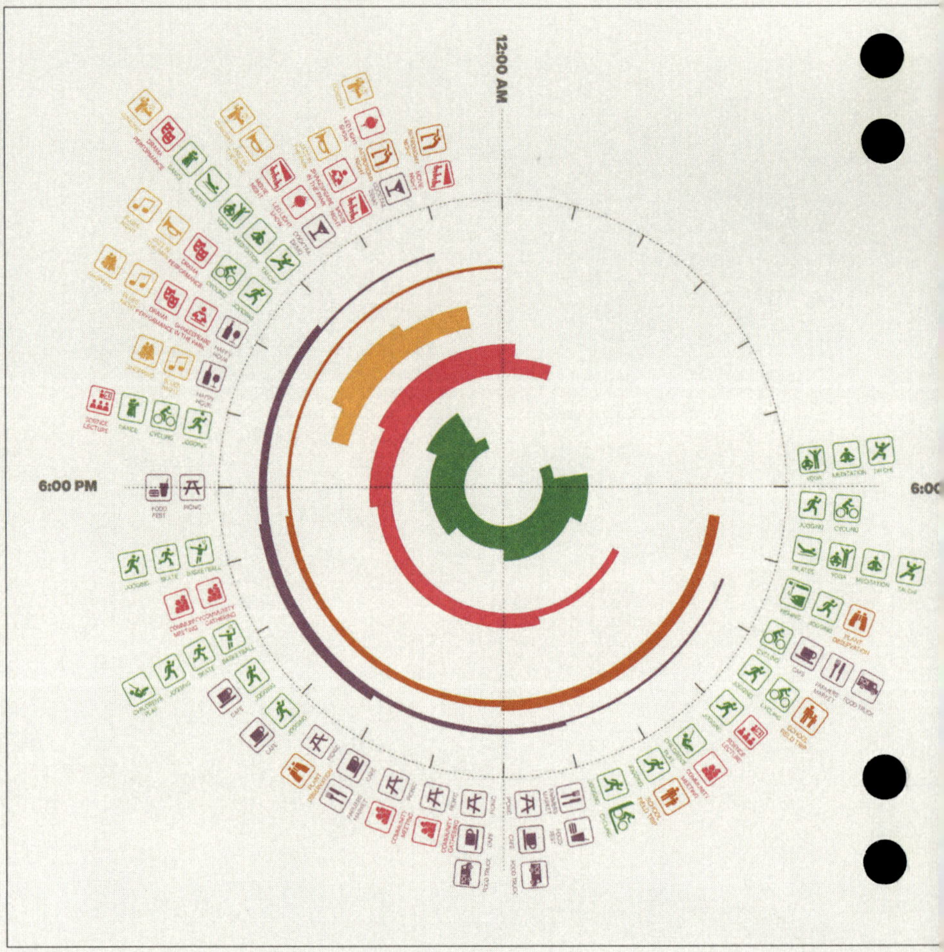

LEGACY PROJECT; 'AFTER THE GAMES' OCCUPATION

CONCEPT

Selected in an invited competition with five well-known international architecture firms, Archi-Tectonics won the 2022 Asian Games project with a bold and innovative design, fusing landscape and building program into a tridimensional landform. Like pebbles in a river, two iconic stadiums and various other building objects form the gravitational nodes for a fluid park landscape for the surrounding city of Hangzhou. In collaboration with !Melk landscape design, Mobility in Chain, and Thornton Tomasetti engineers, we created a multi-functional sports park with a Table Tennis and a Field Hockey stadium, a semi-recessed fitness center and visitor center with green roofs, a shopping concept as a connective "valley village" and multiple parking garages, with a total construction area of 188,000 m^2.

SO.109

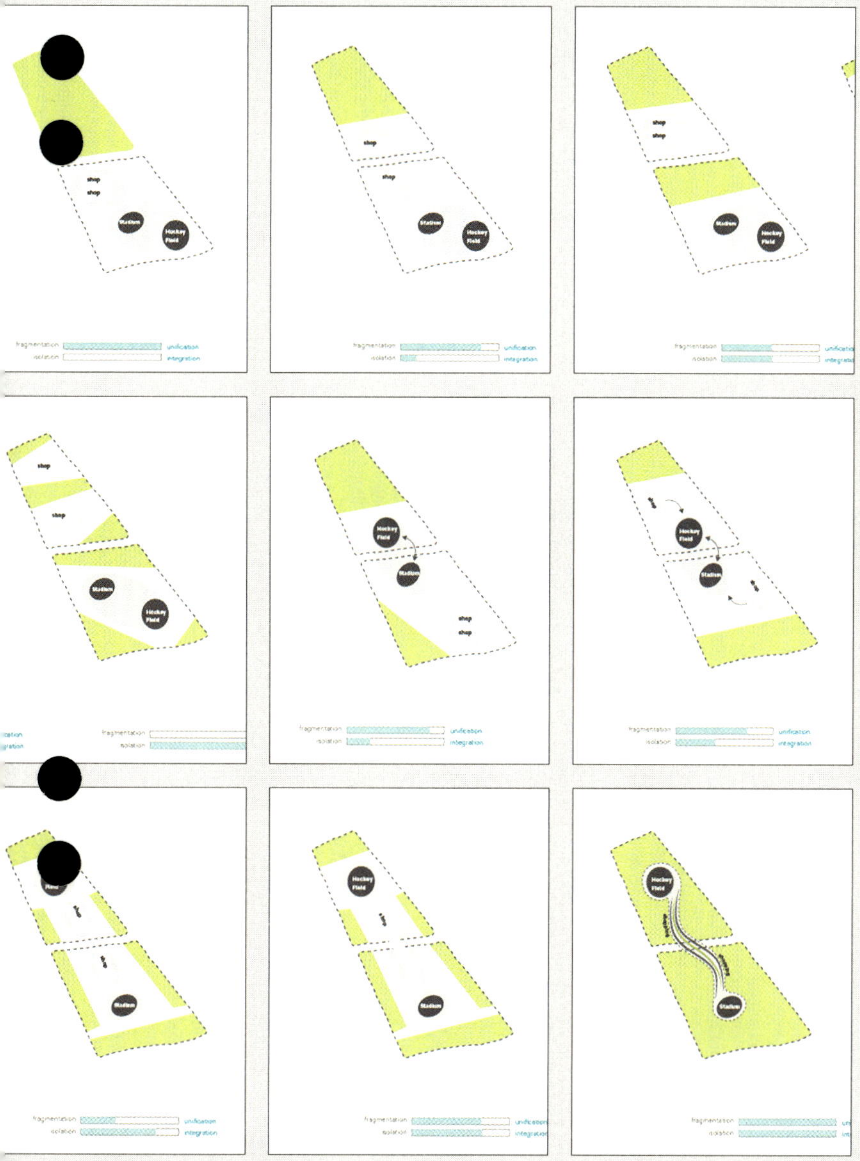

SO.110

BREAKING THE RULES

Early in the design, guided by a rigorously analytical process, the design team made the calculated decision to not follow the competition rules exactly. Rather than locating the stadiums at the bisecting road in the middle of the park, the two stadiums are placed within the park sections, thus operating as gravitational nodes that generate new activities, and allowing for the emergence of intrinsic poetic qualities and tectonic innovation. This leads to stadium designs that are unapologetically modern and technologically advanced, while generating objects and spaces of genuine authenticity. Rather than thinking of the stadium as an inert object in the landscape, we envisioned the stadium as a multi-dimensional body or hybrid, seamlessly integrating the event spaces through a sequence of layers and thresholds into the surrounding park landscape.

ASIAN GAMES PARK 2022

HANGZHOU

SO.111-112 SO.113

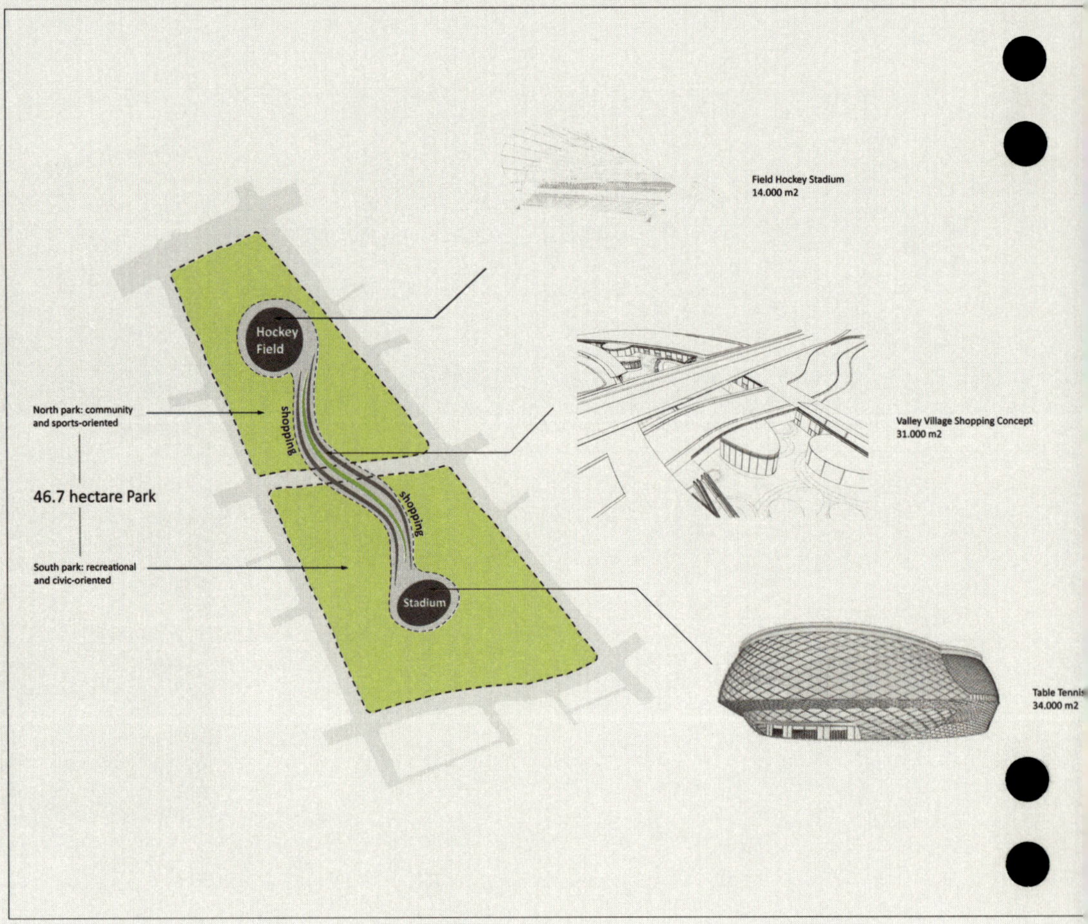

SPONGE CITY: ZERO-EARTH STATEGY

Sustainability, resource management, and energy efficiency were primary drivers of our design. The site had to accommodate no less than 188,000 m² of built structures, including 60,000 m² of underground parking, a 36,000 m² shopping mall, as well as fitness and community centers. The Sponge City concept, meant to control floods, was translated into an environmentally innovative ecosystem with wetland restoration, porous pavement, and the re-introduction of native plants and an extensive tree canopy. The implementation of a zero-earth strategy resulted in an intensely topographical

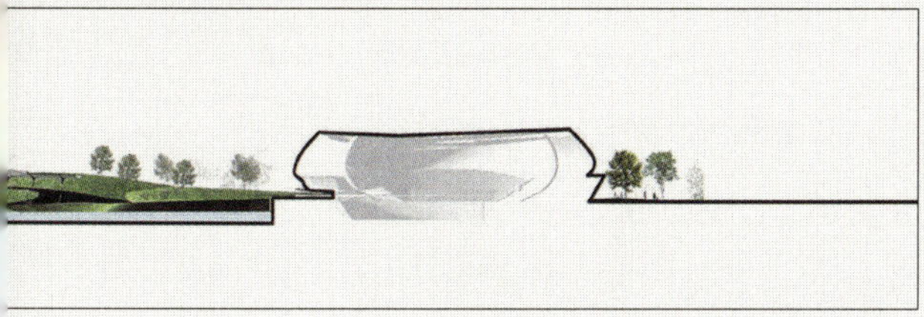

ZERO-EARTH STRATEGY

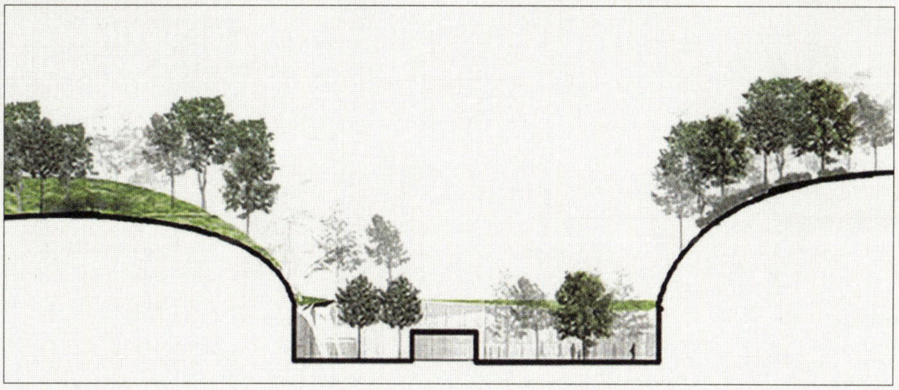

landscape forming the horizon between above- and below-ground.

The Zero Earth strategy—re-using excavated earth to build up the topography of the site—helped create this undulating 116-acre park landscape, while also achieving extreme density. We placed the majority of the program fully or partially underground, resulting in meandering valleys, crevices, hills, and floating green roofs. The park acts as a "green lung" for the city: trees are the ultimate urban multitasker, performing the functions of air filter, sponge, humidifier, heat shield, wind block, and carbon sink.

VALLEY VILLAGE

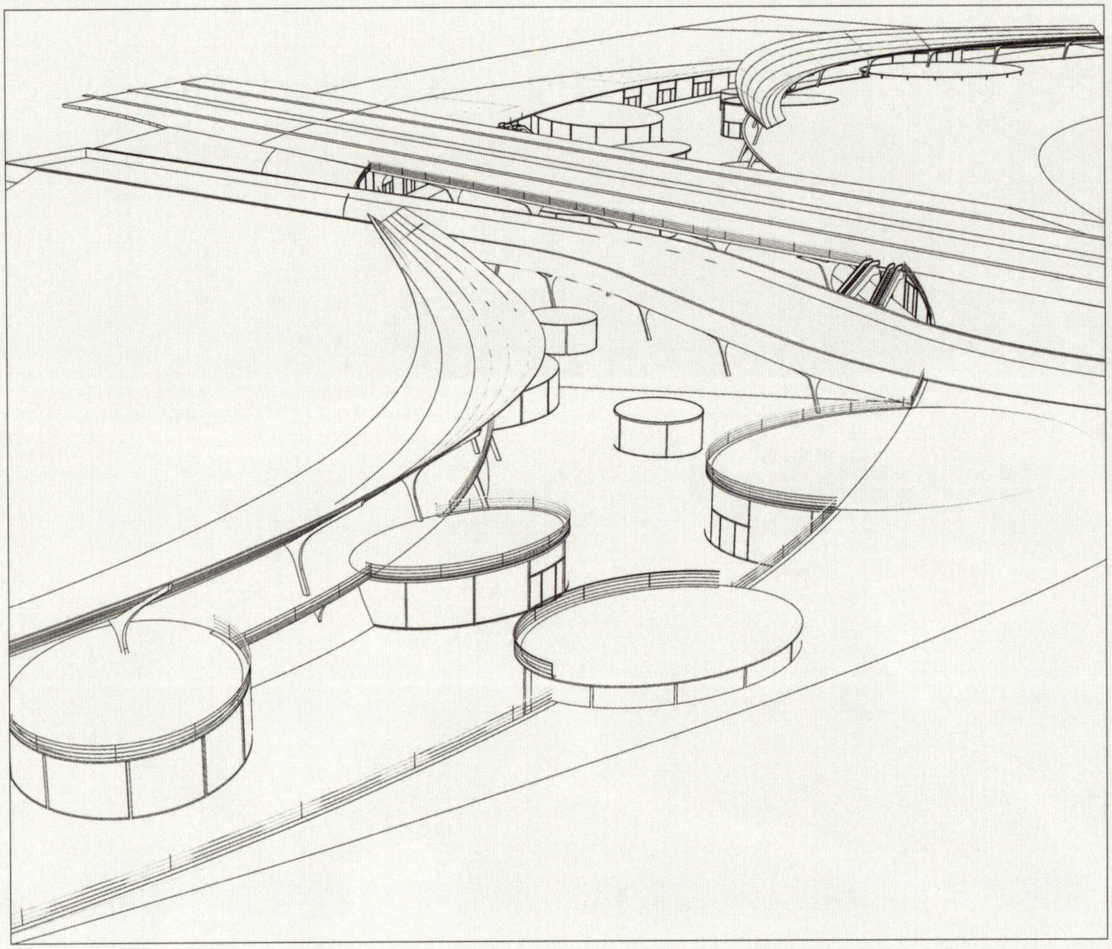

BETWEEN THE NODES: VALLEY VILLAGE

The excavation for the Valley Village mall under the road and the river created a link between the two stadiums and park segments. The introduction of a viaduct and an aqueduct make possible this undulating commercial spine with vegetation, shops, restaurants, kiosks, and underground parking. The zero-earth strategy reuses the mall's excavated soil to create green hills on the surrounding below-ground parking garages. This fluid and natural connecting device guarantees seamless circulation during the Asian Games and ensures the future success of the project as a lively urban space.

The shopping artery features long shading devices with transparent photovoltaic panels that make the Valley Village self-sufficient. Skylights throughout the park allow for natural ventilation and daylight penetration to all underground structures.

VALLEY VILLLAGE SHOPPING

SECTION CUT

TABLE TENNIS STADIUM

琮

CONG

INTERSECTING SOLIDS

Inspired by "Cong" jade stones, historic artifacts prevalent in the Hangzhou area characterized by a peculiar merging of cubic and cylindrical shapes, our initial investigations for the Table Tennis Stadium focused on exploring the formal opportunities of non-platonic hybrid forms and geometries. We incorporated the inherent conflict of the stadium form, the incongruence of multiple, non-stable geometries, as the very "seed" of the design.

But rather than attempting to resolve the competing parameters through a process of rationalization and optimization towards a single, unified body, we allowed these eccentricities and

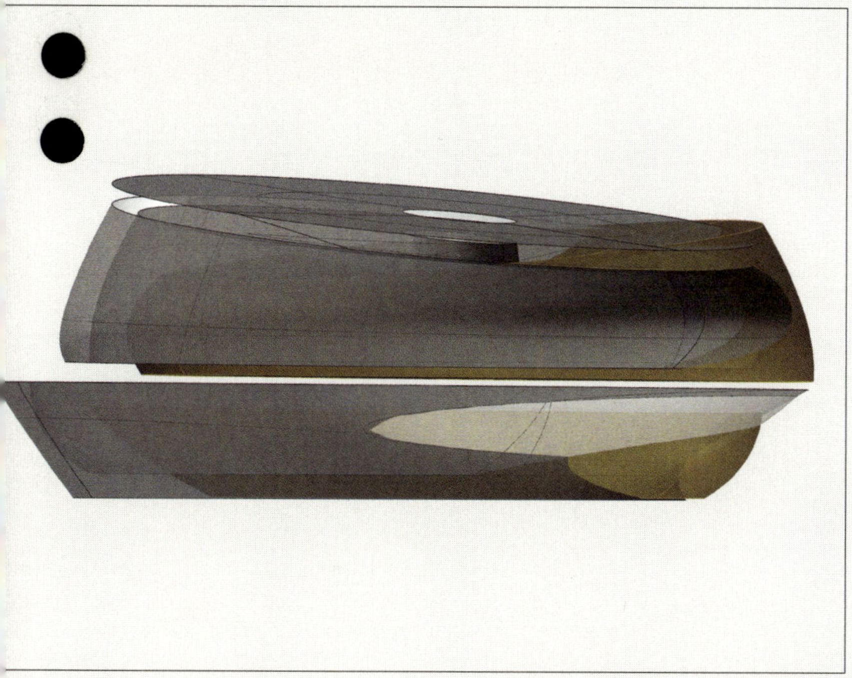

HYBRID SHAPE FACILITATES CHANGE

asymmetries to form a series of spatial iterations, "proto-spaces" with varying degrees of geometric shifts, permutations, and recombinations.

The resulting form is part thing, part object; sublime, massive, and streamlined like an ocean liner, but also ambiguous, complex, and twisted. Smooth spatial gradients fold and invert at their extremes to form abrupt (local) changes of scale and texture (qualities). The amalgam of materials and spaces is both fluid and crystalline, weightless and cavernous. A strange beauty that evokes awe and curiosity, inviting a tentative, tactile approach as much as rational understanding.

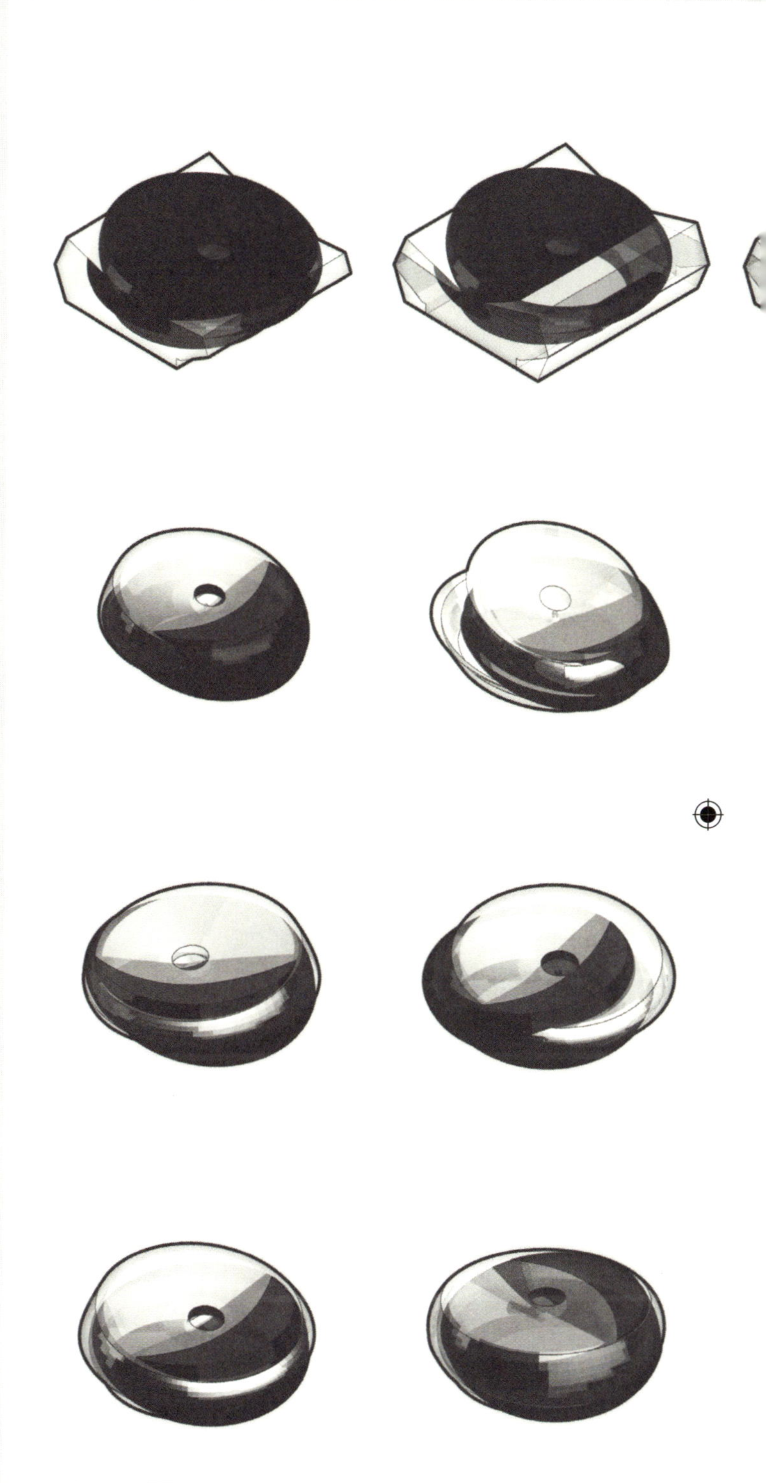

FORM STUDY FOR INTERSECTING VOLUMES AND SHIFTS

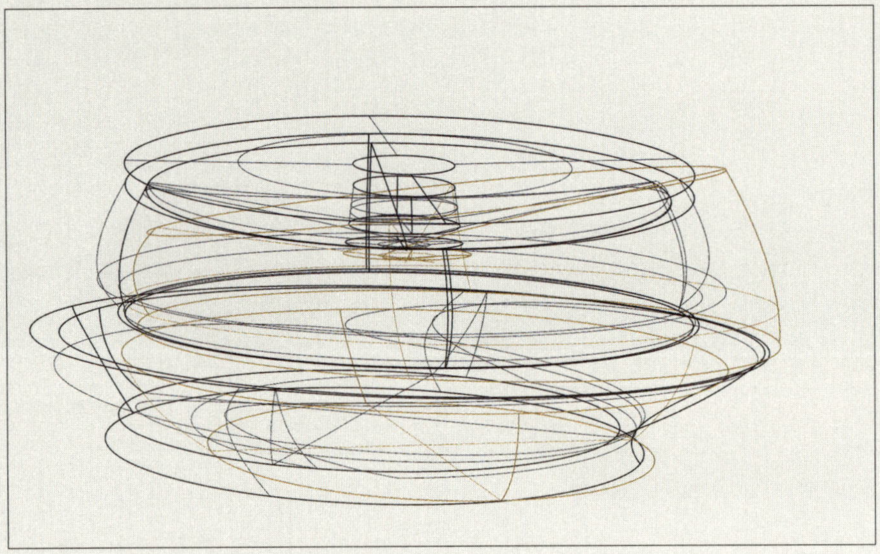

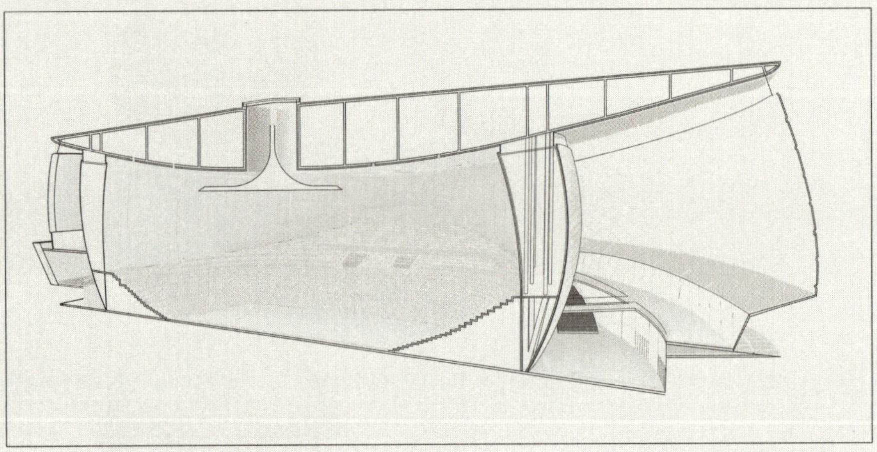

INTERSECTING SOLIDS

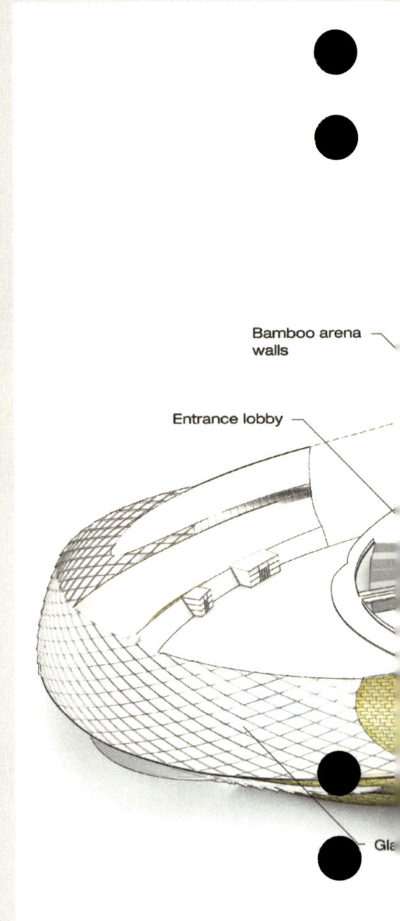

OPTIMIZATION VERSUS POTENTIALITY

In conventional stadium design the programmatic and spatial conflicts are resolved through a process of gradual optimization, seeking to establish a stasis between competing geometries and parameters, such as visibility, circulation, security, VIP privileges, access, and egress. The aim of this operation is to achieve an equilibrium, the largest common denominator to contain all forces within a simple, ideal body.

The design of the Table Tennis Stadium explores an altogether different path, conceptually as well as

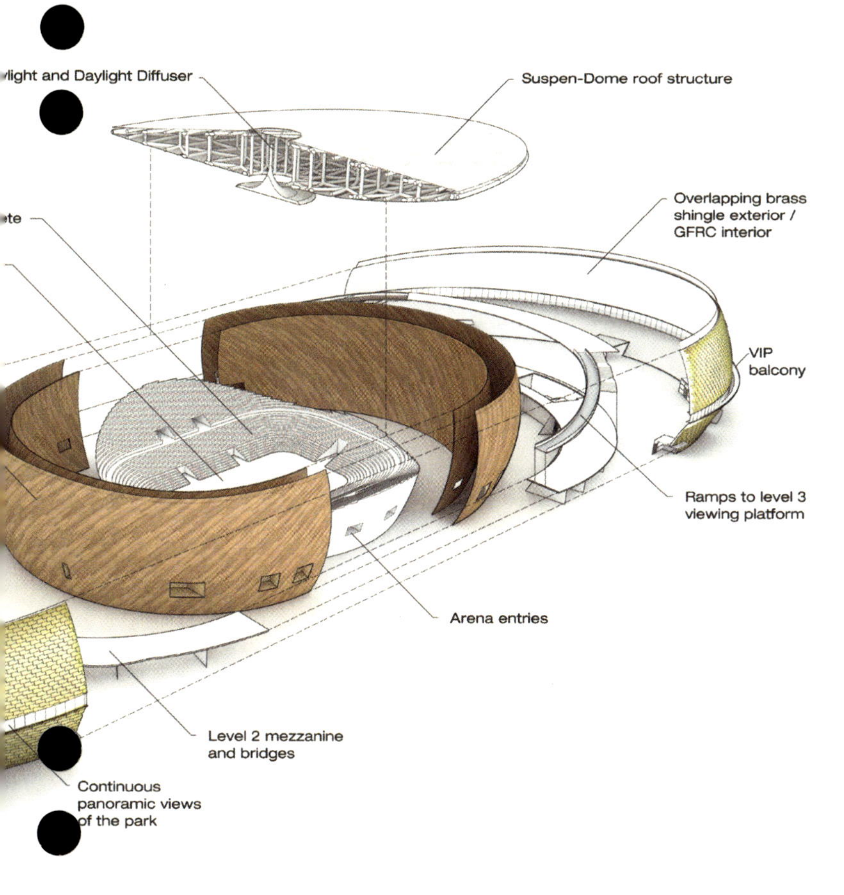

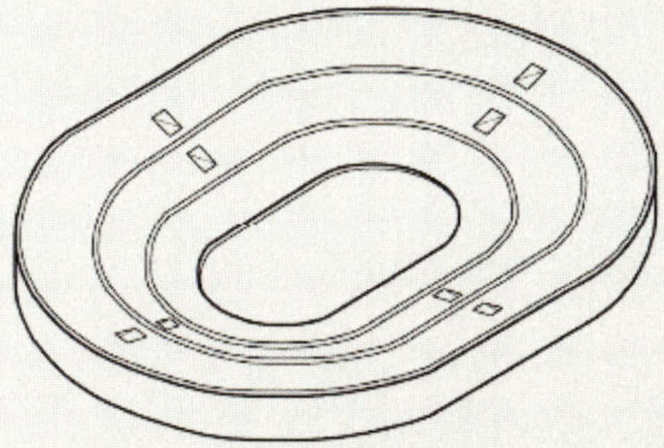

Arena typology

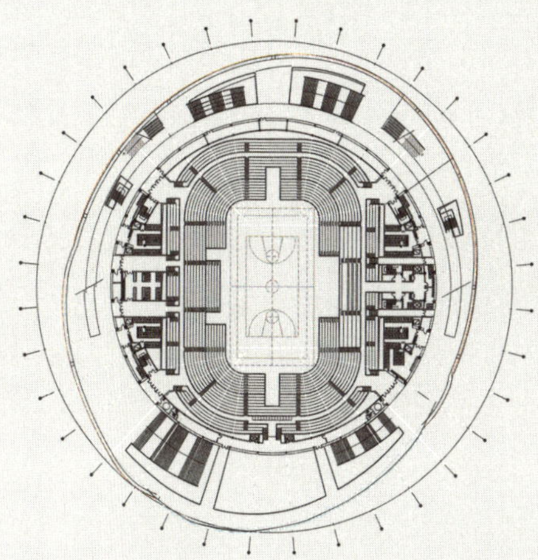

ROTATIONAL PLAN

formally. It utilizes the incongruences and competing parameters of program and geometry as an opportunity to generate an environment that conforms with temporal, local or future intensities, therefore privileging maximum potentiality over a unified, singular, and neutral form.

By definition, potentiality is the "latent quality that may be developed and lead to future success or usefulness."[1] It does not measure the degree of adaptation to current demands but the building's capacity to inform utility *beyond* the known parameters, to inspire altogether new forms of engagement and meaning—not what the stadium is, but what it *could* be. This does not preclude a neutral architectural form or lack of definition—quite the opposite. The architectural object is given autonomy and character to evoke a distinct and particular affect.

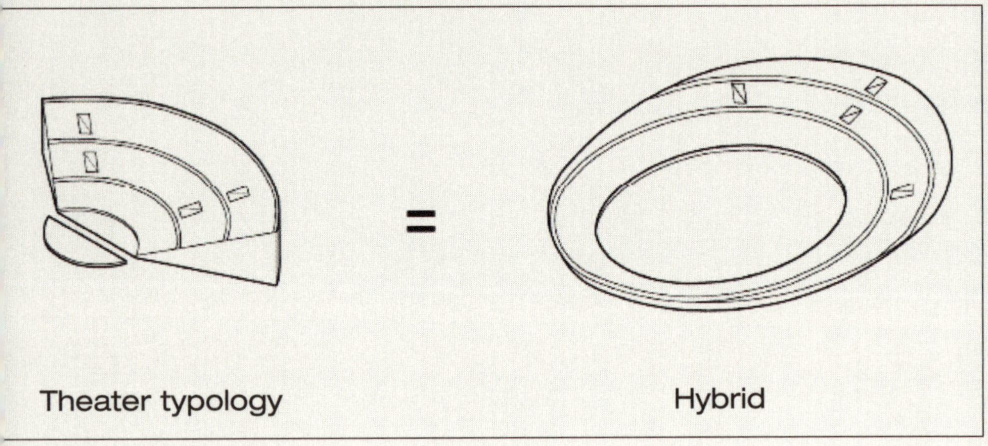

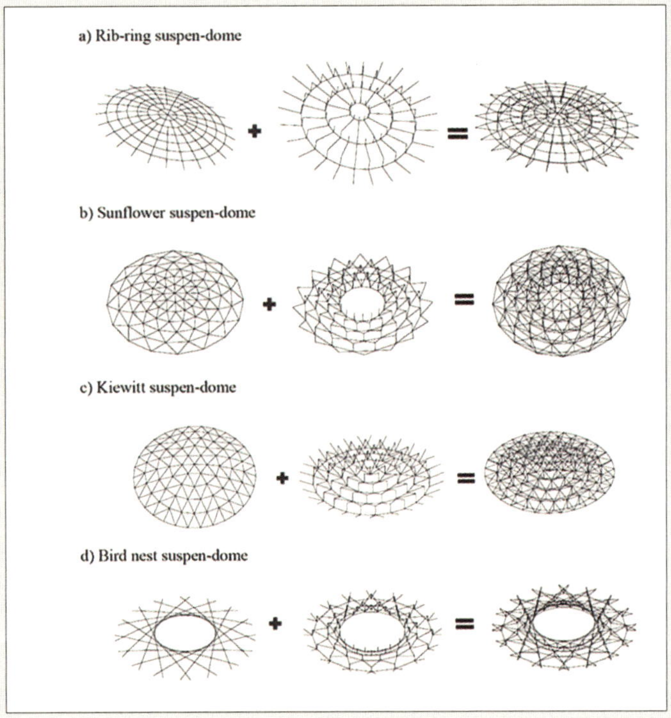

SUSPENDOME TYPOLOGIES

HYBRID

A hybrid grandstand geometry was developed that merges arena and amphitheater seating, accommodating various performance types within one congruent, organic form. Its gradual rise forms a uniquely shaped spectator space, terminating in an undulating line of intersection against the bamboo-clad concave sphere of the inner arena bowl. In the theater modus, the typical central viewing layout preferred for sports events had to transform into an asymmetric, stage-centered configuration, drastically re-establishing preferred seating locations and viewing angles. But not only the spectator space is intrinsically fluid and dynamic; the increasing importance of secondary programs within the stadium "body" has led to an altogether altered definition of the building's function and performance. A contemporary stadium is no longer merely a container for viewing sports events,

SO.132

SO.133

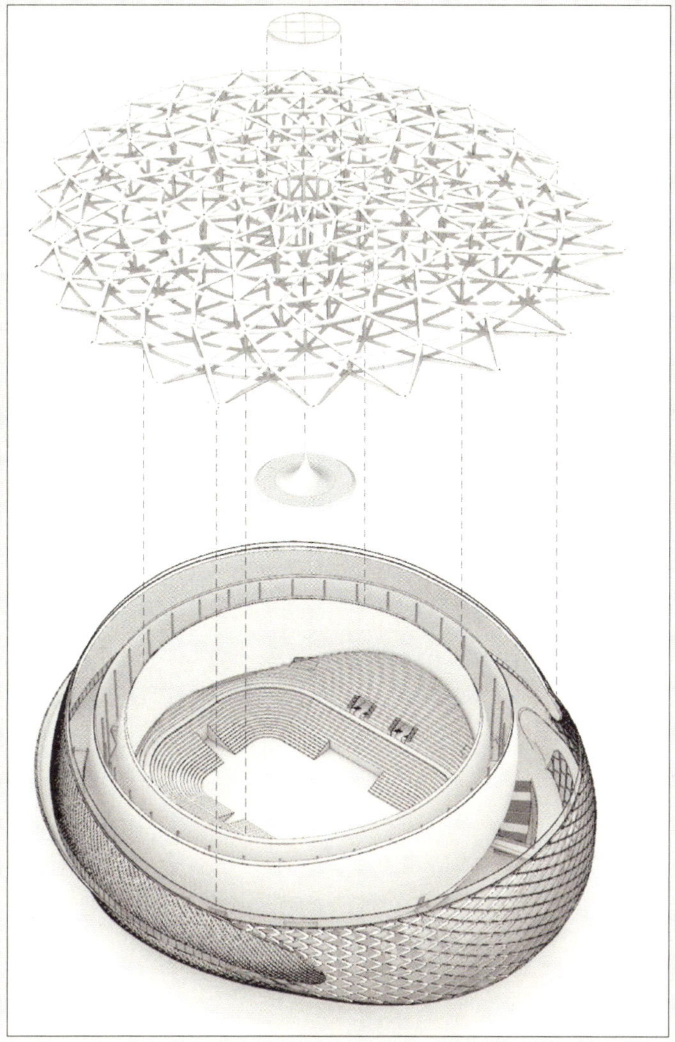

it has to accommodate numerous parallel programs and modes of representation within and outside of its physical boundaries, such as restaurants, VIP lounges, retail and media areas, security zones, instant replays, all competing for access and attention. The synesthetic quality of these layers of experience is what creates the event, differentiates it from seeing it at home. The stadium body can thus no longer be conceptualized as a fixed body, but an agglomeration of simultaneous event geometries, boundaries and focal points; a complex and dynamic cluster of latent qualities and forms, enmeshed within a system of urban and landscape networks and nodes. Its diagram is unstable, impermanent, and non-essential; a cloud of wobbly orbits observed at a moment in time.

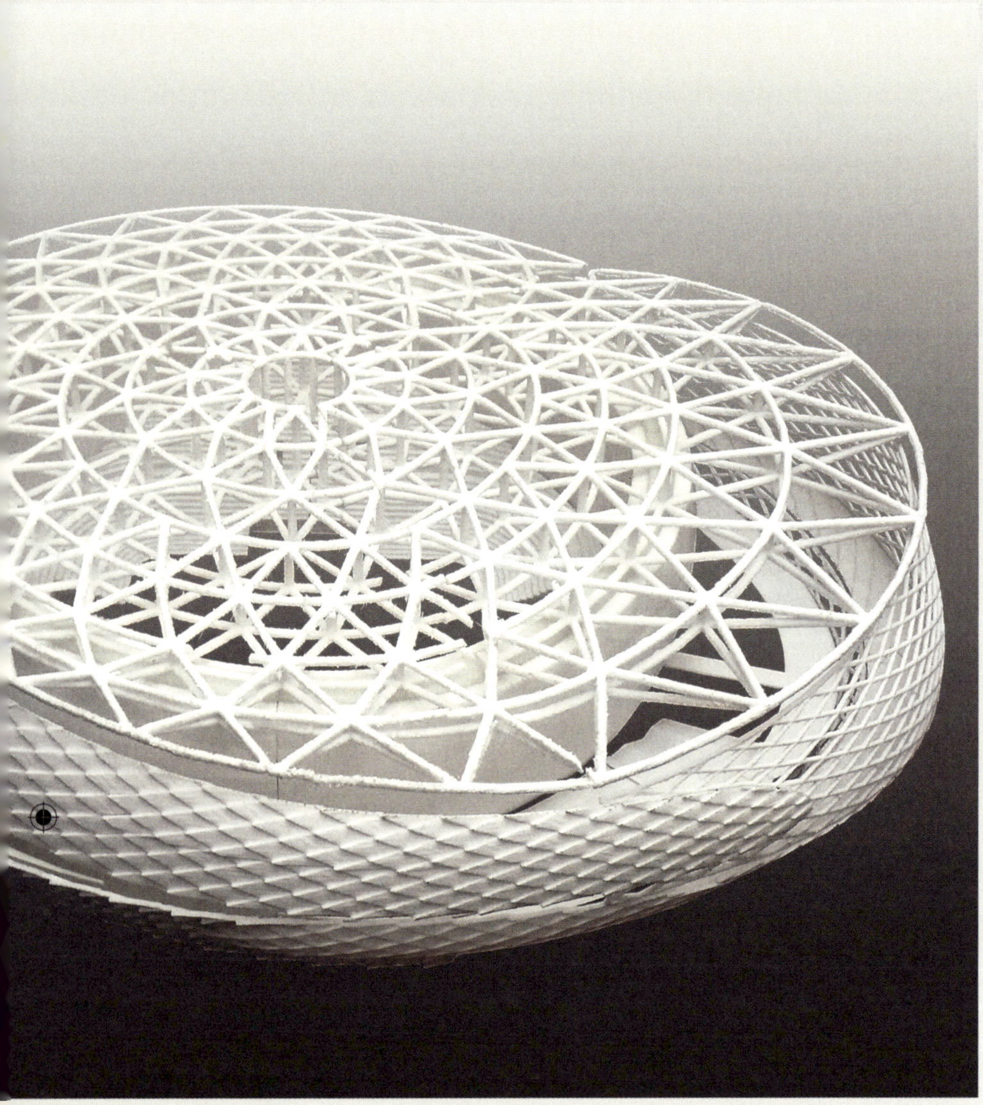

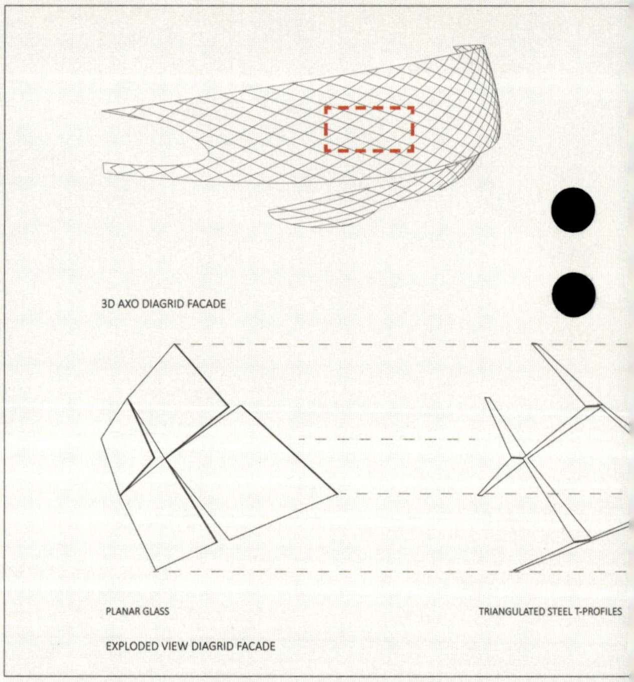

WOBBLY ELLIPSES

The stadium form is one of the most iconic architectural objects. Its characteristic, massive shape, bulging from its context like a colossal alien vessel, imposes scale and order; a sublime attractor in the urban field of gravity. Its self-referential nature, paired with representing a spectacle that celebrates physical power and dominance, has led to an emphasis on expressions of wholeness, idealization, and singularity in stadium design.

But the event of today is no longer the athletic competition these archetypical structures used to embody. Mediated, augmented, and multiplied, the physical spectacle is now just a fragment of the overall experience. The immediacy of the visceral, physical space—quite literally the experience of the

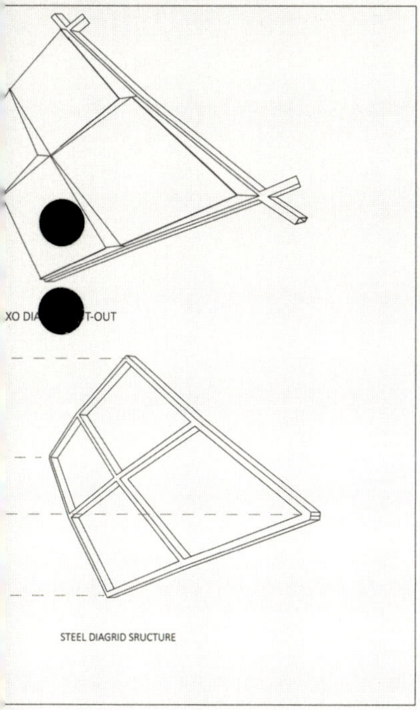

SUPERSIZE DIAGRID WITH
PLANAR GLASS SHARDS

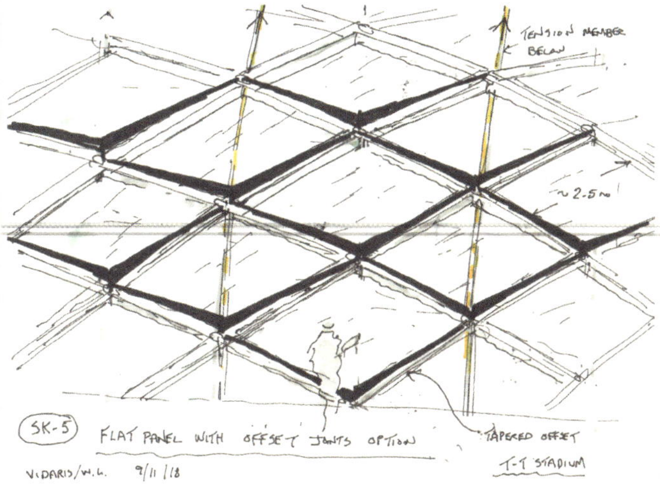

DRAWING BY WILLIAM LOGAN, VIDARIS

architectural "performance"—is what differentiates visiting a sports event from mediated reality, lending the architectural object new agency and meaning. Consequently, the Asian Games Table Tennis Stadium is proposing a new morphology that emphasizes latent qualities over idealized, universal forms. A "body within a body," the stadium seeks to eliminate the dichotomy of event-space and architectural permanence. Its geometries could best be described as intersecting clouds of influence, orbits rather than finite, platonic shapes; their diagrams are no longer based on circles and spheres, but eccentric ovoids. Wobbly ellipses shift in and out of alignment around multiple, dynamic focal points, negotiating boundaries and programs, blurring architecture and landscape, container and contained.

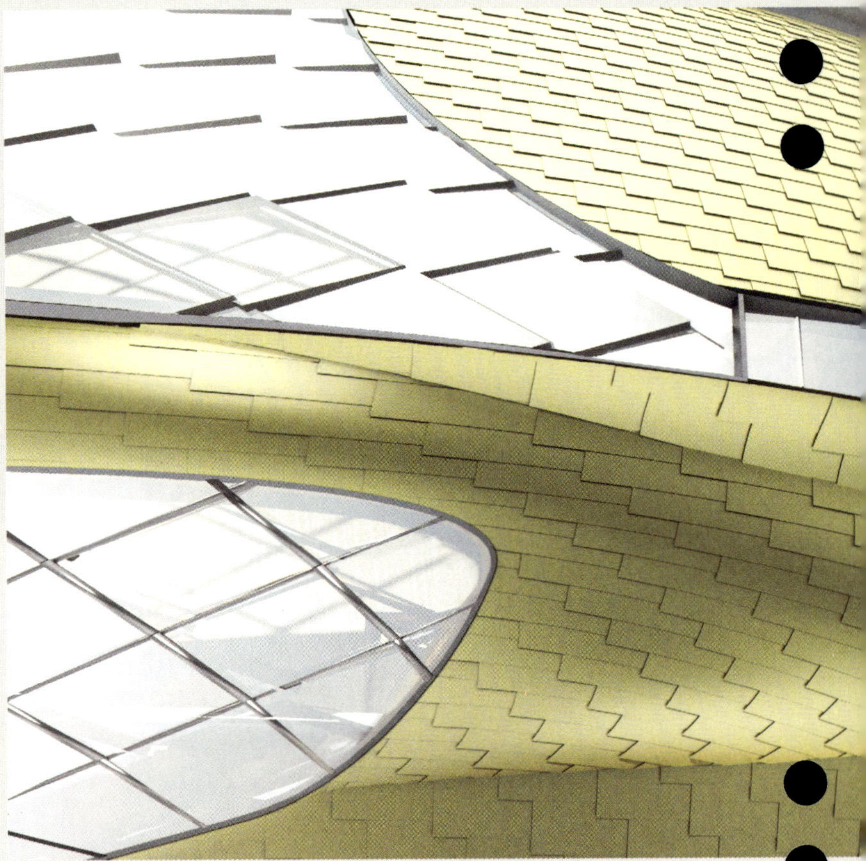

BIM OPTIMIZATION OF THE 5,000 BRASS SHINGLES, SHAPES REDUCED IN JUST 85 VARIANTS

UNSTABLE GEOMETRIES

The two-dimensional stadium shape is, at its most basic level, a hybrid derived from combining circular and rectangular geometries. The Greek word *stadion* does in fact not signify a building but a vector (line)—the measure of length of 600 human feet, the distance of the original Olympic foot race in Olympia. Only the addition of spectator seating, the "arena" program, adds three-dimensionality to the equation, superimposing a second set of dynamic geometries based on visual perspective, thus creating an inherently unstable balance of spectator and event geometries. While the geometry and movement on the playing field is determined by the regulations of the sports event, the form of the arena "bowl"

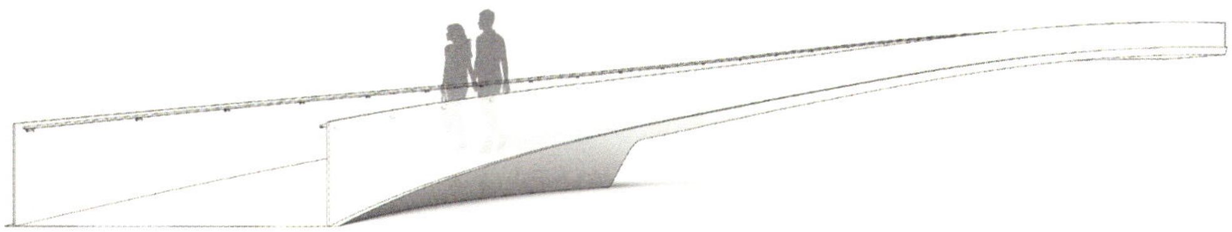

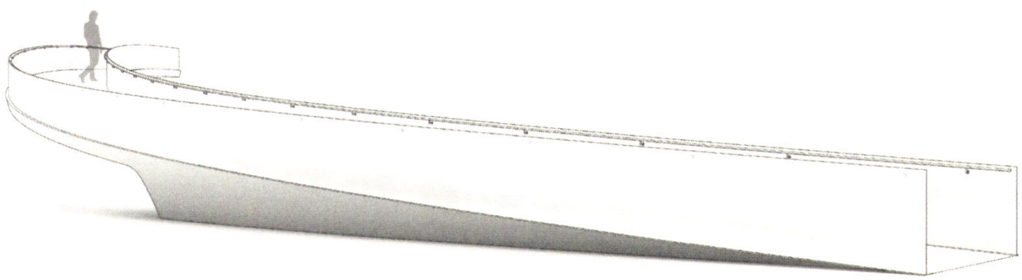

ROTATIONAL PLANS EXEMPLIFIED BY LONG CURVING RAMPS

follows a carefully calibrated calculation of sight lines, viewing angles, and seating rake, as expressed in the "C-value," defined as the vertical distance from a spectator's eyes to the sightline of the spectator directly behind.

DIAGRID

Two intersecting surfaces negotiate the bulging volumes; a natural aging brass shingle system and a steel diagrid with glass shards. The diagrid creates an exterior structural system in which all perimeter vertical columns are eliminated, as the diagonally intersecting metal lattice negotiates the double curve of the facade. It is covered with glass shards with a

ASIAN GAMES PARK 2022

SO.144-151

HANGZHOU

SO.152-153

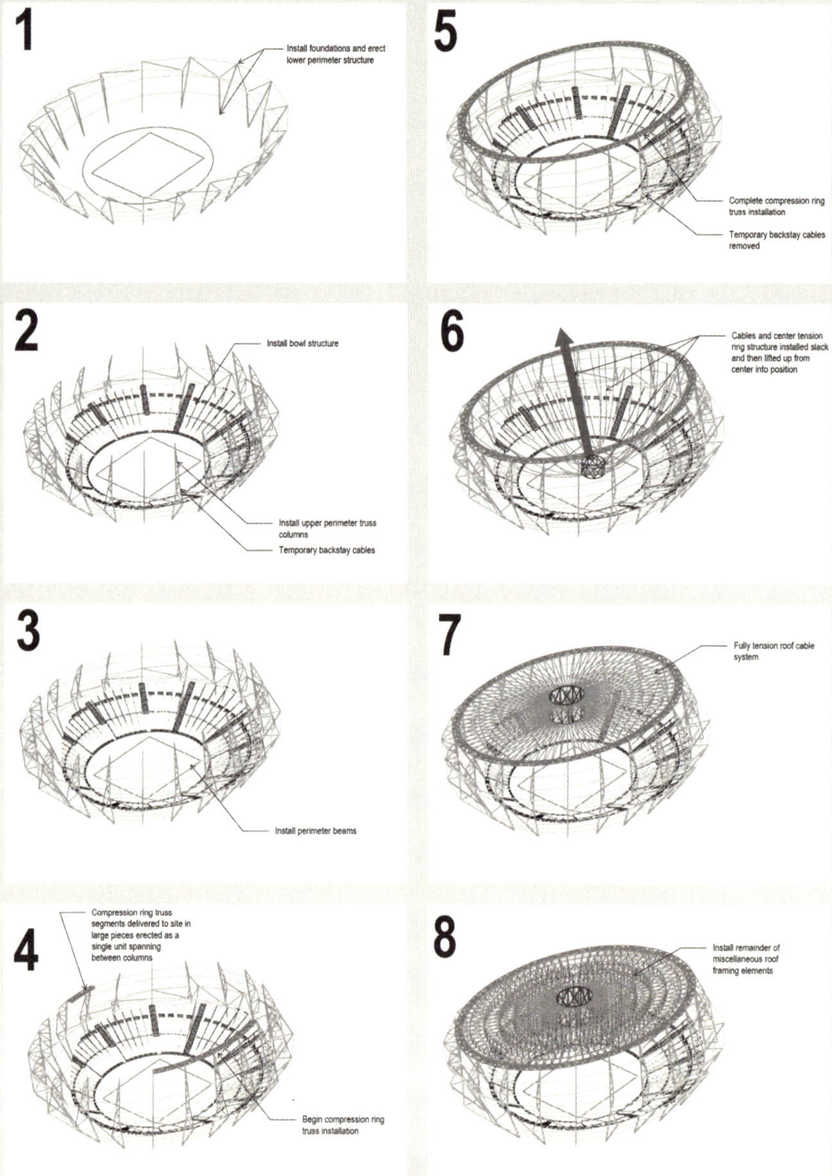

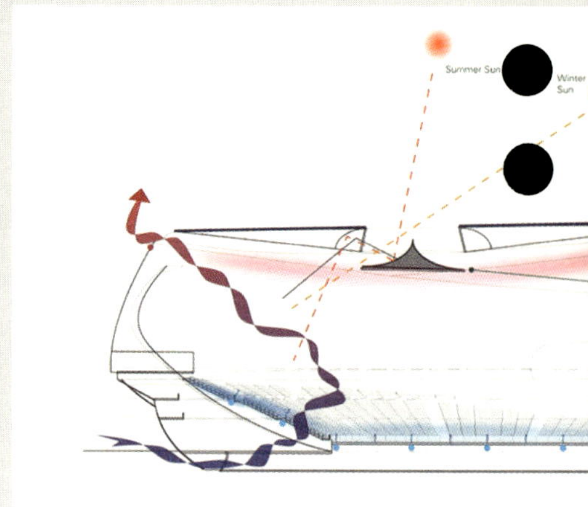

These intersecting volumes integrate several s

- Smart orientation and facade minimize solar
-The roof incorporates a daylight diffuser pane
natural light into the arena

STRUCTURAL ANALYSIS THORNTON TOMASETTI / SCOTT LOMAX

diameter of close to 7 meters. We collaborated with curtain wall consultant William Logan of Vidaris to develop a diagrid with planar glass facilitated by silver "eyelids," giving the facade an almost a fish scale look.

SUSPENDOME

A suspendome roof structure is one of the latest engineering innovations and a type of large-span spatial structure optimized for sports buildings. Its ellipsoid shape is the highest around the open skylight in the middle and tapers to the ends as cantilevers. By pre-stressing the roof members the span is drastically enlarged. The pre-stress defines

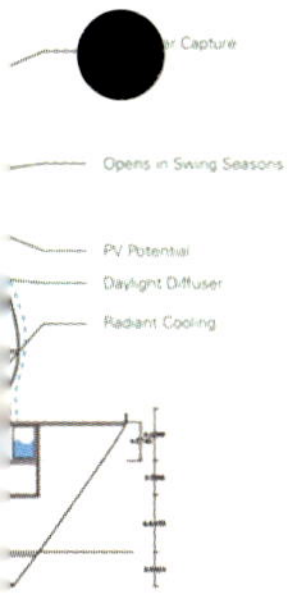

strategies.

a soft

BIM MODELING

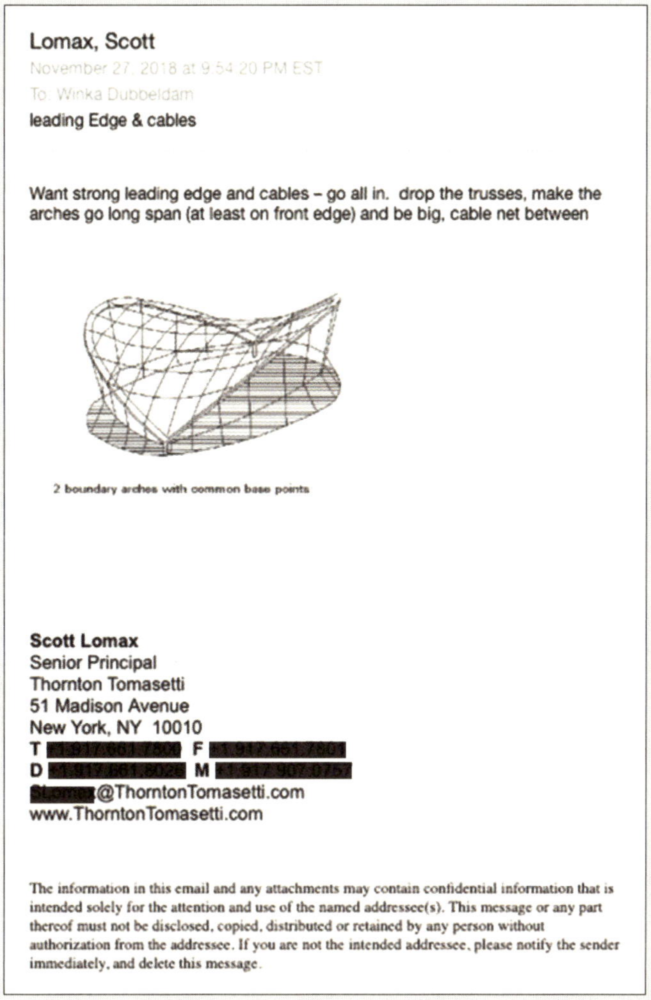

Lomax, Scott
November 27, 2018 at 9:54:20 PM EST
To: Winka Dubbeldam
leading Edge & cables

Want strong leading edge and cables – go all in. drop the trusses, make the arches go long span (at least on front edge) and be big, cable net between

2 boundary arches with common base points

Scott Lomax
Senior Principal
Thornton Tomasetti
51 Madison Avenue
New York, NY 10010
T [illegible] F [illegible]
D [illegible] M [illegible]
[illegible]@ThorntonTomasetti.com
www.ThorntonTomasetti.com

The information in this email and any attachments may contain confidential information that is intended solely for the attention and use of the named addressee(s). This message or any part thereof must not be disclosed, copied, distributed or retained by any person without authorization from the addressee. If you are not the intended addressee, please notify the sender immediately, and delete this message.

the deformation and the internal force of the upper reticulated shell structure. Based on these parameters, the ideal shape of an arena "bowl" would be an ovoid with a parabolic cross section. Merging the spectator and performer geometries is therefore at its very core a "negotiated" oscillation, with no possible single, privileged vantage point. Even the optimum shape can only provide the best average view. This was further optimized by creating the hybrid seating formation between arena and theater seating, ensuring its future use.

SO.159

SUSPENDOME INSTALLATION
IN JUST 15 SEGMENTS

THE MASSIVE

The 350,000-square-foot Table Tennis Stadium appears relatively small in the vast 116-acre park and wetland, acquiring an almost scenic beauty. Only once inside, the supersized stadium will reach its "massive" effect; the structure looms over the visitors, its radial stairs, ramps, and mezzanines accommodate large crowds to simultaneously enter and flow into the sports event. Our concept for the Asian Games Park and Stadiums emerged from a unique combination of innovative design methodology and local cultural heritage. By utilizing vernacular artifacts as "seeds" for our parametric formal investigations, we created a poetic, multi-layered hybrid stadium nested within in the vast park landscape, as a multi-functional, luscious, and inviting Sports Park, for leisure, exercise, and entertainment.

SO.162-163

OCTOBER 2020

APRIL 2021

FIELD HOCKEY STADIUM

DIAPHANOUS WING

Balancing the solidity of the concrete seating arena and the stadium's diaphanous shading wing above, the field hockey stadium functions both as an optimized Asian Games performance module as well as a landscape sculpture. As the Field Hockey Stadium's 5,000-seat sculptural concrete arena rises up, it creates simultaneously a space below for the curved glass lobby. The players' field is set in a recessed oval grass plain, designed to double as

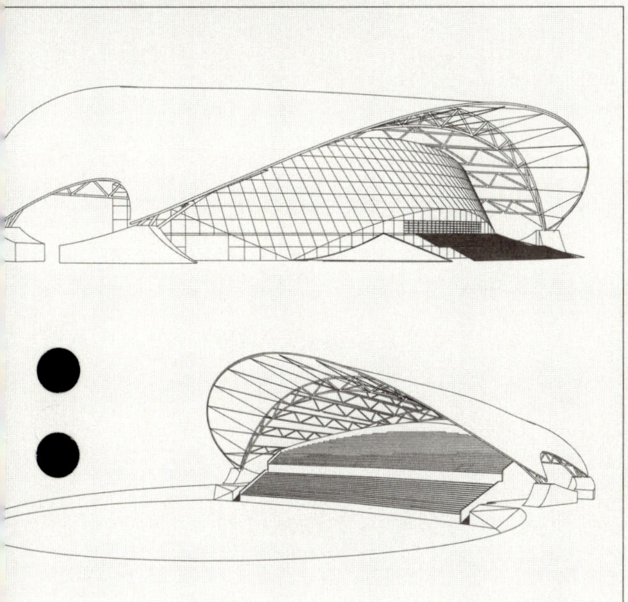

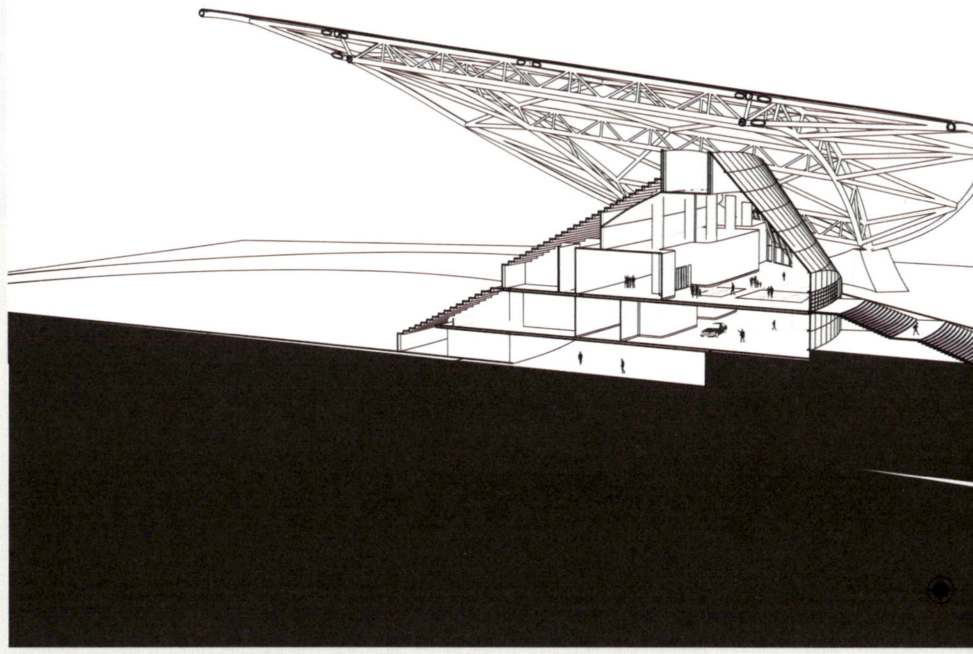

SECTION CUT 125-METER SPAN ROOF

a landscape feature. In plan the grass oval intersects with the 125-meter long lightweight and diaphanous oval wing, similar to the the *Seed of Life*, or the Vesica Piscis.

The massive wingspan's material ecology was inspired by the strength and elasticity of the similarly diaphanous traditional Meinong oil paper and bamboo umbrella. Bamboo, which is local to Hangzhou and found in the surrounding large forests, combines extreme physical strength with the appearance of lightness. The outdoor stadium's self-supporting 125-meter span thin foil forms a luminous weather and sun protection canopy above the Field Hockey arena. Placed into a circular depression within the landscape, the hockey field is integral part of the surrounding park and thus naturally translates between the geometric turf of the playing field and the surrounding hills.

125-METER SPAN WITH JUST ONE TRUSS

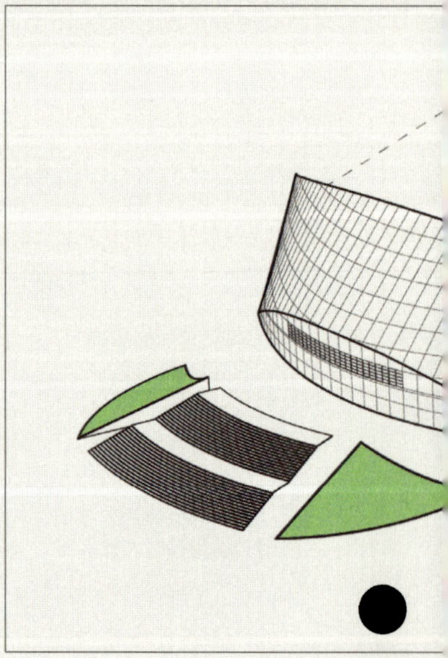

CROSS-FERTILIZATION

While the stadium building typology is commonly dominated by a "high tech" design language and materiality, here the focus was on the creation of a user experience that was not only intelligent and sustainable, but also highly atmospheric and emotionally appealing. Beautiful natural and recycled materials, such as bamboo, recycled brass or faceted glass, are brought to life by the stadium's

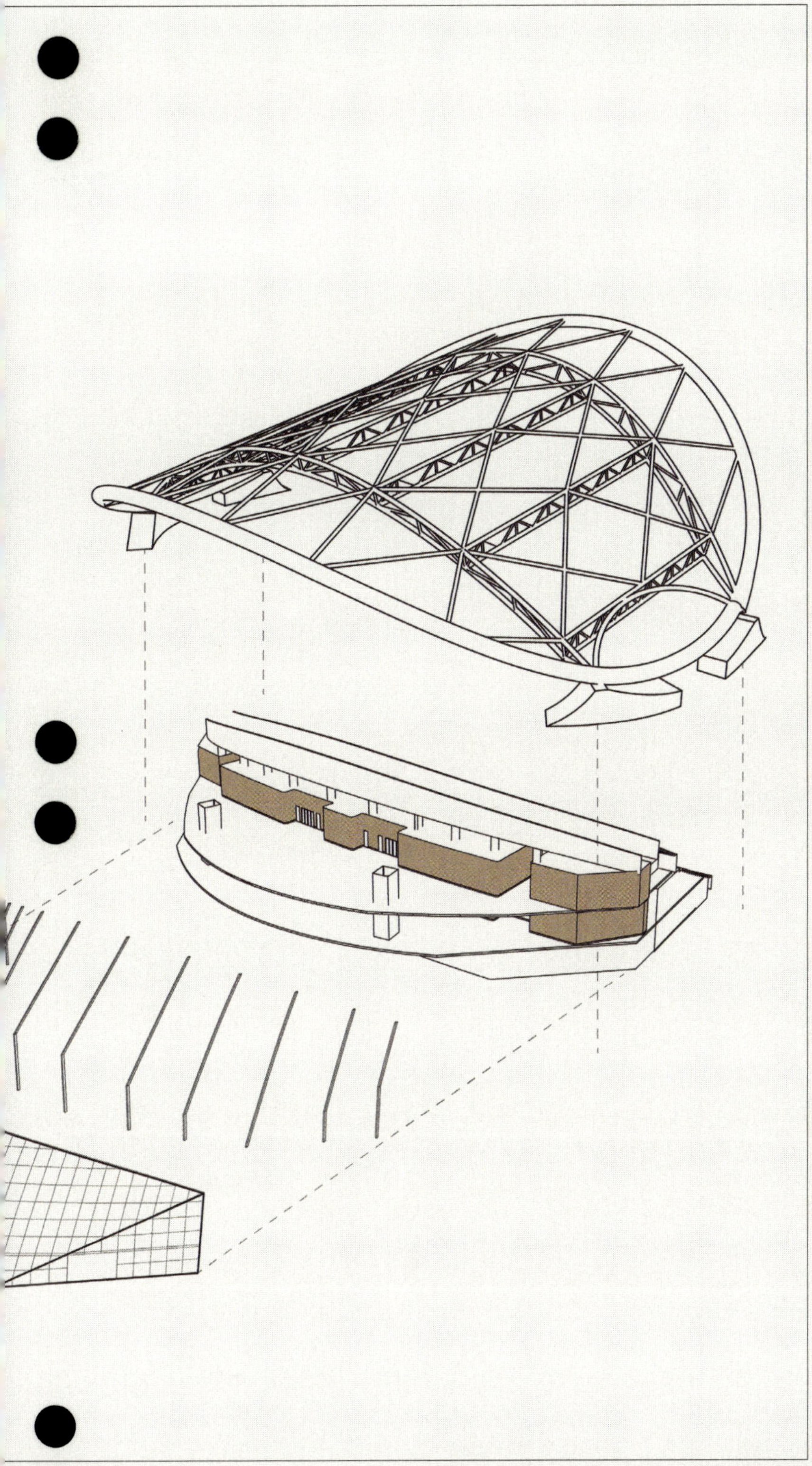

EXPLODED VIEW FIELD HOCKEY STADIUM

SECTION CUT 125-METER SPAN ROOF

APRIL 2021

complex curvature resulting in intense contrasts of light and shadow. This "cross-fertilization" between design aesthetics allowed for the creation of strange or unknown building typologies that defy conventional categorization, and thus greatly expand their flexibility and hybridity that accommodates varying programs, as well as potential future adaptations.

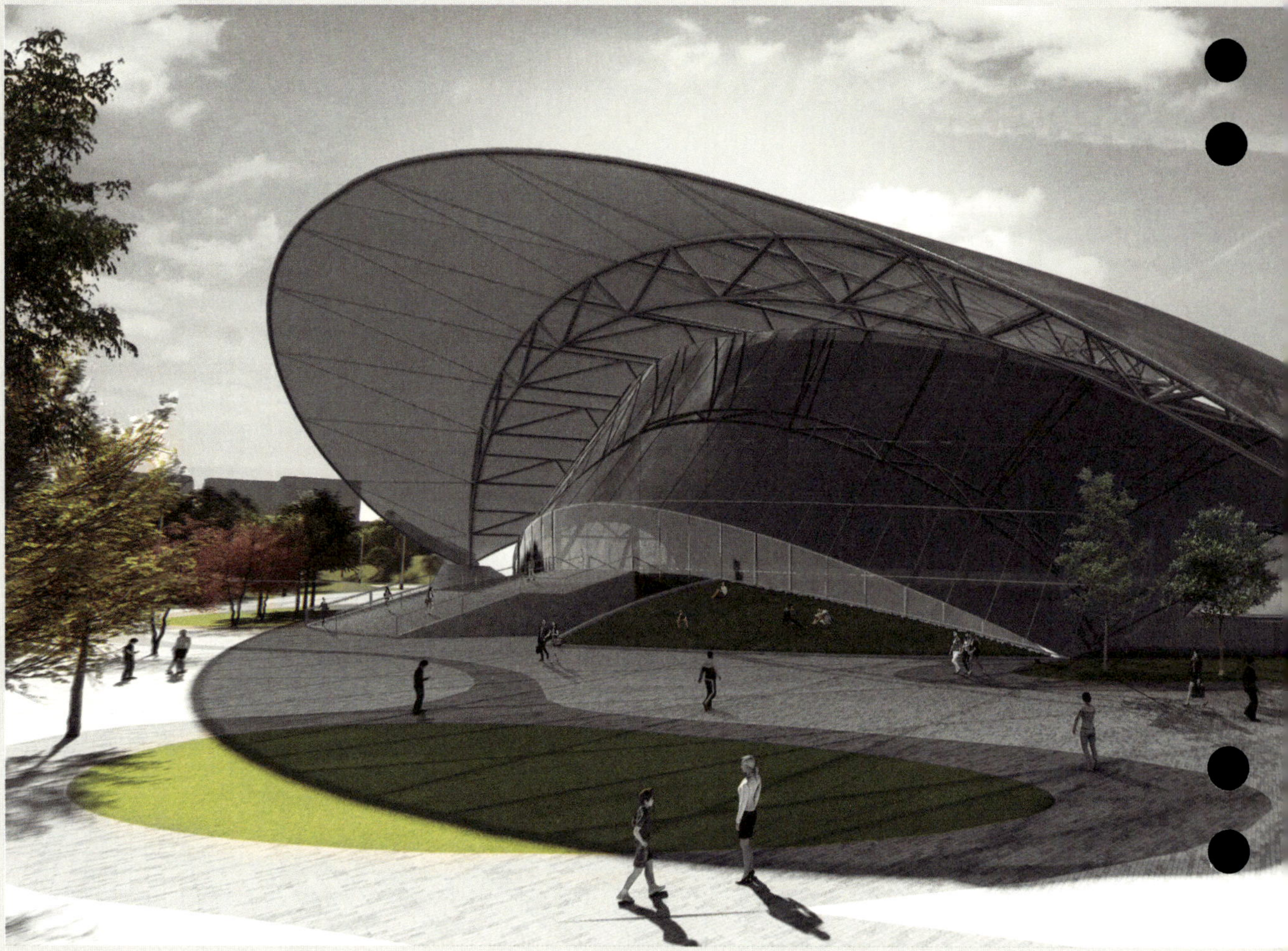

SEED OF LIFE / VESICA PISCIS

The aerial view reveals the intersection of the large ellipse roof and similarly ellipsoid field, a figure resembling the *Seed of Life* diagram; a sacred geometry first used as "overlapping circles," or the intersection of two disks with the same radius, dating back to the 7th or 6th century BCE, when it was found on the threshold of the palace of an Assyrian king in Khorsabad, and later in geometry used by, for example, Euclid and Da Vinci. This universal geometry is used here to exemplify the hybrid use of the stadium: first as the Asian Games Field Hockey stadium, later as a recessed landscape feature that allows easy access from the park, and doubles as outdoor concerts, theater, and other park events.

PROTOTYPING AND FEEDBACK LOOPS

During the design process, the intensive use of prototyping and instant feedback loops with manufacturers allowed for a fast analysis and adjustment of design parameters between the many international teams. Extensive BIM modeling allowed for non-linear working methods, coordinating the many layers of information, a method more akin to product development in industrial design. The team managed to deliver a fully integrated and developed design within a very short timeframe. Especially given the nature of real estate developments in China, we believe this high-tech, dynamic teamwork model can outperform traditional methods of architectural production, and offers new opportunities for growth.

SO.173-174

JUNE 2020

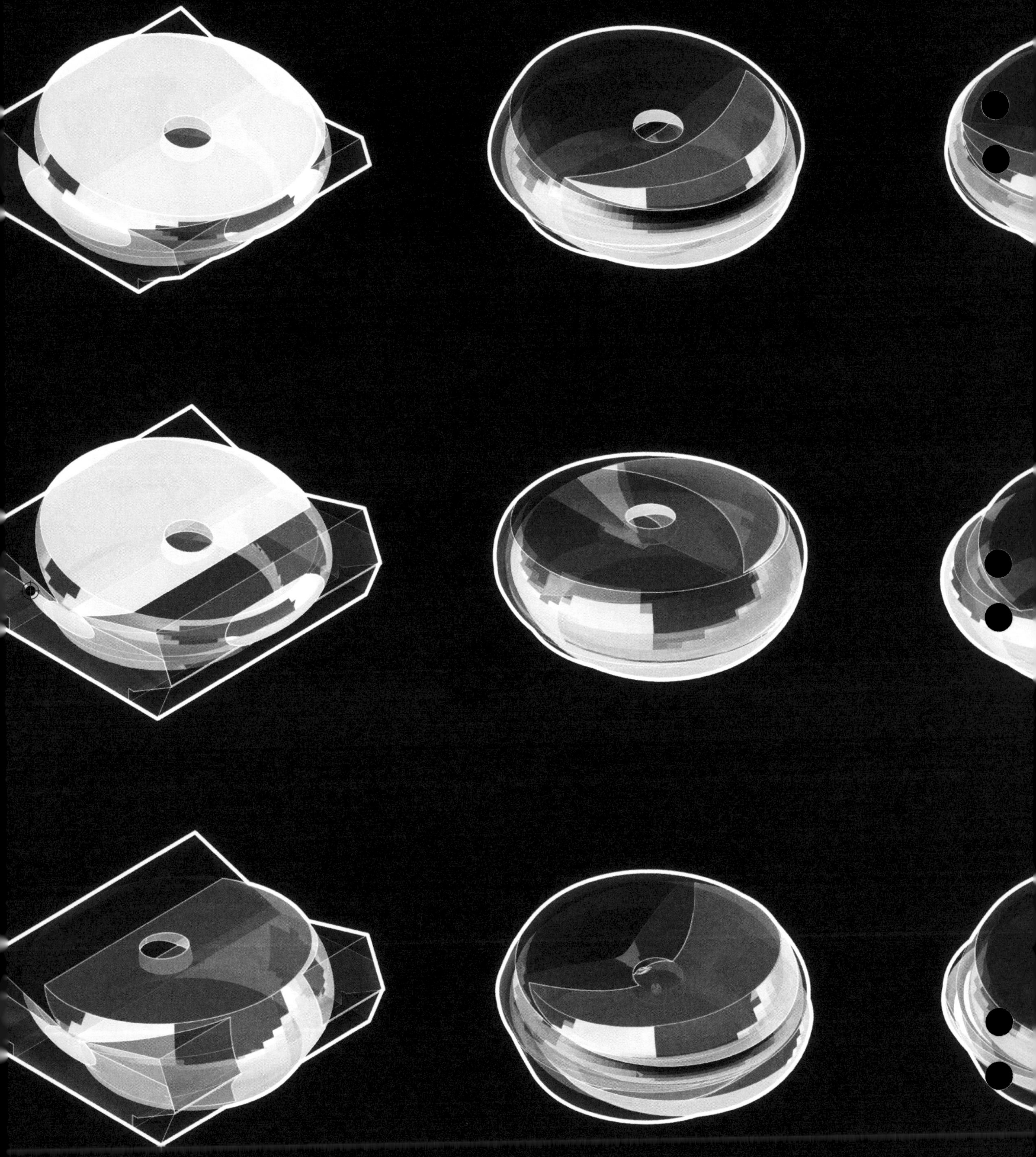

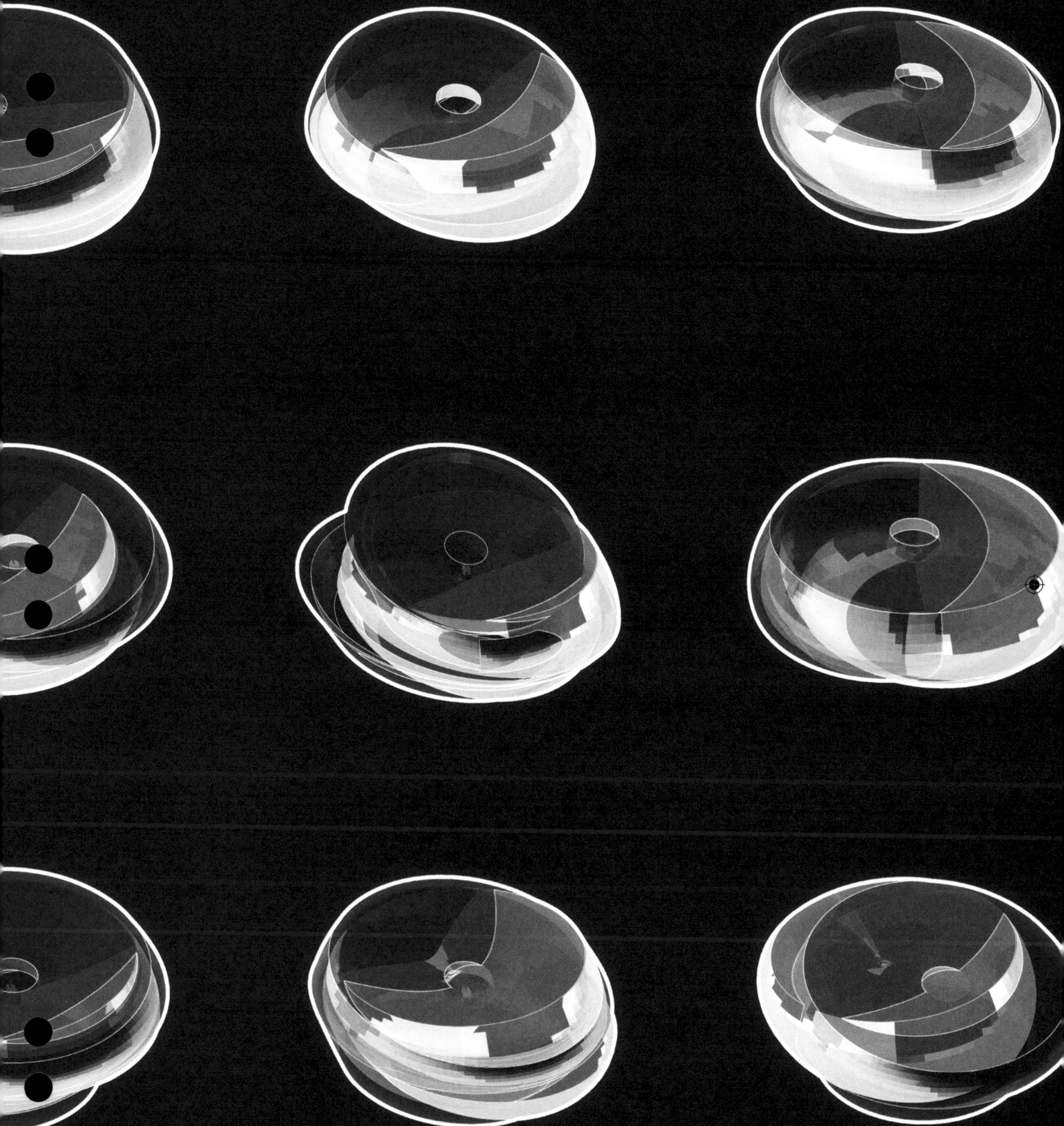

华东院

SO.104-105

The Asian Games are held every four years in the even years between the Olympic Games. With 12,000 athletes competing, it is the largest sporting event worldwide. (https://inside.fei.org/fei/games/cont-reg-games/Asian)

SO.106

SO.107

SO.108

SO.109

SO.110

SO.111-112

SO.113

SO.114

The 116-acre park serves as a "green lung," which acts in a similar manner as the urban tree canopy in a city like Chicago, where it has been measured to remove 15 metric tons of carbon monoxide, 84 metric tons of sulfur dioxide, 89 metric tons of nitrogen dioxide, 191 metric tons of ozone, and 212 metric tons of particulates annually, according to David Nowak, project leader of the U.S. Forest Service's Urban Forest Ecosystem Research Unit. (https://www.fs.fed.us/ne/newtown_square/news/NE_news/2002/articles/e_magazine_lung.pdf)

SO.115

China has been noted for its effort in adopting the Sponge City initiative. In 2015, China was reported to have begun a pilot initiative in 16 districts. The country plans for 80 percent of its cities to harvest and reuse 70 percent of rainwater. (https://en.wikipedia.org/wiki/Sponge_city)

SO.116

SO.117-119

SO.120

SO.121

SO.122

SO.123

SO.124-125

SO.126

SO.127-128

SO.129

SUSPENDOME

Long span space structures came into existence in the 1970s based on the discovery of new lightweight and high-strength materials such as steel. (https://benthamopen.com/)

SO.130-131

SO.132

SO.133

SO.134

SO.135

The pattern on the facade resembles fish scales. The term derives from the Old French *escale*, meaning a shell pod or husk. These protective scales provide camouflage through reflection and coloration, as well as hydrodynamic advantages. Scales also prevent the fish from becoming dehydrated. This "climate" aspect was extremely interesting to us.

SO.136-137

SO.138-139

SO.140

BIM

Building information modeling creates computer files (often but not always in proprietary formats and containing proprietary data) which can be extracted, exchanged or networked to support decision-making regarding a built asset. (https://en.wikipedia.org/wiki/Building_information_modeling)

SO.141

SO.142-143

SO.144-151

Structural engineer Thornton Tomasetti created a daringly large suspendome supported only on the inner dome and cantilevering out to the facade.

SO.152

SO.153

SO.154

SO.155-156

SO.157-158

SO.159

SO.160

SO.161

SO.162-163

SO.164

SO.165-166

SO.167

SO.168

SO.169

SO.170-171

SO.172

SO.173-174

In Latin, *vesica piscis* means "bladder of a fish," reflecting the shape's resemblance to conjoined dual air bladders. The vesica piscis appears in Euclid's *Elements*, where it forms the first step in constructing an equilateral triangle using a compass and straightedge. (https://en.wikipedia.org/wiki/Vesica_piscis)

SO.175-185

---

1 "Definition of potentiality". *Oxford University Press*. Lexico.com. 11 February 2021. https://www.lexico.com/definition/potentiality.

S.02
ANOMALIES

Anomaly: Something anomalous, a deviation from the common rule, type, arrangement, or form; something that strays from the usual method or arrangement.

oddity
peculiarity
abnormality
irregularity
inconsistency
incongruity
deviation
aberration
quirk
freak
exception
departure
divergence
variation
rarity
eccentricity [1]

1 Definition from Oxford languages

ANOMALOUS PARTS

In his 2016 book *Assemblage Theory*, Manuel DeLanda claims that almost everything in the universe is an assembly, a thing made of parts, and usually parts can be removed and substituted by sufficiently similar parts without changing the basic character of the object. Gilles Deleuze defined assemblies as "a multiplicity which is made up of heterogeneous terms and which establishes liaisons, relations between them, across ages, sexes and reigns—different natures. Thus the assemblage's only unity is that of co-functioning: it is a symbiosis, a 'sympathy'."[2] It is crucial to DeLanda's theory that the part-to-whole relation

2 Gilles Deleuze and Claire Parnet, *Dialogues II* (New York: Columbia University Press, 2002), 69.

is a continuum, and that not only alliances, but, more importantly, contagions are formed.

The anomaly here is seen that "contagion" but also picks up on Deleuze's notion of sympathy: we claim the Anomaly as a symbiotic system of a standard "normal" system with inserted strange objects. They form the 10 percent irregularity in the otherwise standard system; this non-standard is where the structure's identity is found, its intelligence and its performative aspects.

THE PRECISE FIT

While still unusual in architecture, thinking in iterations and progressive optimization is common practice in industrial design, where innovation is considered the essential goal of the creative process. Architects often undervalue the techniques of industrial design: the meticulous fine-tuning of lines, curves, and edges in full-scale prototypes, the integration of innumerable parts and aggregates, and advanced material technologies and assembly methods. But architecture would greatly benefit from this approach, allowing for intense and radical change in design, detailing, and production processes. As the non-sequitur to the "standard," the Anomaly also constitutes a precise fit, be it as the "other" in the system. This is where innovation happens; qualities and characteristics of still undefined objects are discovered, and building character and identity emerges.

BREAKING THE RULES

The dependency on a singular, often legalistic relationship between architect and contractor has limited architecture's ability to adapt and innovate, and produced the building industry's tendency to resist change and the unknown. It also obscures the fundamentally collaborative and non-linear nature of the design process, in which architects, manufacturers, and contractors utilize teamwork and feedback loops to develop highly customized, efficient, and intelligent technologies and structures. As Jane Bennett suggests, a thing's "efficacy or agency depends on the collaboration, cooperation, or interactive interference of many bodies and forces."[3] The work presented here utilizes intelligent manufacturing to develop the project's smart components directly in a tight architect-manufacturer collaboration, with 1:1 prototypes in which engineering and detailing is further defined, and efficiency and pricing is optimized—all before the contractor is involved. The anomaly as component is not only "other" but also smarter and stranger.

3 Jane Bennett, "The Agency of Assemblages," in *Vibrant Matter: A Political Ecology of Things*, (Durham: Duke University Press, 2010), 21.

SIKI IM PAVILION

"Many accused her of being too little into fashion, but probably Amber is simply a result of this time, when the mixture of themes the 'interference' by other disciplines, is part of fashio Some wrote her a letter, oth sent her a postcard or just printed her name on a little piece of paper. In the last fe days, in Holland everyone is talking about Amber, as the insiders call her, or simply the 4th Arnhem Mode Biennale."

– Manuela Martorelli, *Vogue Italia*, 2011

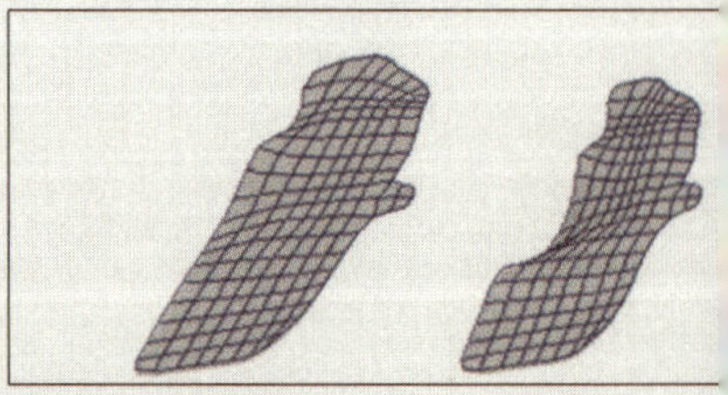

For the Dutch Arnhem Fashion Biennale "Amber," treated by its curator as a person, we were asked by fashion designer Siki Im to design the pavilion for his collection. Siki had been an Archi-Tectonics studio collaborator in the past, and as Winka is Dutch, the response was a fast "yes." Realizing the amazing congruity between fashion and architecture production methods, we asked Siki for his favorite article of clothing and its pattern as the originator for the design of the pavilion. Siki selected a men's blazer; its pattern was then morphologically transformed by us in the 3D Maya software into the pavilion concept.

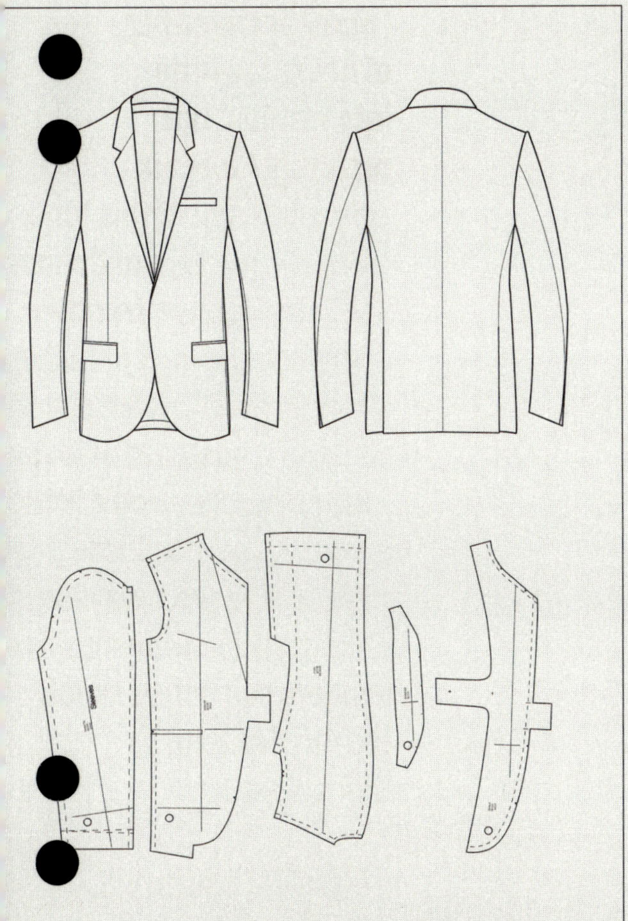

PATTERN MAKING: 2D DESIGN TO 3D GARMENT

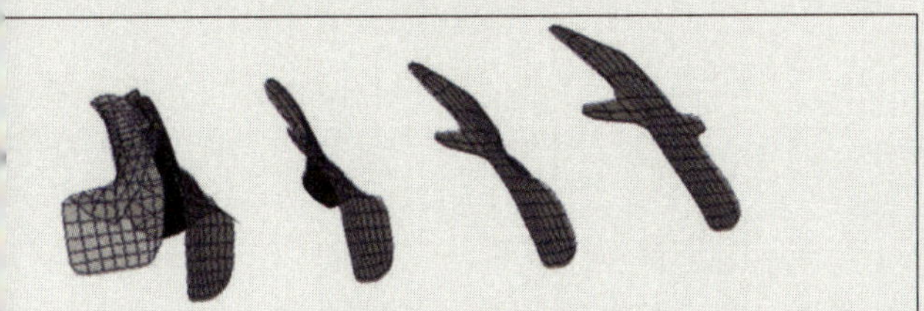

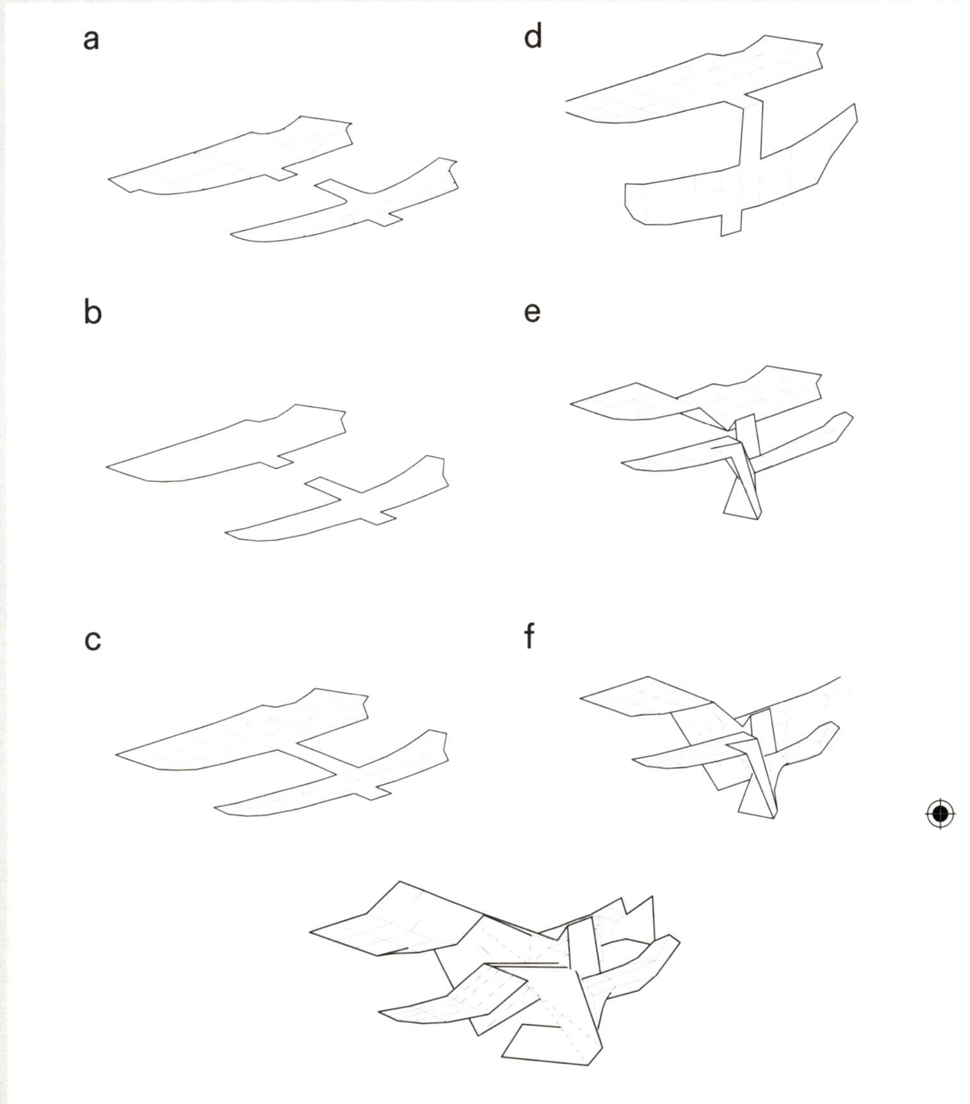

TRANSFORMATION: 3D MODELING IN MAYA

"The blazer is probably the most complex and most time-consuming garment of menswear. It has history and it has future. [...] Winka Dubbeldam and I wanted to create a physical space, which allows us to evoke intangible spaces. These spaces and emotions have the same sensibility and quality as I hope my collections provoke and inspire."
— Siki Im on the design of the pavilion.

By reversing the process of tailoring a blazer, we created components that were three-dimensional and together formed the pavilion, which literally enveloped the visitor as the jacket would. The arms formed separate elements that held the mannequins dressed with Siki's collection. The chosen material was Concrete Canvas, a concrete-impregnated fabric made in England and originally used in the 1970s to create bomb shelters. The pavilion provided seating in its canvas folds, incorporated a retro black and white monitor showing Siki's fashion show, and most importantly, offered a podium to display his collection. Its intense materiality, its excessive thick seams, and peculiar shape gave the pavilion its own "strange" character, making it stand out from all the other, much more aesthetic and "pretty" pavilions.

AN.07

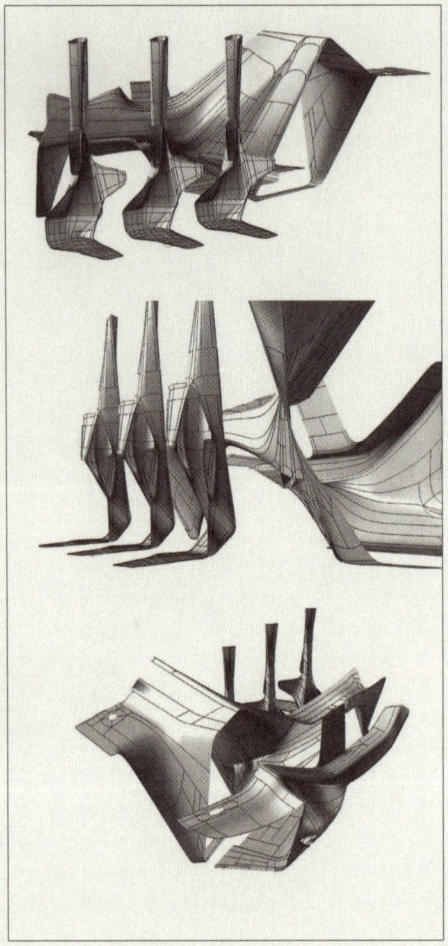

AN.08

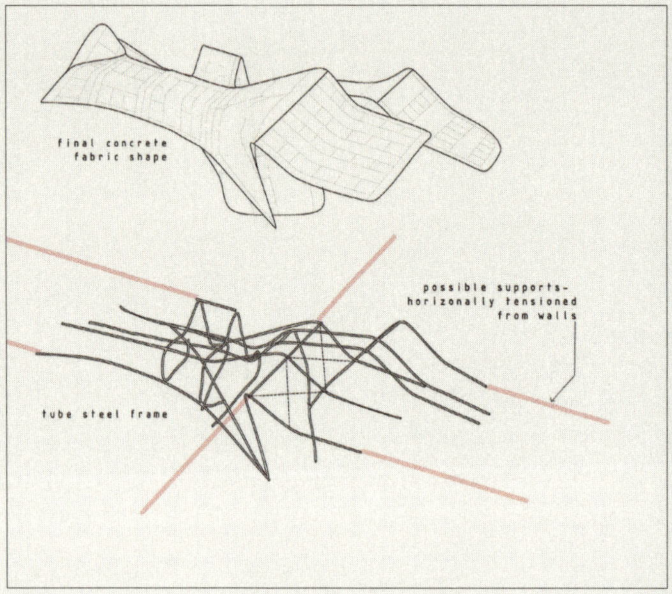

STRUCTURE IS TREATED LIKE A REBAR FRAME

AN.09

In the Dutch newspaper *NRC* (May 30, 2011), Georgette Koning noticed this "strange object," quoting the Mode Biennale's artistic director on the most memorable item in the show being our pavilion, "a monumental installation of concrete that you can walk in. In the 'jacket' you then hear sounds and you see [Siki Im's] fashion pieces on a small integrated monitor."

"The outside is not a fixed limit, but a moving matter animated by peristaltic movements, folds and foldings that together make up an inside: they are not something other than the outside, but precisely the inside of the outside."
— Gilles Deleuze, *Foucault*, "Foldings, or the Inside of Thought," trans. by S. Hand (Minneapolis: University of Minnesota Press, 1988).

AN.10

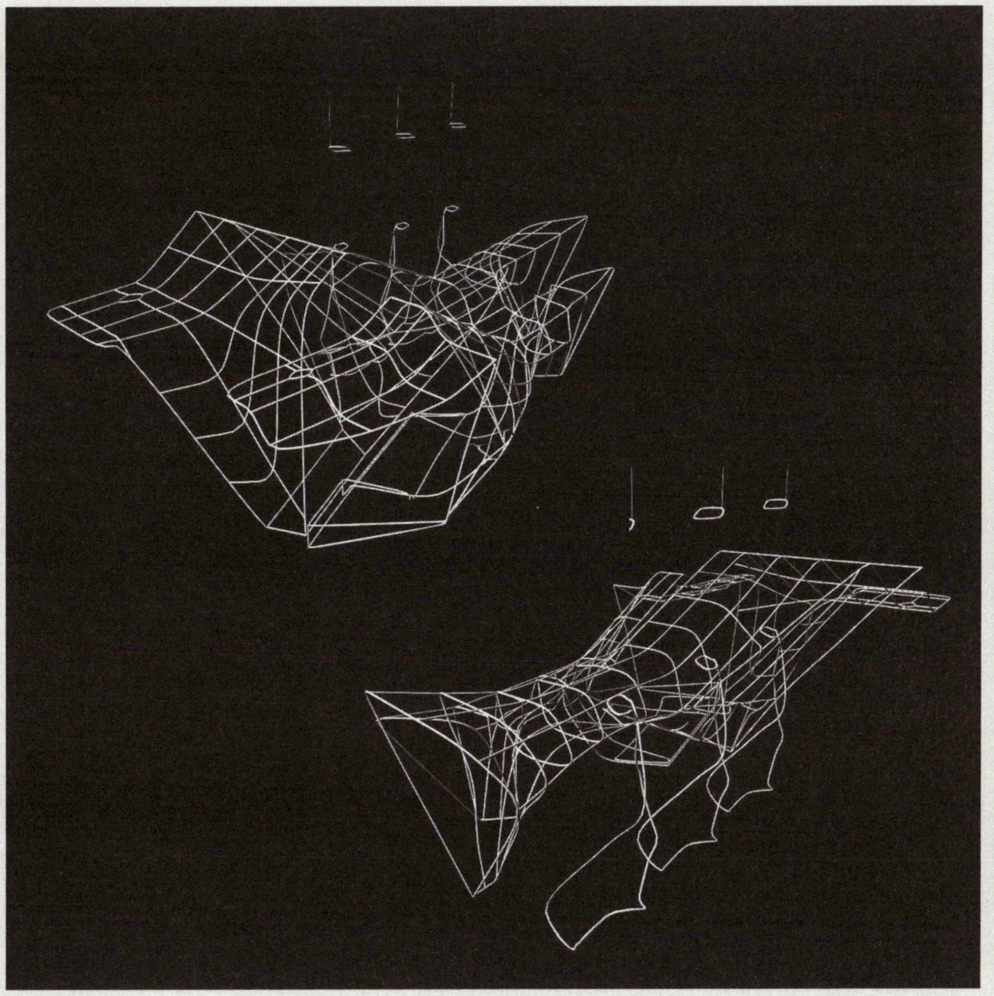

AN.11

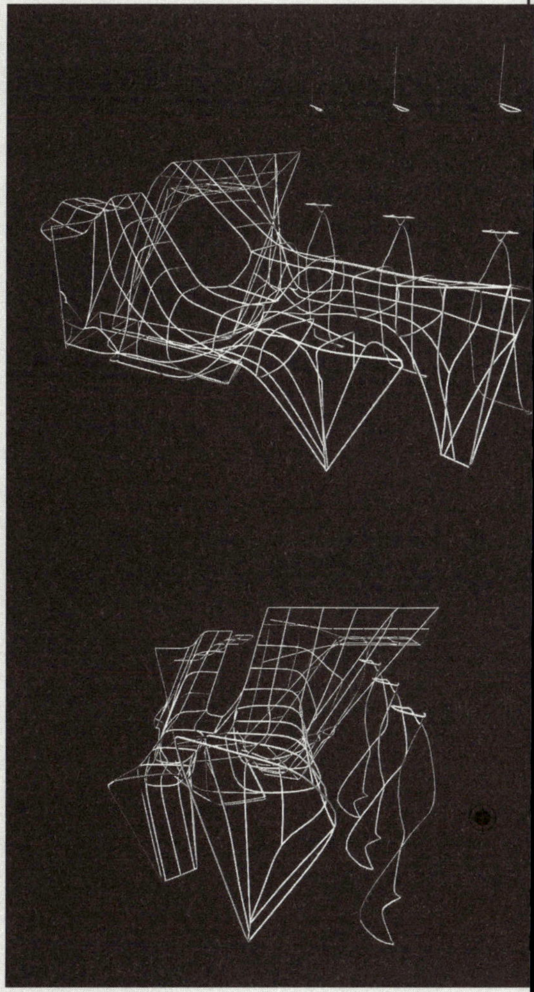

DECONSTRUCTED BLAZER

Why the blazer pattern, rather than a more abstract design? Siki Im stated:

"The tailored blazer best illustrates the full dichotomy of my design process, which rests between humanity and science, old and new, solidity and openness. Fashion is not just about garments. It is not just tangible and purchasable but often vague, imaginary, emotional, and sometimes trivial. Architecture is the same: it is not just about mere buildings or physical space but always describes an emotional, psychological, political, and spiritual space—our space. I collaborated with Winka Dubbeldam from Archi-Tectonics to create a physical space, which gives room to several intangible spaces. We dismounted my blazer design and reversed the process until we arrived at the beginning stage: patternmaking... The architecture of the fold creates a blur by questioning the inside and outside, the solid and void, the public and private, you and me."

AN.15

iki im
3/28/11
Hide
SI
e:
o: JOFF
c:
harlie
hris
wan Meijerink
inka

joff,

kewise!
eat news about the discount.
i talked to winka and they already experimented with the concrete canvas. it is very
ard and stiff. so it might be you dont really need a totally structured steel
onctruction. we could also hand certain parts with steel cables.

is great that you will get some samples and then you can see yourself. winka will
end more section drawings to make the shapes more readible. can you maybe talk to
structural engineer maybe?

so we dont mind to be a bit experimental. we could get some great happy accidents.

est,
ki

KI IM DIO LLC
GREE EET 2F NEW YORK NY 10013 WWW.SIKIIM.COM E: T: +
F:

PAVILION CONSTRUCTION

The two-dimensional pattern of the blazer was transformed into three-dimensional shapes in Maya to start creating the pavilion.

We looked for a construction material reminiscent of fashion and of a fabric. We contacted Concrete Canvas, a company based in the United Kingdom that produces concrete impregnated ½-inch thick fabric.

AN.16

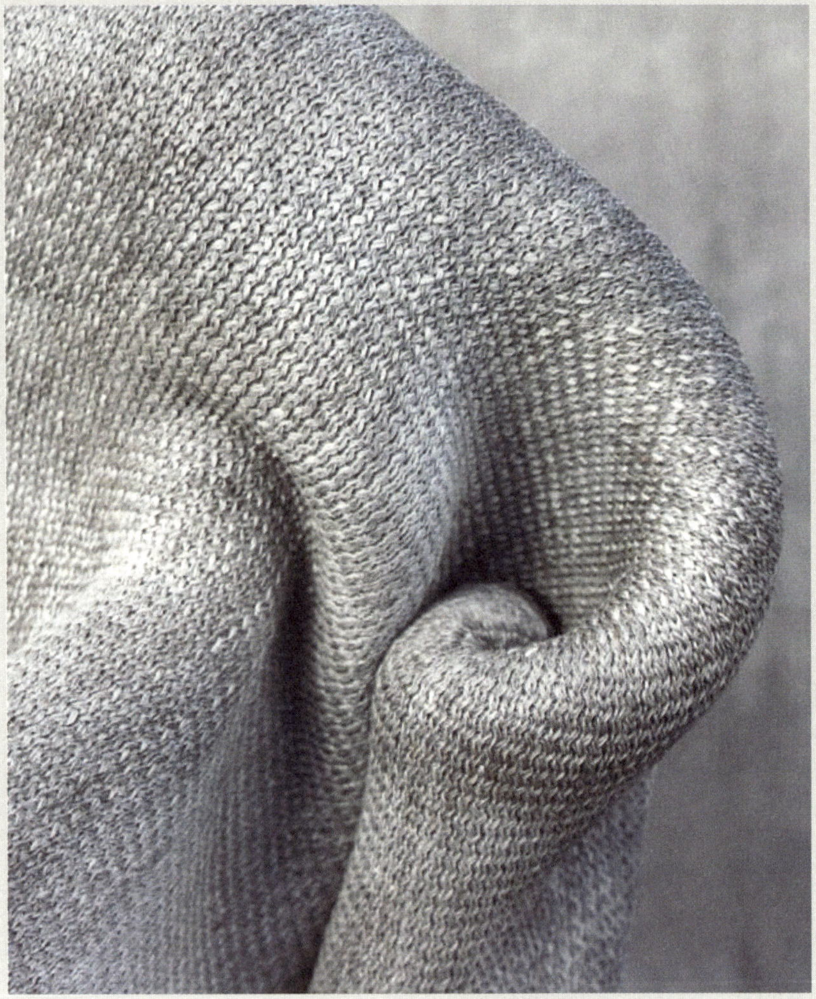

AN.17

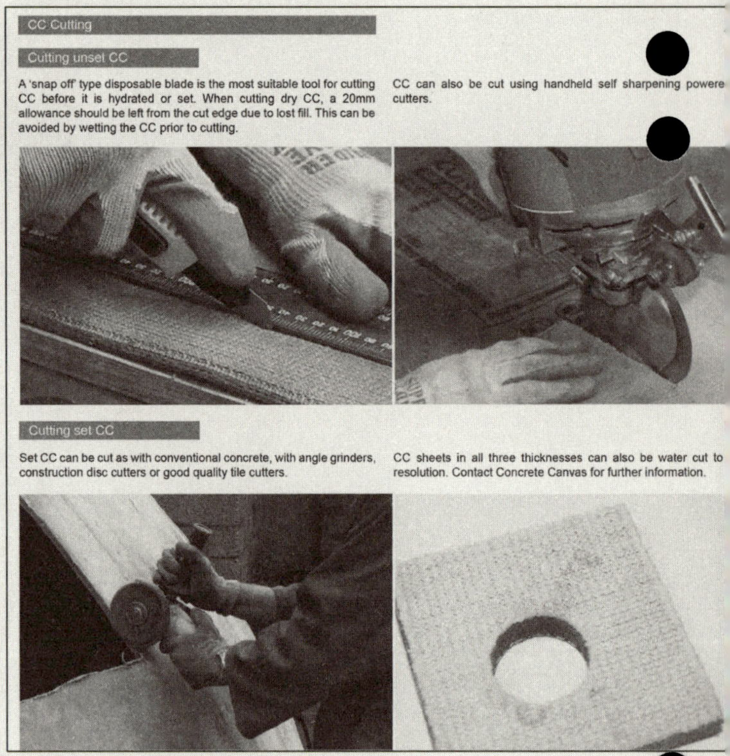

CC Cutting

Cutting unset CC

A 'snap off' type disposable blade is the most suitable tool for cutting CC before it is hydrated or set. When cutting dry CC, a 20mm allowance should be left from the cut edge due to lost fill. This can be avoided by wetting the CC prior to cutting.

CC can also be cut using handheld self sharpening powere cutters.

Cutting set CC

Set CC can be cut as with conventional concrete, with angle grinders, construction disc cutters or good quality tile cutters.

CC sheets in all three thicknesses can also be water cut to resolution. Contact Concrete Canvas for further information.

CONCRETE CANVAS MANUAL

DEPLOYABLE SHELTERS

Among other uses, the material was historically marketed as ideal for bomb shelters, which could be deployed by two people in under 24 hours, making the material optimal to provide quick defense in your own garden! While once a popular construction, DIY bomb shelters have lost momentum and hence the company turned to other potential uses, such as retaining walls. After hearing about the possible use for the fashion pavilion, the Concrete Canvas company was extremely interested in collaborating, as architects could be another new market for their product. They were happy to sponsor the pavilion, donating the concrete cloth mostly pro-bono.

AN.18-19

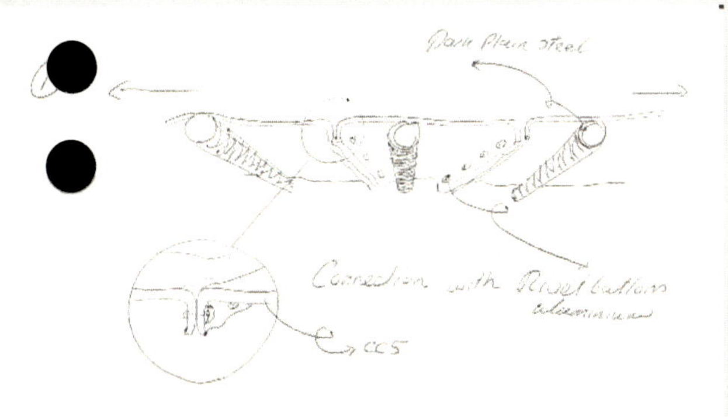

he Concrete Canvas cures in the shape of the inflated inner and 24 ours later the structure is ready to use. Access holes can be cut to low the installation of services.

AN.20

AN.21

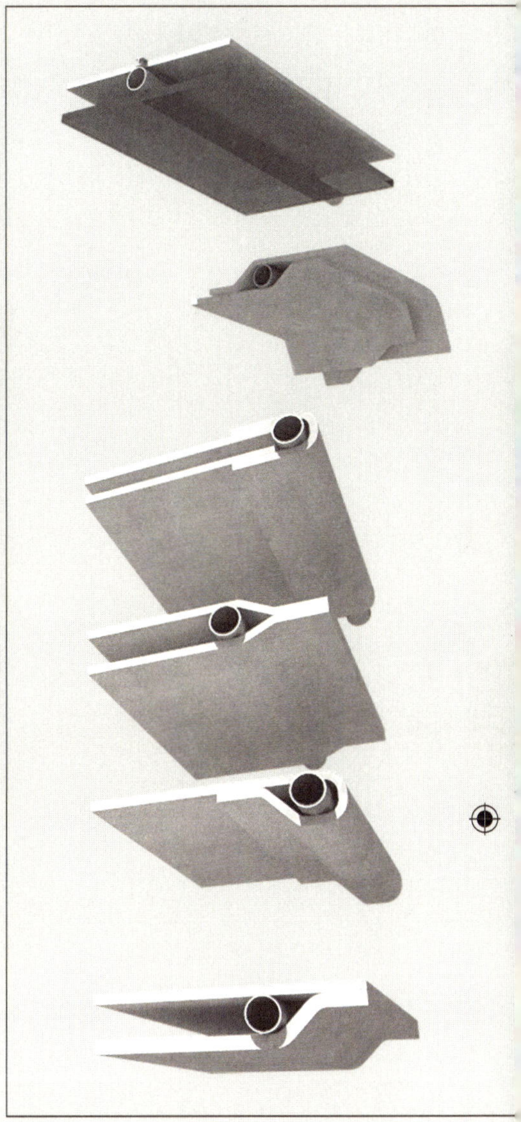

MANUAL OF SEAMS

SEAMING / AGENCY

With the unusual and heavy building material of Concrete Canvas, it was challenging to find a contractor who would take on the construction of the dynamic pavilion shape. Ultimately, the Amber organizers hired an extremely capable sculptor, who was willing to take on the challenge. Extremely relieved to find a collaborator, it seemed crucial to rethink the process. The installer was given agency and control in the construction process. Rather than providing him with traditional construction details, we developed a manual of "seam typologies." The fabricator was provided with a choice of five different seaming options, different methods for the fabric's seam connections, and he was free to use whichever option he felt was most appropriate for each particular connection.

AN.22

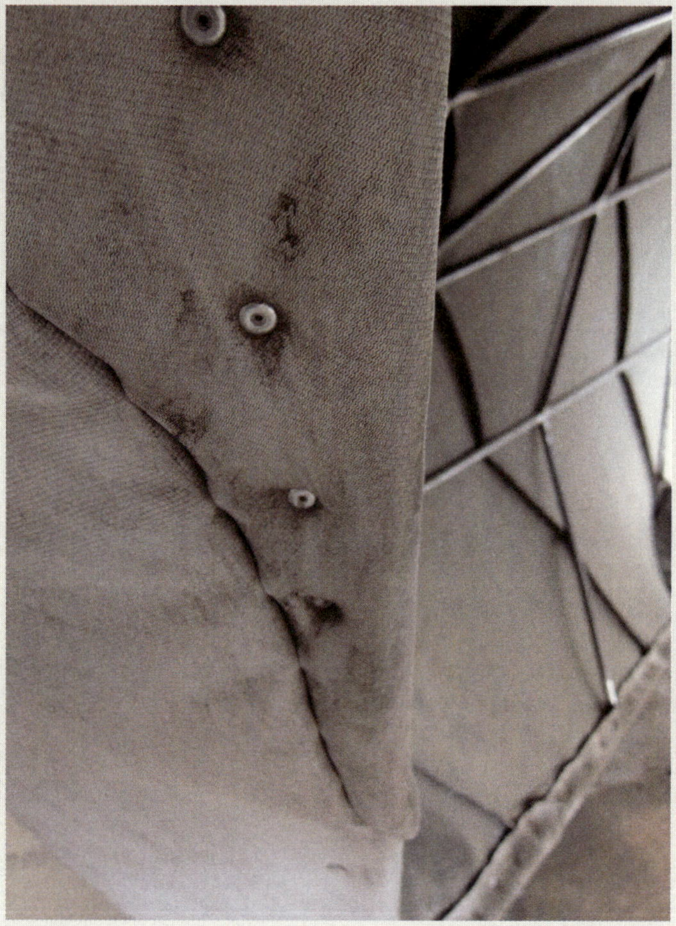

AN.23

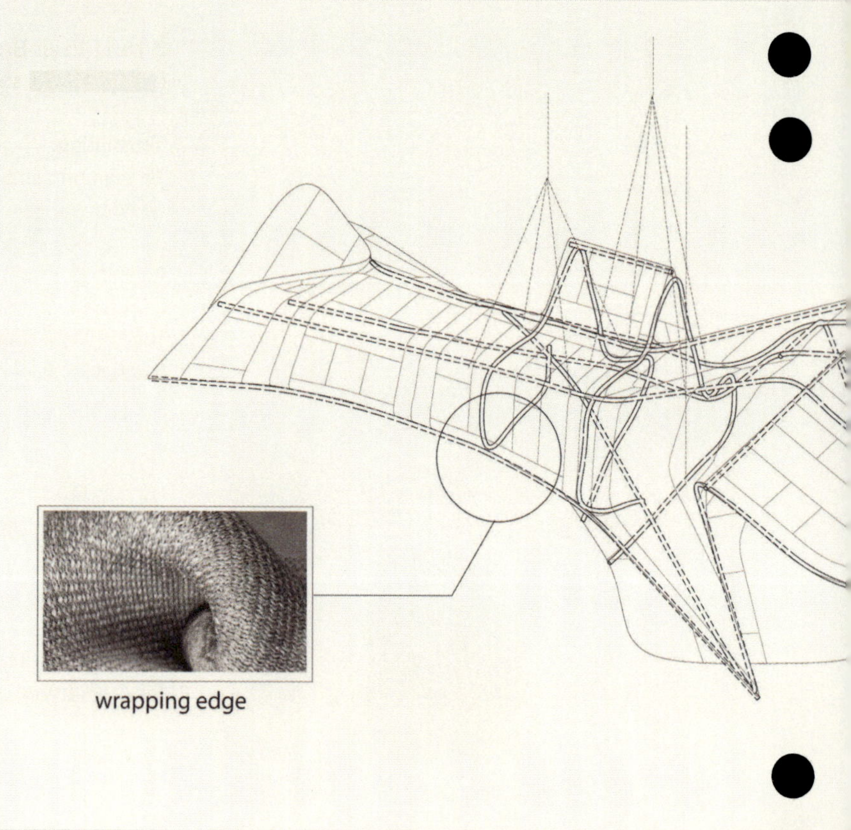

AN.24

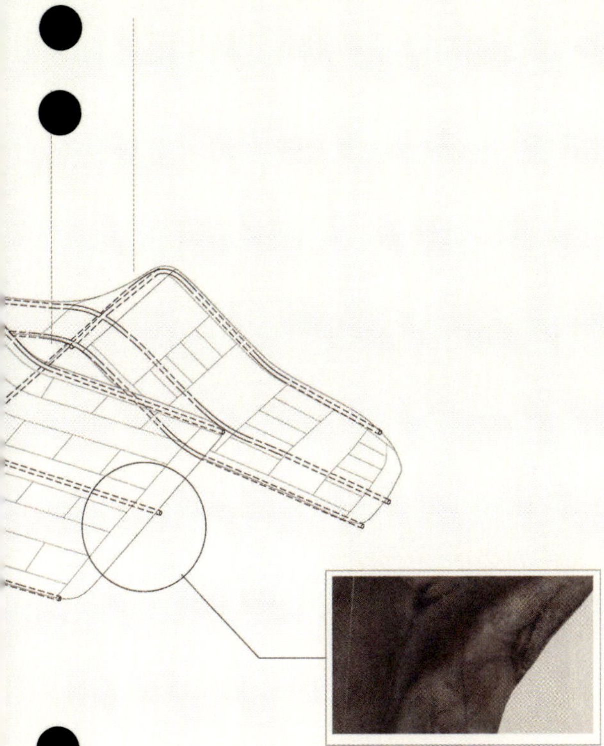

straight cut

2/16/11 Peter Brewin at CC +44 144 384 19 84
(Peter Brewin states that these are simply suggestions, not him nor CC have any liability)

Tensioning:
To maintain straight planar form, canvas can be tensioned before wetting. To tension, two wooden battons are screwed together at the end 25mm. of the CC strip (one on bottom, one on top). Tension with ropes/cables. Wet while tensioned, let dry for 3 days while tensioned. Then cut the end 25mm off.

With any thickness material (5mm, 8mm, 13mm), 1m span should be good between structural frame members (if not cantilevered).

With 5mm CC, all framing should be left in.

Tensioning will always have at least a very small parabolic curvature, but to make a perfectly flat, wetted CC should be placed on a negative formwork. In past, expanded polystyrene (white foam) has be CNC milled.

Seams:
For seams, Stitching to taping is suggested because "hog-rings" are very industrial (used for ditch-lining).

Surfaces:
CC has two surfaces, a concrete fabric surface and a PVC surface. To make both sides concrete, must be double layers
(future correspondence, ask about possible removal of PVC surface)

To create concrete texture on underside:
To create concrete texture on underside, it would have to set in place after drying. CC must be wetted with concrete fabric surface up (PVC down), or with it vertical (note: proper saturation is needed).
Another option is that CC can be wet in a tub/pool, and then set into place (within a 1 hour working time).

EFFICIENCY / LOW WASTE

Temporary pavilions have a history of producing construction waste near that of permanent structures. In the case of the Siki Im Pavilion, however, the rapid construction process of the Concrete Canvas entailed minimal waste, low-cost of installation, and a highly customizable surface. It serves as one of the more unusual examples of our efforts to promote sustainable building practices. Typically, ten times faster to install than conventional concrete solutions, Concrete Canvas is essentially concrete on a roll.

Concrete Canvas is a flexible fabric that hardens when hydrated. Although water dependent, Concrete Canvas is also waterproof. Hydrophilic fibers line one side of the cloth and draw water into the concrete mixture so that the cloth transforms into a solid and hard surface.

AN.25

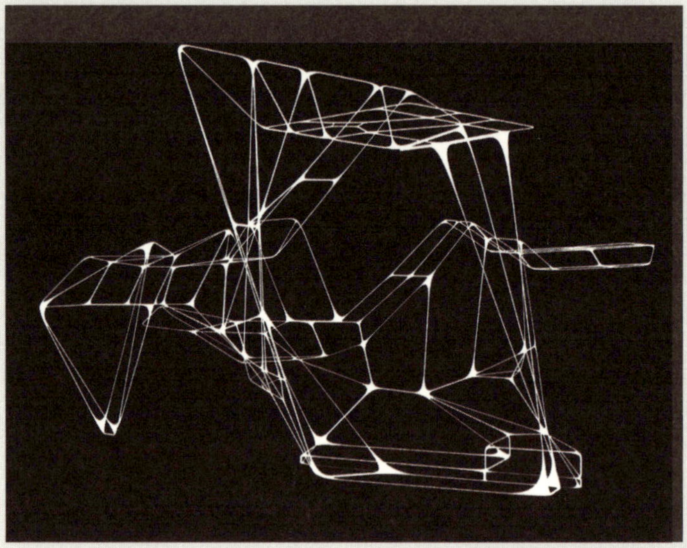

A GRID-SHAPED SYSTEM OF REBAR CREATES THE OBJECT OUTLINE

AN.26

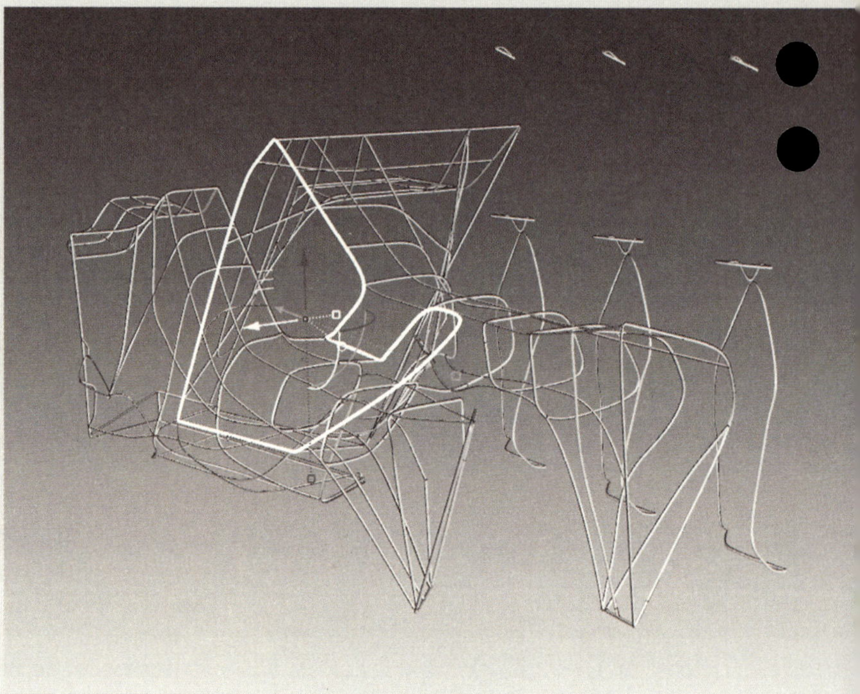

REBAR VERSUS COLUMN

Thinking about the erection of the heavy concrete cloth, we developed a new structural support system for the concrete-impregnated fabric. Rather than a traditional structure of columns and beams, we developed a woven "rebar" frame, reminiscent of normal concrete installation. This woven frame would create the three-dimensional outline over which the concrete fabric could be folded. After the installation, the installer would simply spray the canvas with water and the Concrete Canvas hardens in a few hours to an ultra-thin, ½-inch structural shell.

AN.29

SITE INSTALLATION

AN.30

MATERIALITY AND INSTALLATION

As per the manual provided by Concrete Canvas, "CC shelters are rapidly deployable hardened shelters that require only water and air for construction," and, in our case, a few strong installers with protective gear, persistence and creativity. The manual continues, "essentially it's a building in a bag".

Just as conventional thick canvas, Concrete Canvas can be cut with scissors before installation. Once hardened, it can be cut with angle grinders, construction disc cutters, or good quality tile cutters.

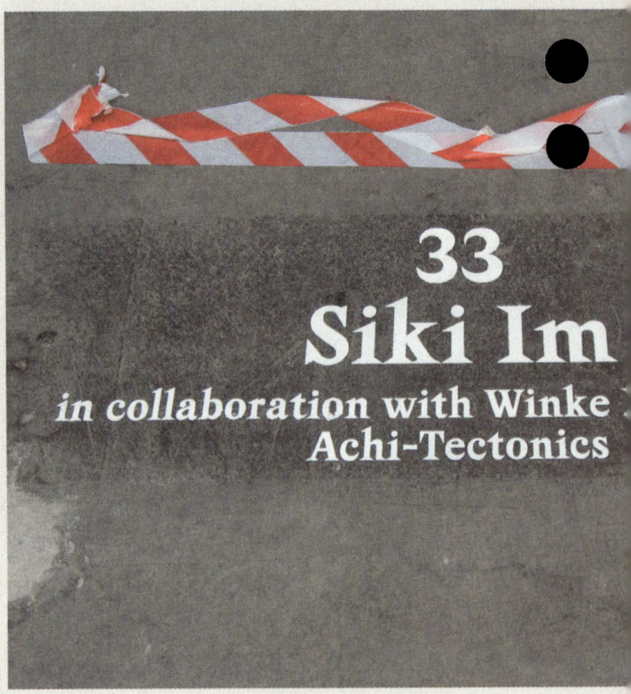

FASHION AND ARCHITECTURE

Manuela Martorelli from *Vogue Italia* noticed the connection between architecture and fashion in the pavilion:

"If the structures of the Dutch archistar Rem Koolhaas for Prada dominated the scene for their minimalism, the installation of the young designer Siki Im is striking for his architecture created from the deconstruction of a men's blazer pattern and made by concrete canvas—the material used mainly for refugee camps—designed in collaboration with Winka Dubbeldam.

The fact that Dubbeldam (of Dutch origins but living in the U.S.) studied at Columbia University when Bernard Tschumi was Dean and later on she did work for him and for another pillar of contemporary architecture, Peter Eisenman, says everything about Siki Im's background, who was a part of Dubbeldam's team before becoming a fashion designer."

AN.34

WHAT IS THIS THING?

AN.35

STRANGE OBJECT; STRANGE ATTRACTION

AN.36

AN.37

AN.38

AN.39

THE GAZE

AFFECT / WAR MACHINE

With its historical connection to bomb shelters and its alien and somewhat gloomy atmosphere, the pavilion resembled for many a "war machine." The Biennale's organizers, however, declared the pavilion their favorite, and affectionately named it the "Cuddly Elephant," because of its unusual texture, delicate folds, and its soft, smooth gray skin. Several visitors were found touching, stroking, and even sniffing its delicate curves. The pavilion's alien character was developed through a set of unusual decisions; to start with the process of taking a two-dimensional fashion pattern, inflating it to 3D in Maya, and building it from Concrete Canvas. This design method is dependent on the decision to aim for invention rather than aesthetics, and the appreciation for the unusual or even the ugly and the inappropriate. Peter Eisenman's notion of "affect" explains this same outcome—he aims to give priority to the experiential or perceptual in the finished product at the expense of the conceptual origin. The Biennale's visitor's behavior of touching the pavilion seems a clear indicator of this affect or strange character.

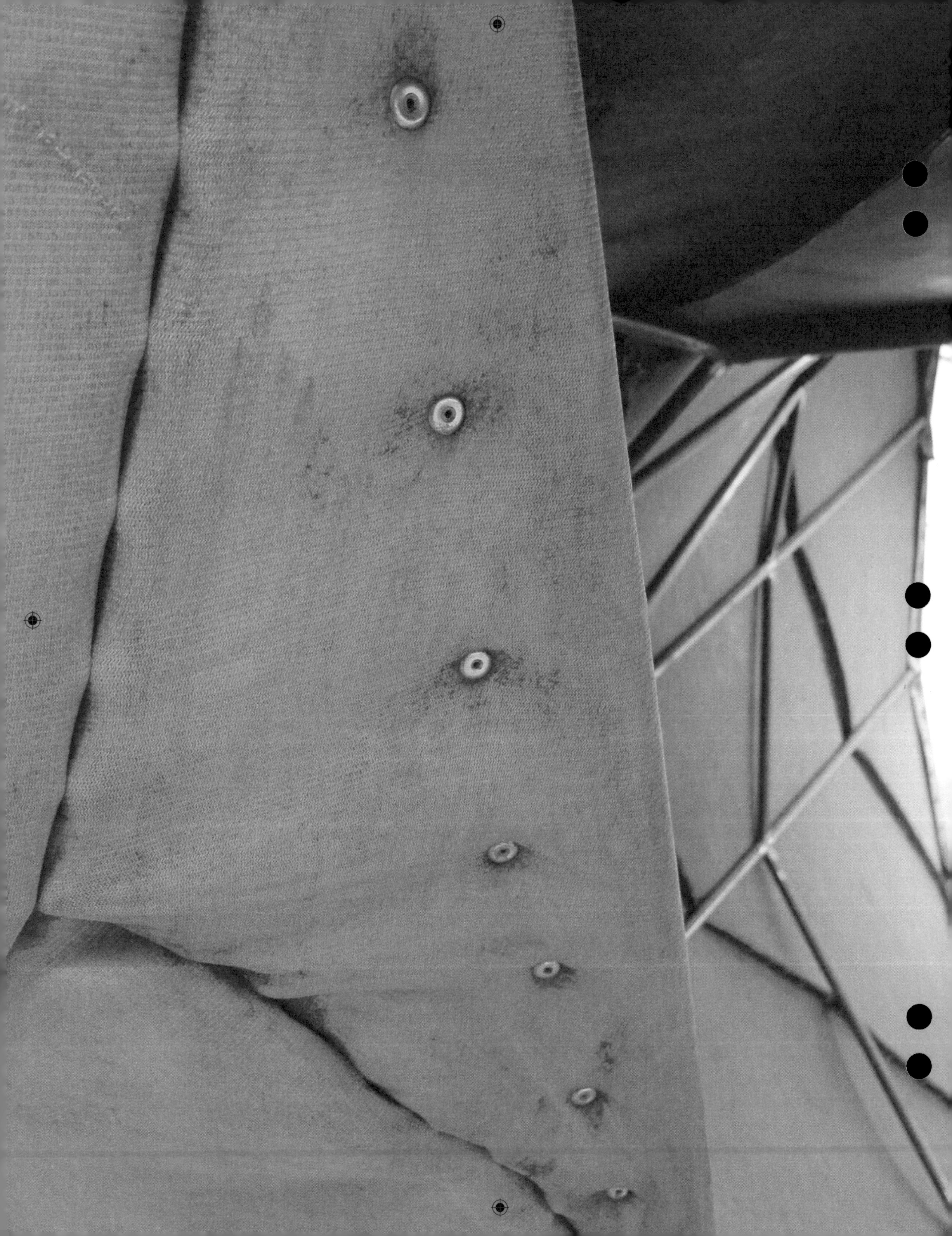

AN.02

AN.03-04

AN.05

"A pattern is the template from which the parts of a garment are traced onto fabric before being cut out and assembled [...] The making of industrial patterns begins with an existing block pattern that most closely resembles the designer's vision. Patterns are cut of oak-tag (manila folder) paper, punched with a hole and stored by hanging with a special hook." (https://en.wikipedia.org/wiki/Pattern_(sewing))

AN.06

AN.07

AN.08

AN.09

AN.10

AN.11

AN.12

AN.13-14

AN.15

AN.16

AN.17

AN.18

"What Are CC Shelters?

CC Shelters (CCS) use inflation to create a surface that is optimised for compressive loading. This allows thin-walled concrete structures to be formed which are both robust and lightweight. CCS are constructed from Concrete Canvas CC13, bonded to the outer surface of a plastic inner. Once inflated, it which forms a Nissen-Hut shaped structure. CCS are deployed in four stages: delivery, inflation, hydration and setting." (https://www.concretecanvas.com/cc-shelters/)

AN.19

AN.20

AN.21

A manual is a book of instructions, especially for operating a machine or learning a subject; a handbook. Here created to give builders "agency," a choice of seams for them to choose from.

AN.22

AN.23

AN.24

Email from Concrete Canvas with erection instructions. The pavilion was assembled by a sculptor rather than a contractor in the end.

AN.25

AN.26

AN.27

AN.28

AN.29

Concrete CANVAS consists of a 3-dimensional fiber matrix containing a specially formulated dry Concrete mix that hardens when hydrated to form a thin, durable concrete layer.

AN.30

Due to the dusty aspect of the concrete impregnated fabric, the workers wore hazmat suits (hazardous materials suits) a piece of personal protective equipment that consists of an impermeable whole-body garment worn as protection.

AN.31

AN.32

AN.33

AN.34

AN.35

AN.36

AN.37

AN.38

"In critical theory, sociology, and psychoanalysis, the gaze, in the philosophical and figurative sense, is an individual's awareness and perception of other individuals, other groups, or oneself." (https://en.wikipedia.org/wiki/Gaze). Here at "Amber" people were fascinated by this unusual creature and its peculiar texture and material presence.

AN.39

AN.40

AN.41

Siki watching his video. Born in Cologne, Germany, Siki Im moved to the U.K. and studied architecture at the Oxford School of Architecture. After working as an architect, he started his fashion career in New York City and was Senior Designer for Karl Lagerfeld and Helmut Lang. In September 2009, Im introduced his first solo collection and subsequently won the Ecco Domani award for Best Menswear in 2010. The following year, he was awarded with the Samsung Design & Fashion Fund and in 2015, he received the Vilcek Prize.

AN.42

AN.43-47

BLAAK TOWER

STIBNITE

Named after the Latin *stibium*, the old name of the element antimony (Sb), a stibnite is one of the most exceptional natural crystals, typically formed into sharp prismatic clusters. Centuries ago, antimony compounds were powdered for use as medicine and cosmetics, often known by the Arabic name kohl. In the West, the earliest known description of the metal is found in a book from 1540 by Italian metallurgist Vannoccio Biringuccio.

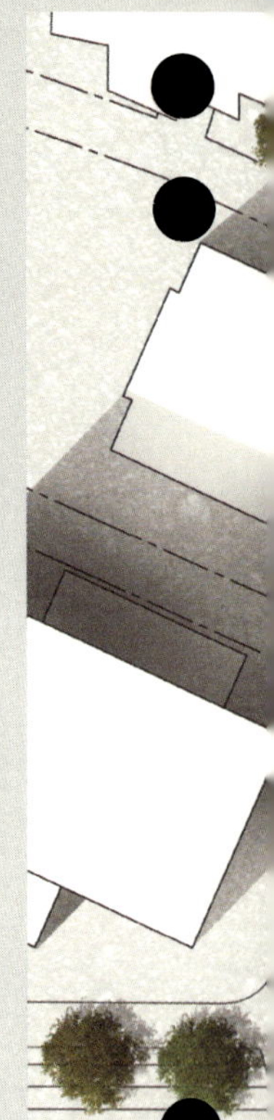

STIBNITE FORMATIONS / THE TOWER AS CITY

For the 200-meter tall Blaak Tower in Rotterdam, the Netherlands, we looked at the self-referential shapes of stibnite formations. These crystalline solids form spontaneously and result in unique forms, despite originating from identical systems. Stibnites are categorized as *orthorhombic* crystals, belonging to one of seven crystal systems.

The tower's slanted, striated surfaces are designed to follow a self-similar formation system

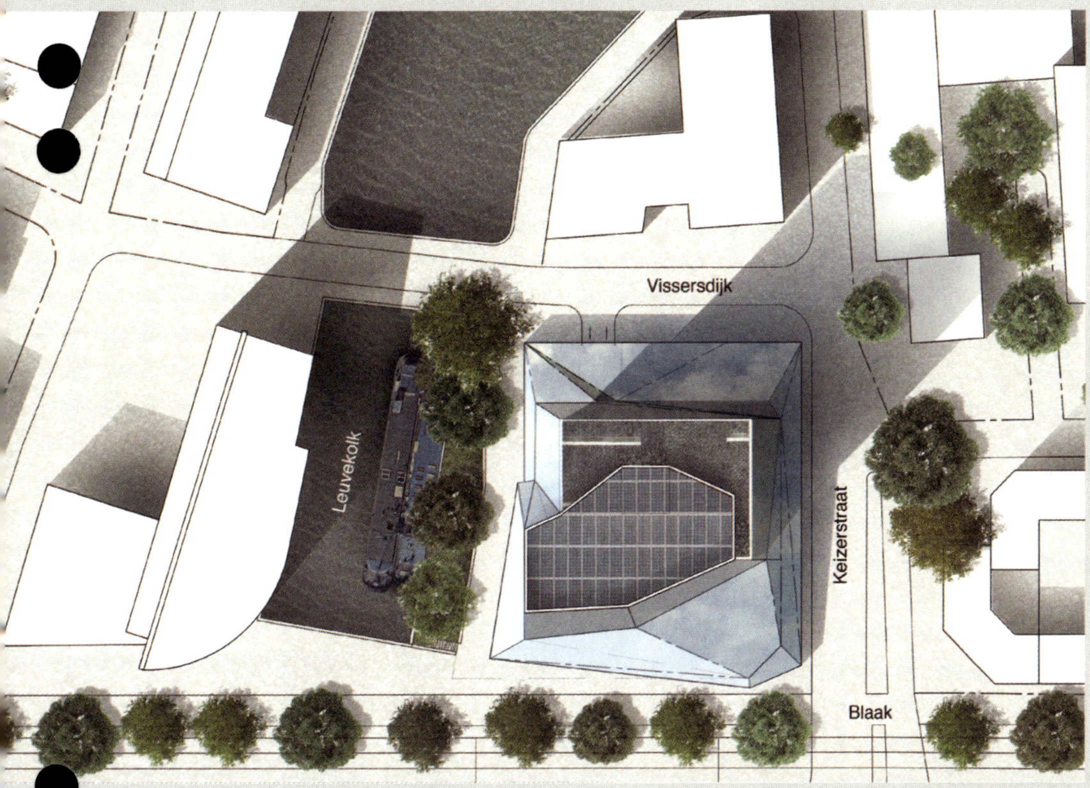

SITE: BLAAK, ROTTERDAM, THE NETHERLANDS

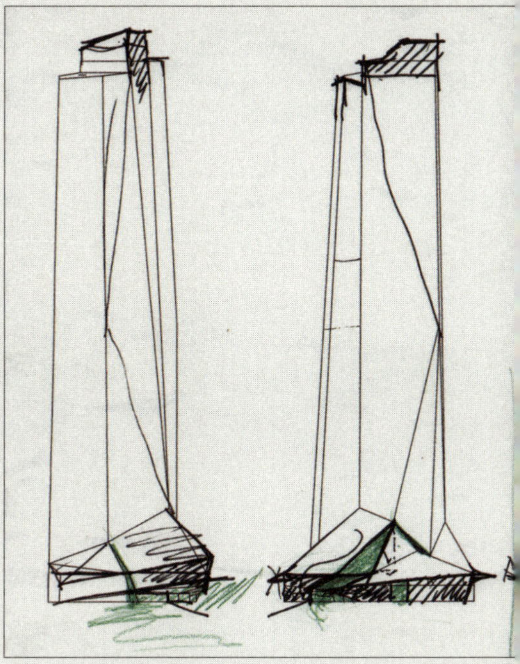

EXTENDED GROUND FLOOR

with a clear logic, while allowing for "anomalies." These anomalies are inserted in the tower's surfaces as fragmented glass crystals with glass striations connecting them. The Blaak Tower holds a mixed-use community of retail, hotel, and residences. It was designed to blur the boundary of public and private spaces through the introduction of a crystalline tapered "skirt" that creates a mix of retail and hospitality spaces on the tower's lower floors, and public skylobbies on the higher levels. The crystalline lobby connects via a solar chimney to the upper green skylobbies, creating a microclimate that tempers and cools the environment and reduces the building's energy use. The resultant energy-efficient and self-sufficient tower creates its own biome and microclimate, which is expressed in its unique elongated crystalline shape.

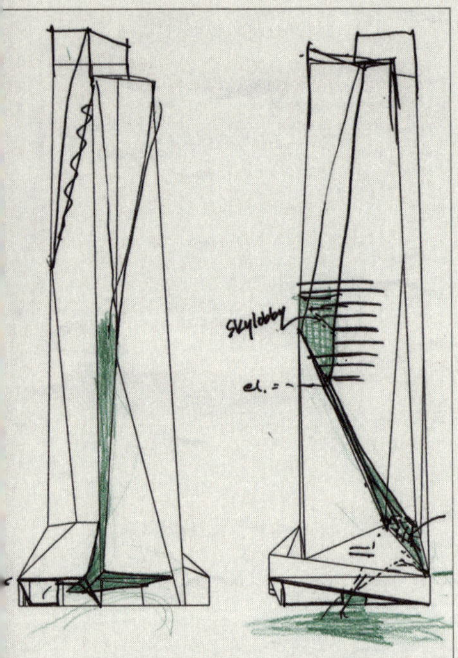

AN.52

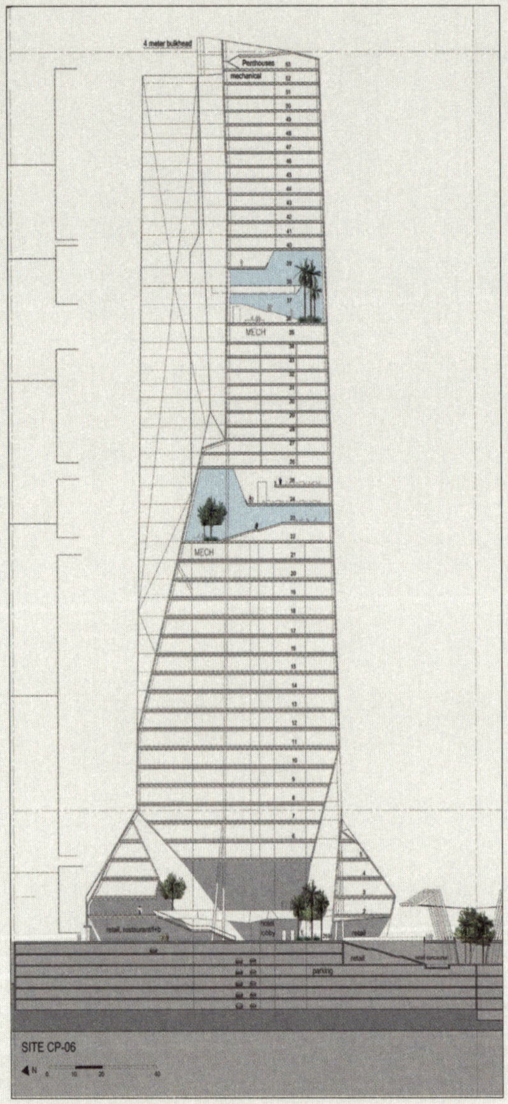

AN.53

SKYLOBBY

The Blaak Tower is an object with built-in variation; the crystalline skylobbies create a 15 percent anomaly in an otherwise simple, structurally glazed curtain wall clad tower. Typically, skylobbies are intermediate interchange floors where people can change from an express elevator that stops only at the skylobby to a local elevator which stops at every floor within a segment of the tower. In the Blaak Tower, however, the triple height skylobbies not only create public spaces—such as a gym, library, meeting rooms, and a restaurant—but also create "green lungs" for the tower, essentially cooling and ventilating the tower from the inside. To optimize the climatological effect of the slender slanted tower, frit patterns are optimized to respond to the orientation of the sun.

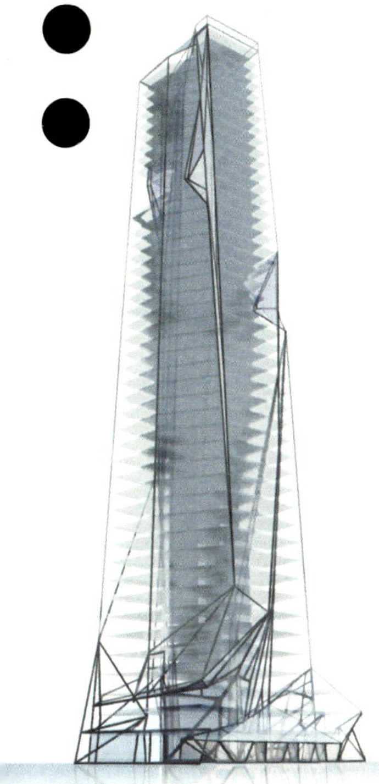

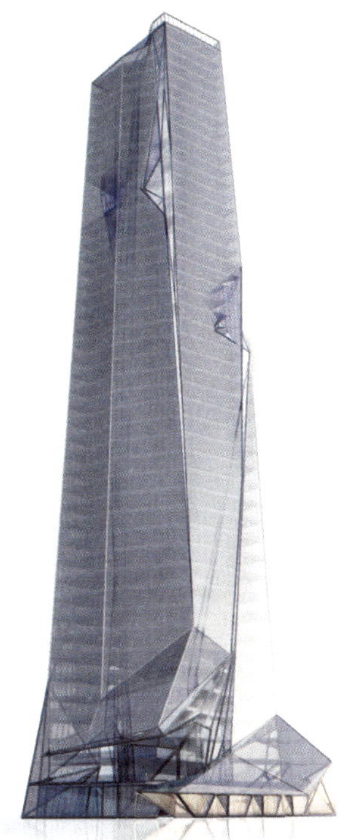

FACADE WITH 15% ANOMALY AS SKYLOBBIES

BREATHING TOWER / CLIMATE VEIL

The tower's silver frit pattern creates a "climate veil" on the tower's facade. The gradient varies from dense on the warmest to transparent on the coolest facades, thus reducing heat gain while still allowing unobstructed views. The tower's design aims to achieve LEED Silver and an estimated rating of at least 75. The combination of the solar chimney, green skylobbies, and the tower's operable windows allows for natural ventilation optimized to the predominantly west wind direction. Essentially, the building is a breathing tower.

AN.55

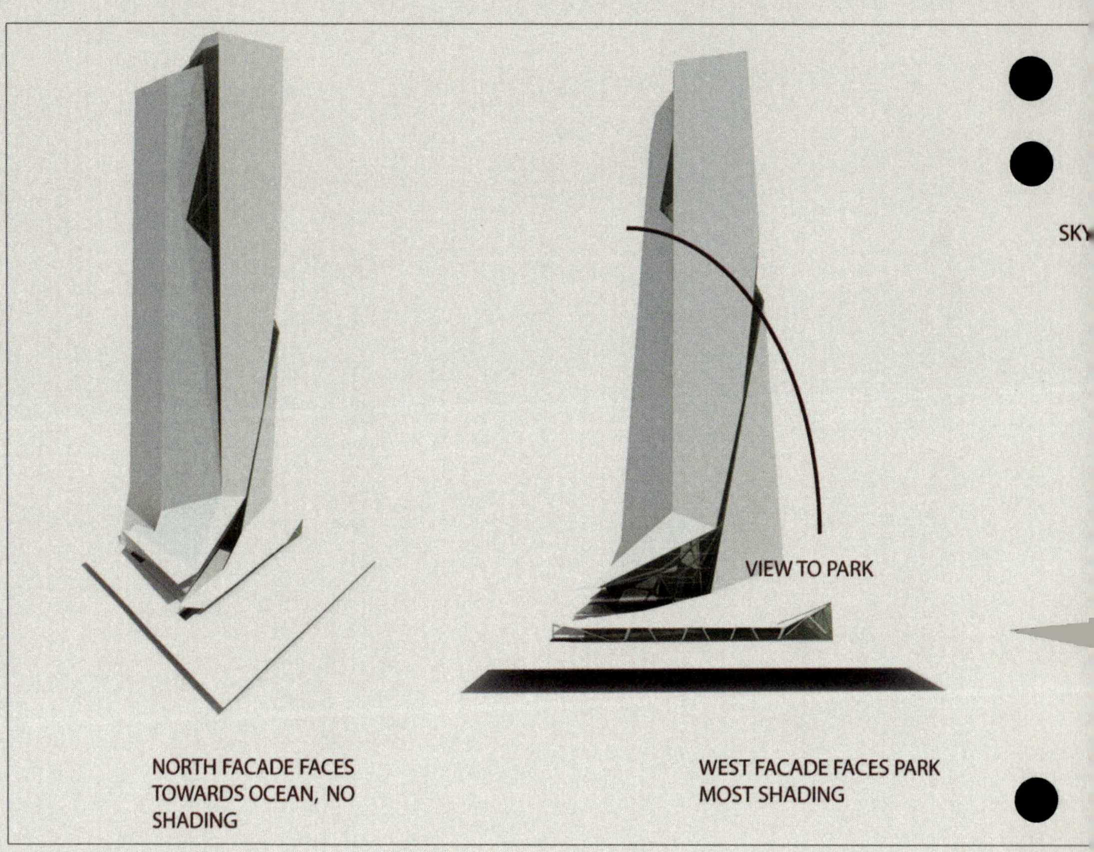

"Within the dazzling gemstone architecture, the interior design embraces the visitor in diaphanous veils of light and color. A rich collection of one-of-a-kind furnishings and luxurious finishes creates a comfortable oasis in the heart of a vibrant city. The expansive floor plan embraces the heritage of this island enclave, providing guests the opportunity to discover the mystery and mathematical beauty of the architectural details."
— Glenn Pushelberg, George Yabu

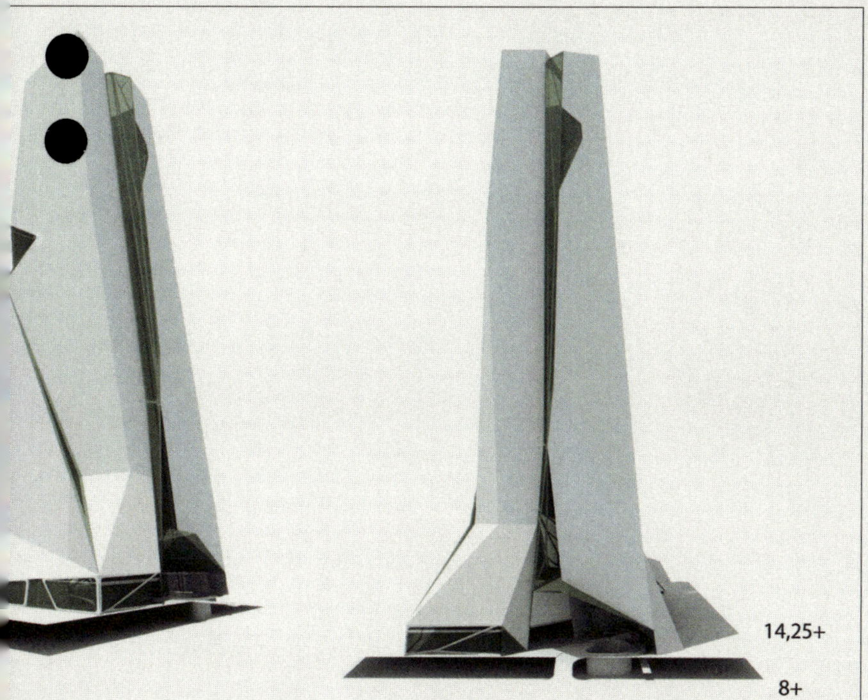

UTH FACADE LITTLE SHADING

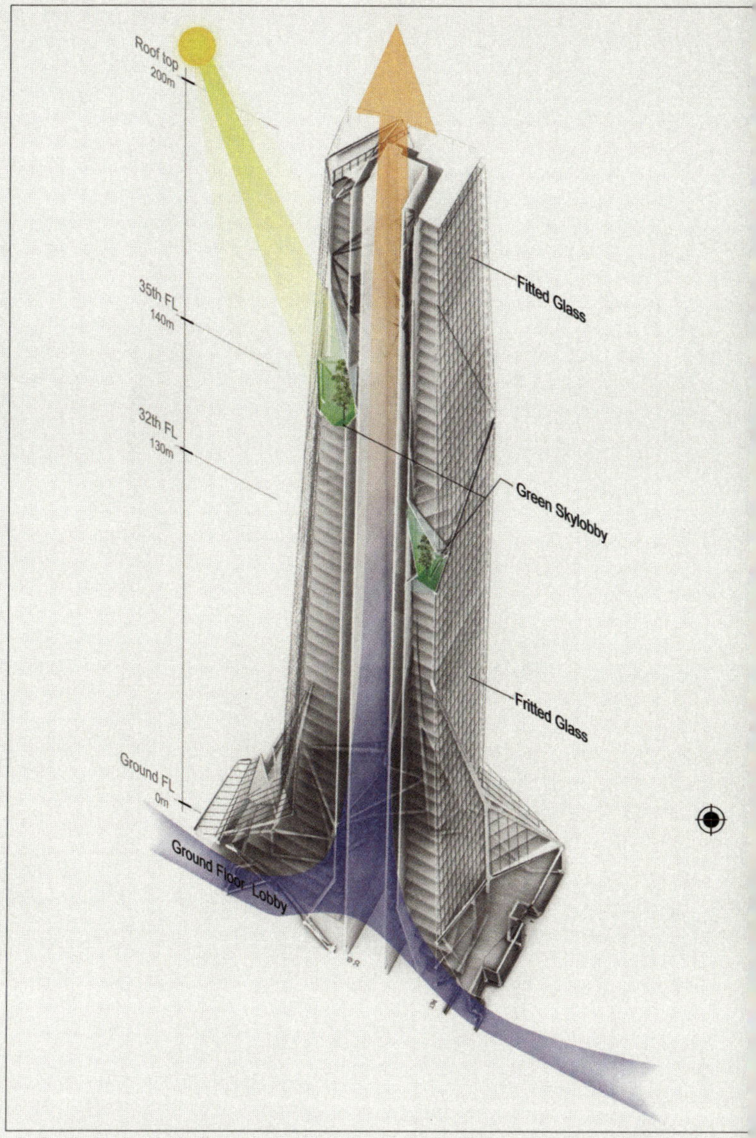

SOLAR CHIMNEY CONCEPT

SOLAR CHIMNEY

An added value was found in connecting the skylobbies with a solar chimney. The lobbies negotiate the tower's facade surface and contain vegetation that allows them to function as green lungs with bio filtration. In this way, the sky lobbies encourage natural cooling and filtration of the air via the solar chimney, thereby reducing the tower's energy use. This hybrid system allows for a simple way to achieve an energy efficient building design. Heat naturally rises—like air from a fire rising through a chimney—creating draft and taking the warm air with it. Draft is generated by creating an opening at the lower lobby "skirt" connected to an opening at the roof that allows for the heated air to be pulled up and out of the chimney, pulling new air in from the outside and drawing cool, fresh air into the building. It also stores the coolness of the night air to moderate warmer daytime temperatures. The efficiency of this process is often much undervalued. For this 200-meter tall tower, the cooling rate in the moderate Dutch climate results in substantial savings.

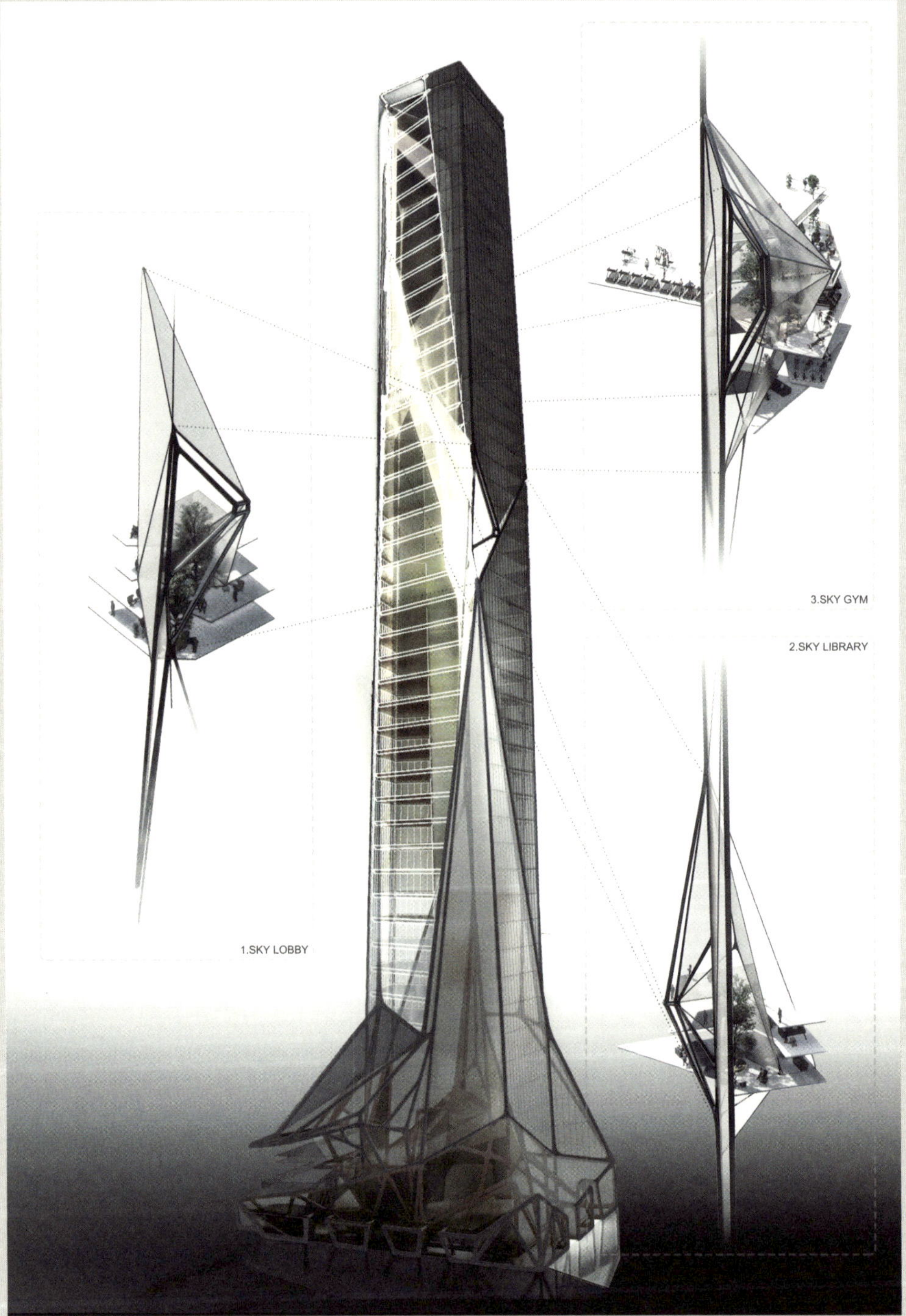
1.SKY LOBBY
2.SKY LIBRARY
3.SKY GYM

1. SOUTH FACADE
2. EAST FACADE
3. NORTH FACADE

2018

MIXED-USE

AN.59

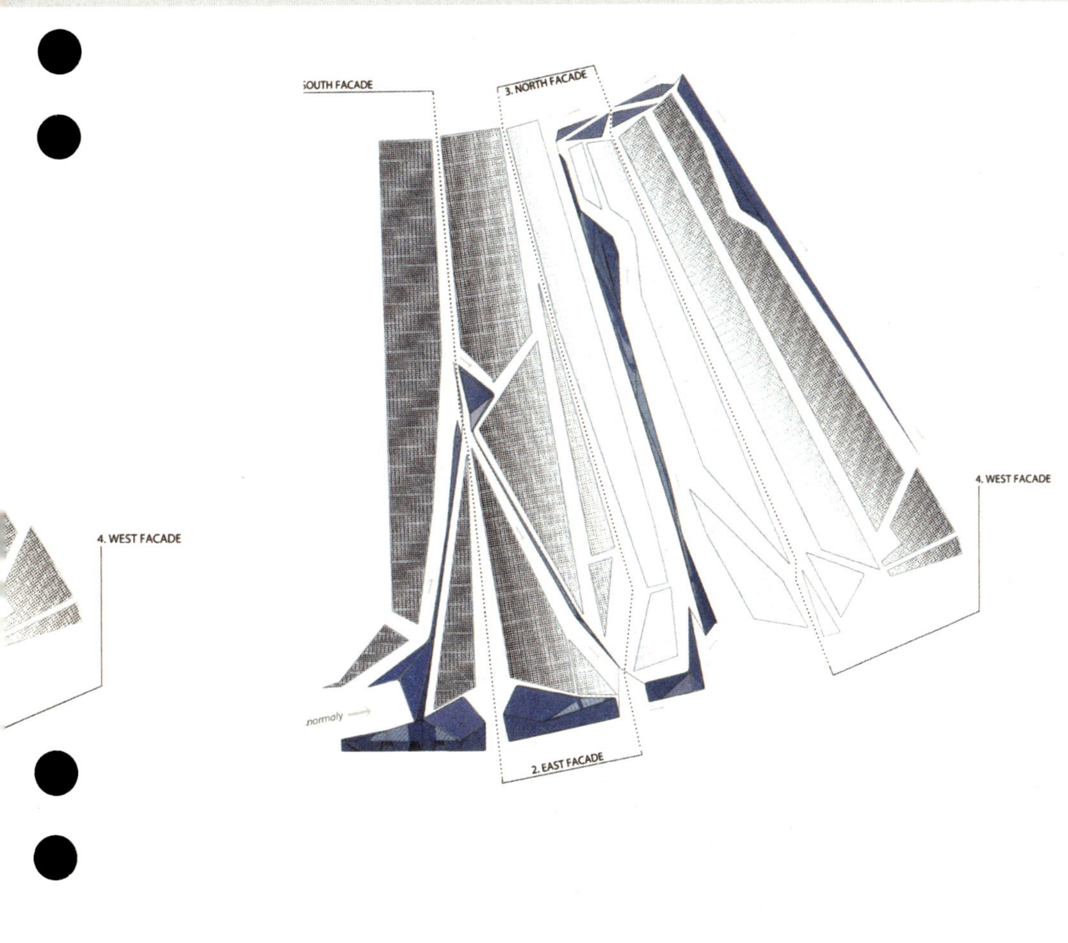

SILVER FRIT PATTERN DENSITY REACTS TO SUN EXPOSURE

LEED SILVER

Recent developments have proven the importance of self-sufficiency. With its mix of private and commercial programs, this tower is a perfect example of such a microclimate. Inhabitants would not have to leave the tower to survive a lockdown, and passive heating and cooling allow for independency. Cantilevering surfaces extend from the facade, expanding its floor area and creating an inviting storefront with naturally lit public retail and hospitality spaces, and above-grade parking. Glass seams connect the street to the upper green skylobbies, and allow natural light deep into the lobby, where we also find the private entrances for the apartments above. The tapered glass surfaces integrate city life into the tower, without the usual separation and control.

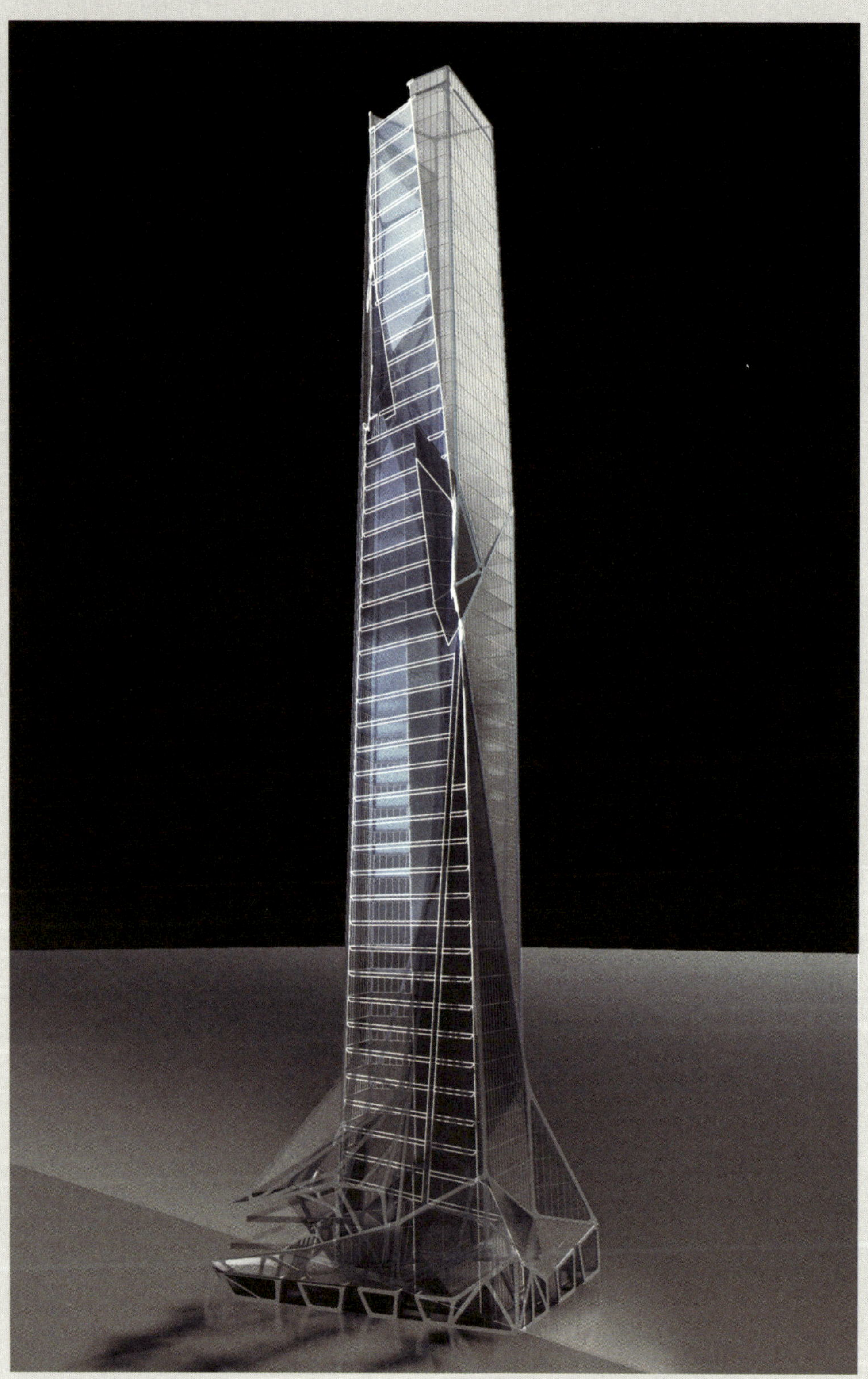

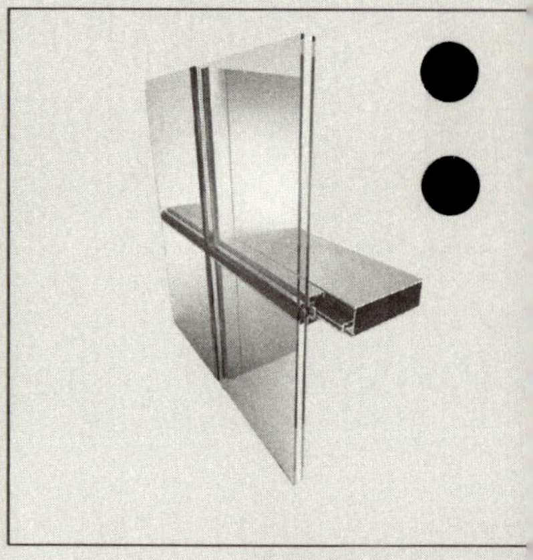

STRUCTURALLY GLAZED CURTAIN WALL WITH VENT WINDOWS FOR NATURAL VENTILATION

AN.63

AN.64

SKYLOBBIES FUNCTION AS GREEN LUNGS FOR TOWER

PASSIVE COOLING AND HEATING

The tower incorporates structural and material innovations, and energy-efficient systems. Proper building orientation minimizes solar gain. It provides ample shade and air movement through outdoor public spaces year-round and indoor spaces in the cooler months which will optimize the building's energy efficiency. Other energy strategies include architectural features and structurally glazed facade systems that reduce solar gain; the use of landscaping to reduce temperatures without energy intensive air conditioning; the use of photovoltaics and fiber optics to light corridors, parking structures, and other internal spaces that require diffuse light; and the use of low voltage LEDs for certain lighting features. Hot water is provided by rooftop vacuum tube solar panels and the reduction of the water demand through the use of high efficiency appliances further limits wasteful use of water.

UNDER ARMOUR

ROBECO

AN.48

Vannoccio Biringuccio, born 1480, was an Italian metallurgist. He is best known for his manual on metalworking, *de la pirotechnia*, which was published posthumously in 1540. The book describes details of mining practice, the extraction and refining of numerous metals, the development of alloys, as well as the use of compounds in explosives. Before its publication, the specifics of metallurgy and especially its potential for military arts were closely held secrets. Biringuccio's book marks the beginning of scientific and technical literature. (https://en.wikipedia.org/wiki/Vannoccio_Biringuccio)

AN.49

Named after the Latin *stibium*, the old name of the element antimony (Sb), a stibnite is a lead-gray mineral. A stibnite is one of the most exceptional natural crystals, typically occurring in sharp prismatic clusters. (https://en.wikipedia.org/wiki/Stibnite)

AN.50

AN.51

An *orthorhombic* system is one of seven structural systems assigned to crystalline solids. Crystals that are categorized as belonging within this particular system, according to the *Encyclopedia Britannica*, are those with three "mutually perpendicular axes that are unequal in length." In other words, crystals in this system are characterized by the right angles of all edges, but the length of edges can vary. (The Editors of Encyclopaedia Britannica, "Orthorhombic system," *Encyclopaedia Britannica* www.britannica.com/science/orthorhombic-system)

AN.52

AN.53

AN.54

AN.55

AN.56

A solar chimney is a passive solar heating and cooling system that can regulate the temperature of a building through the use of natural ventilation. As cool air is drawn into a building through windows and vents, it is drawn toward the solar chimney—essentially, a hollow container within a building. Sunlight heats the cool air at the base in the solar chimney, causing it to rise and release to the exterior. Solar chimneys can reduce energy costs up to 50 percent. (https://energyeducation.ca/encyclopedia/Solar_chimney)

AN.57

Skylobbies are transitional spaces that function as ecological green lung for the tower, voids that clean and filter the air

AN.58

Fritted glass helps reduce facade glare and light transmission to cut down on solar heat gain. Ceramic frit is applied to the glass through a fine mesh screen before the glass is tempered or heat strengthened. Through this process, the frit fuses into the glass surface and it becomes a permanent coating. (https://in.saint-gobain-glass.com/ceramic-fritted-glass)

AN.59

AN.60

AN.61-62

AN.63

Frit itself is a ceramic component that can be laid out into an assortment of patterns, most typically consisting of dots or lines.

AN.64-70

BREWSTER CARRIAGE HOUSE

FILLING A VOID

"It will be a Gilded Age, New York, harking back to old times. This building is an 1850s carriage-making building. No one knows it, yet it is a treasure for American history, unchartered and unwritten about."
— Ross Morgan, Owner

For the longest time, luxury has been identified by excellence and complexity of craftsmanship, and the rarity or refinement of materials used. The Industrial Revolution radically altered this reciprocity, allowing components to be produced cheaply and quickly, while generating synthetic materials that far exceeded the capacities of their natural equivalents. As we find

AN.72-73 AN.74 AN.75

BREWSTER CARRIAGE

ourselves today once again at a paradigm shift in the valuation of resources and modes of production, the notions of manufacturing intelligence, complexity, and material performance have in themselves become signifiers of luxury, creating what has been termed Digital Craft.

The Brewster Carriage House project exemplifies and incorporates both of these transitions, inspiring a unique combination of restored original details as historic references, innovative spatial concepts, as well as state of the art digital design and FTF production methodologies.

A historic landmark, the Brewster Carriage House stands at the intersection of three of New York City's oldest and most diverse neighborhoods: Soho, Nolita, and Chinatown. A former factory for carriage and coach building for New York's high society, the Brewster Carriage Company was founded in 1810 by James Brewster. Its carriages enjoyed national and international status for their quality and exclusivity. Already then customization was an important appeal of the firm's products; Brewster kept records of all family crests and colors of its customers. The Astors' was a blue, J. P. Morgan's dark green, and the Vanderbilts' was a shade of maroon. These reserved, "copyrighted" colors sometimes made it difficult for new customers to select a body color of their choice.

The factory had long been abandoned but was now newly converted into a mixed-use building with a variety of open plan apartments on the upper

BREWSTER CARRIAGE HOUSE
AN.76

NEW YORK
AN.77

floors, commercial spaces on the ground floor, and a restaurant and lounge in its spectacular vaulted cellar. From the outset the client's goal had been to meticulously restore the building's facade to its former glory. Brass number plates and ornaments, and custom-cast glass lenses and their cast iron sidewalk grilles were reproduced by local craftsmen. We gut-renovated the existing factory interiors and added a steel egress stair and elevator core to accommodate the new program, while also introducing a new patterned 3D steel facade lattice screen for the commercial storefronts as well as light-refracting, crystalline glass stair bulkheads providing access to the green roofs and terraces of two duplex penthouses.

AN.78

3D STEEL FACADE LATTICE

UPCYCLING

Fundamentally redefining the significance of material life cycles and the embedded energy content of old and new materials, our sustainable design strategy began with the idea of upcycling, also known as creative reuse: in this case the transformation of existing wood beams [no longer suitable to carry the load of the new use] into building materials of higher quality and environmental value than comparable new products. Wall cladding, windowsills, and bulkheads were all made from these large wood planks. We took every opportunity to introduce materials with a high recycled content, from renewable sources, such as blown soybean-based insulation, or with minimized energy content added through transport and installation, resulting in extraordinary material innovations and energy savings.

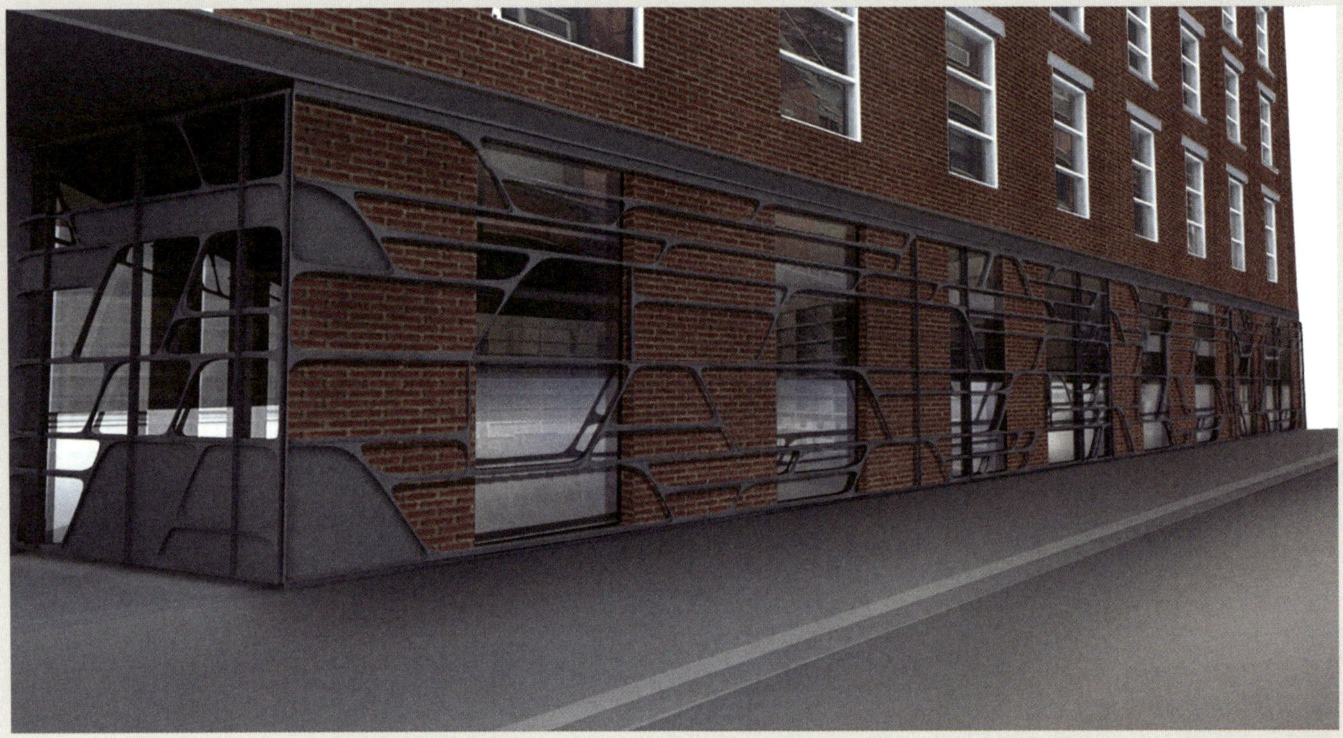

SECURITY MADE INTEGRAL

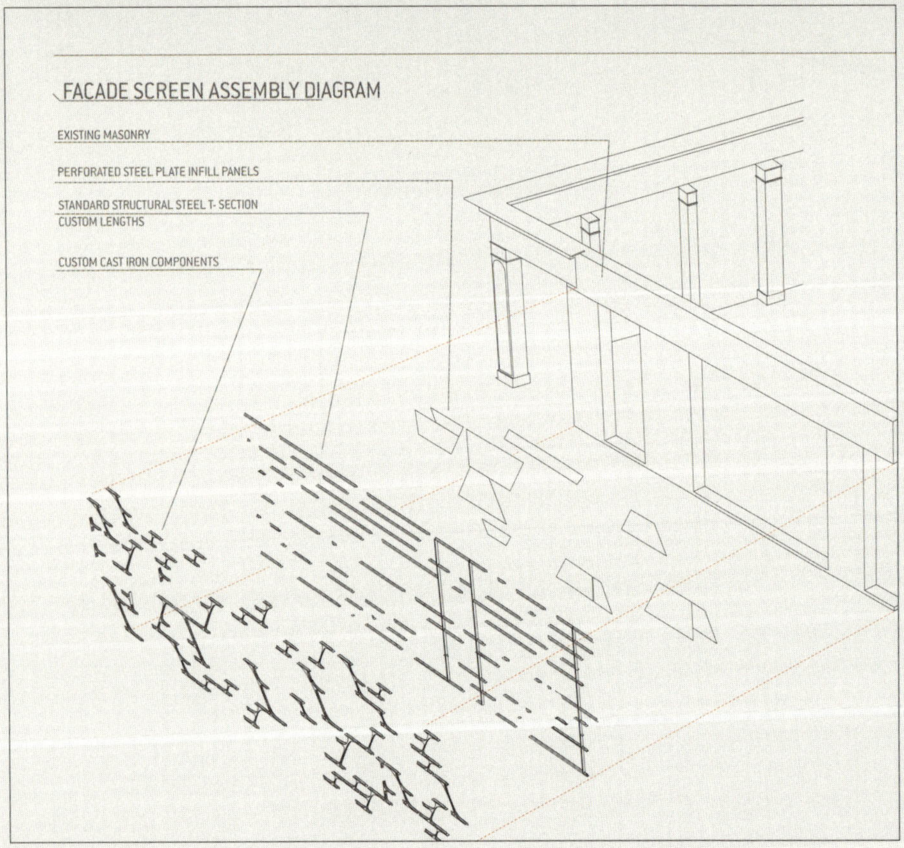

AN.81-82

AN.83

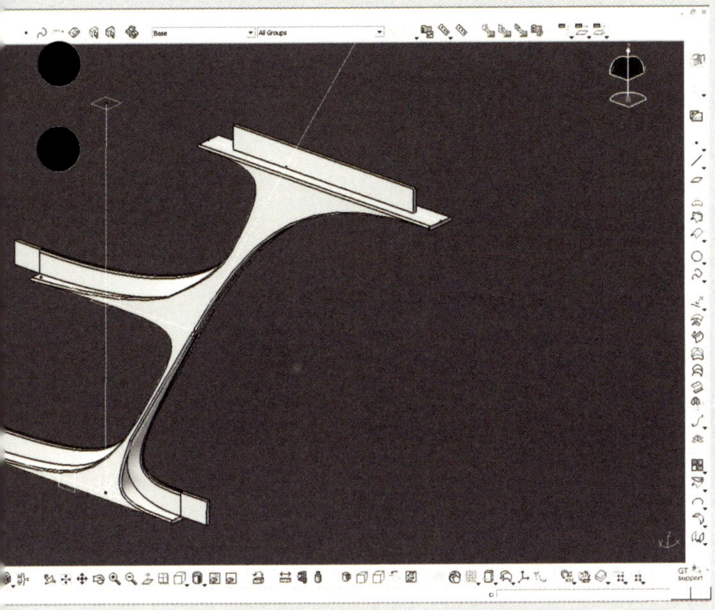

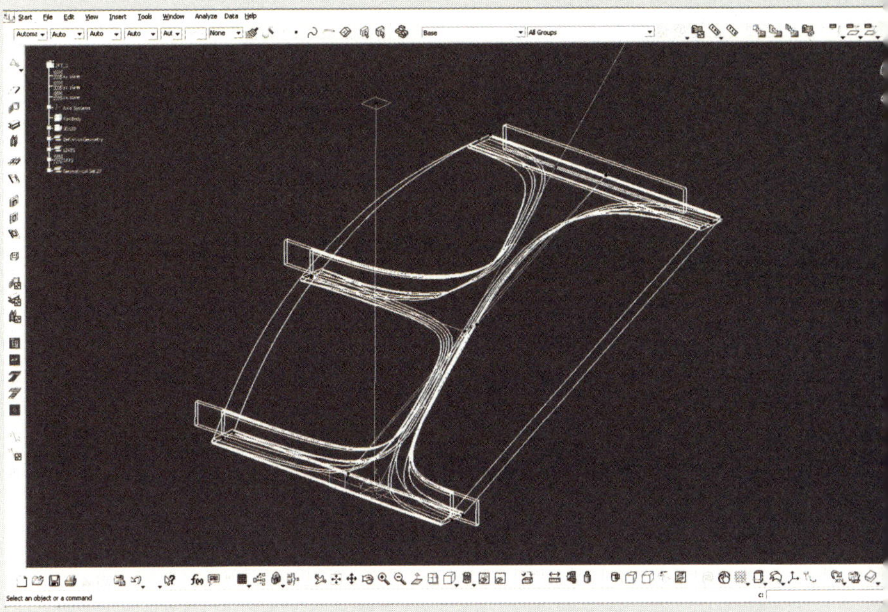

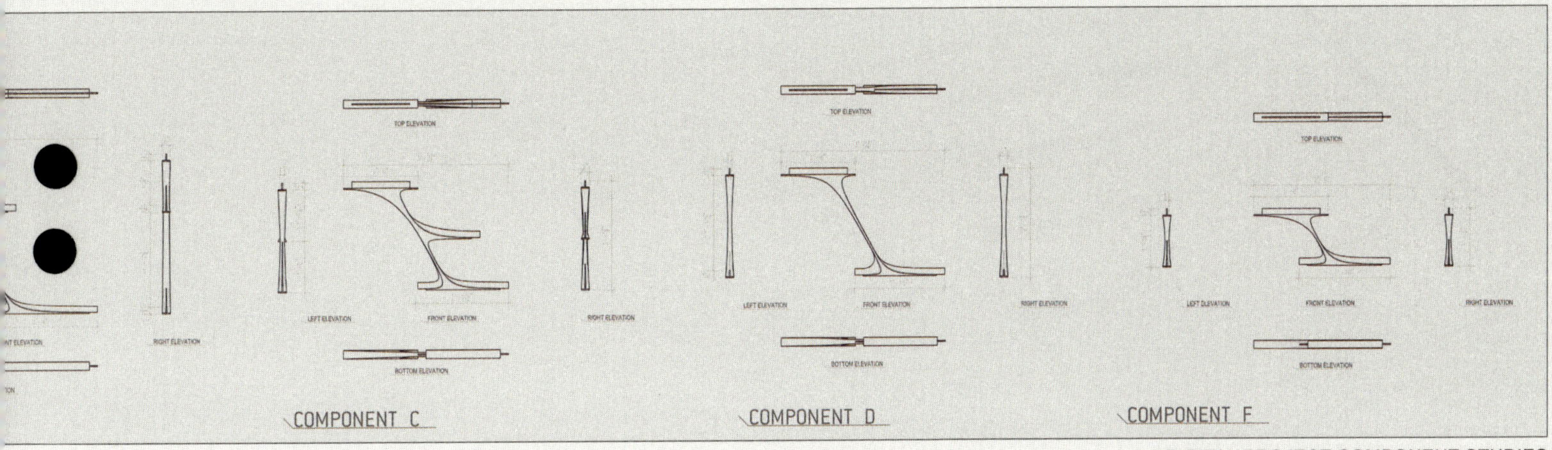

DIGITAL PROJECT COMPONENT STUDIES

FACADE SCREEN / LATTICE / PROTOTYPING

The storefront of the building's ground level commercial spaces was meticulously restored and overlaid with a parametrically designed steel lattice structure, creating a distinctive layered facade that fuses cutting-edge contemporary and historic details, safety, and materiality. Composed of curved steel sections assembled into large components, the lattice is suspended in front of the glazed storefront and wraps the building's corner, thus unifying the south and east facades in a more continuous skin and creating a sense of continuity and flow. This lends the historic brick structure an entirely new character: a diaphanous, precise and elegant quality that contrasts with and enhances the solidity of the masonry solid.

BREWSTER CARRIAGE HOUSE

NEW YORK

AN.84-86

AN.87-88

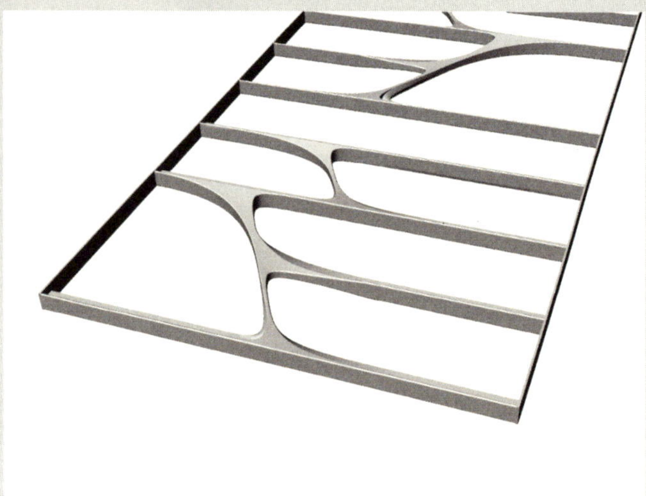

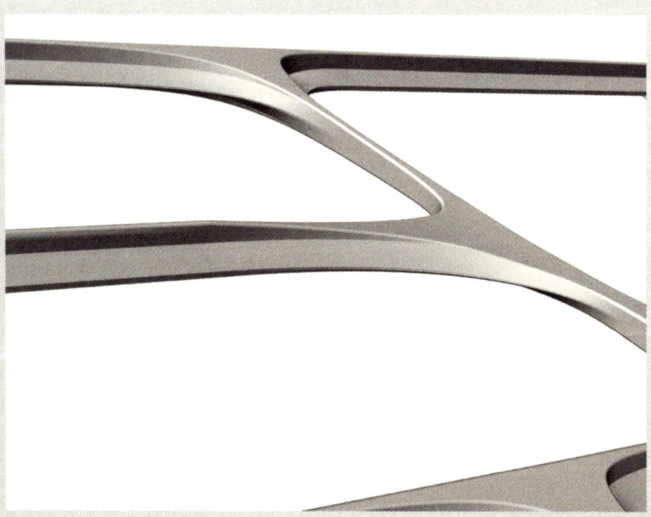

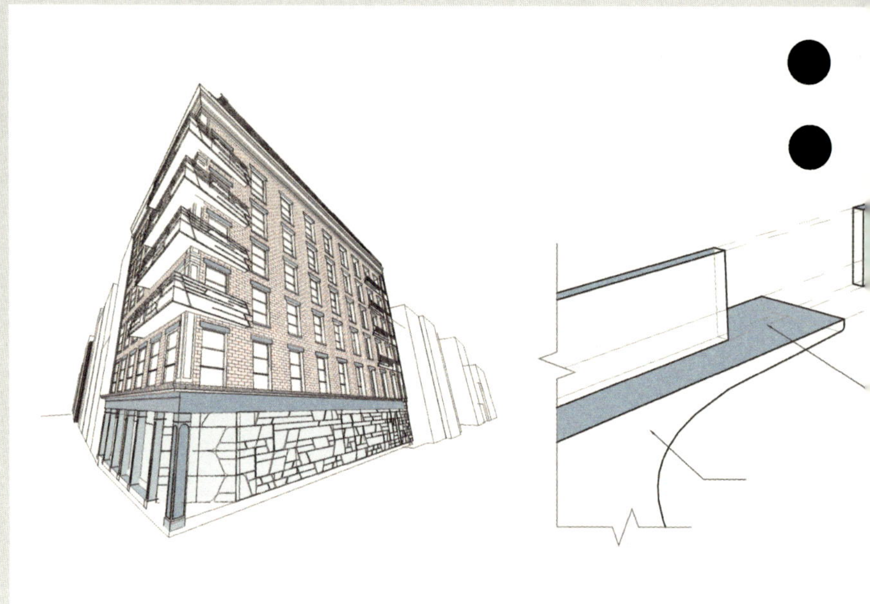

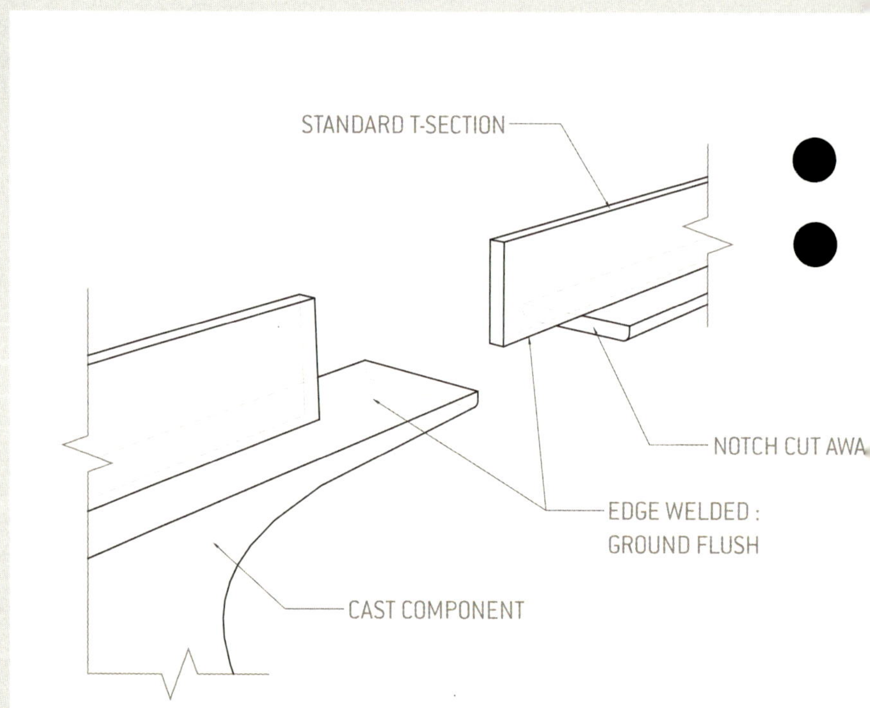

AN.89

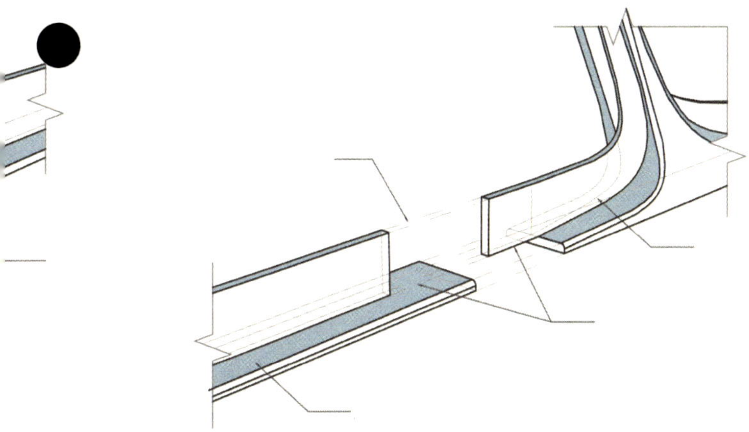

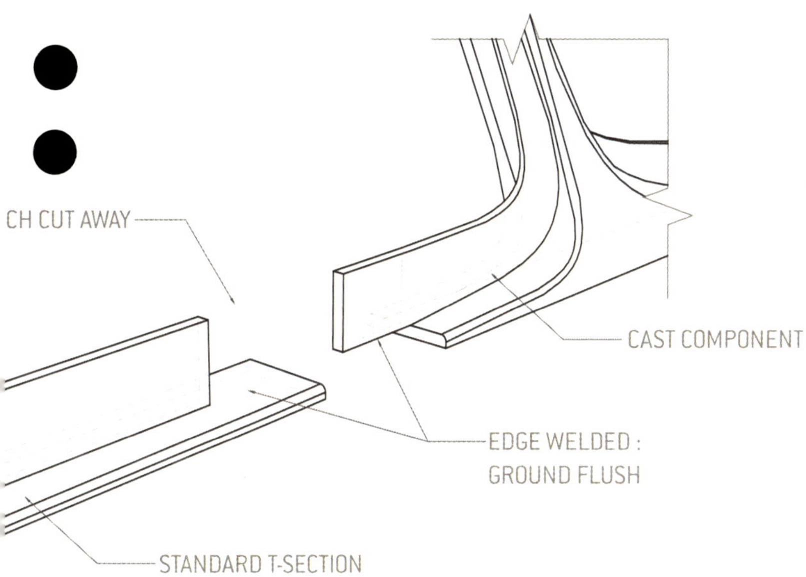

PROTOTYPE

SCREEN FABRICATION

The screen pattern was parametrically designed in Digital Project, a powerful 3D software originally developed by Dessault Systems as CATIA for plane design and adapted for architecture by Gehry Technologies. We were given the unique opportunity to assist in the testing and optimization of the design

tools and parameters, which proved instrumental in developing the lattice design and reducing the number of component variations, thus minimizing manufacturing costs while achieving the desired design complexity. The optimized assembly consisted of only eight standard parts, linked by a series of T-sections cut to varying lengths, resulting in the characteristic fluid pattern that stretches across the facade's surface. The specific deployment of the pattern is based on precise performative parameters of each section within the facade.

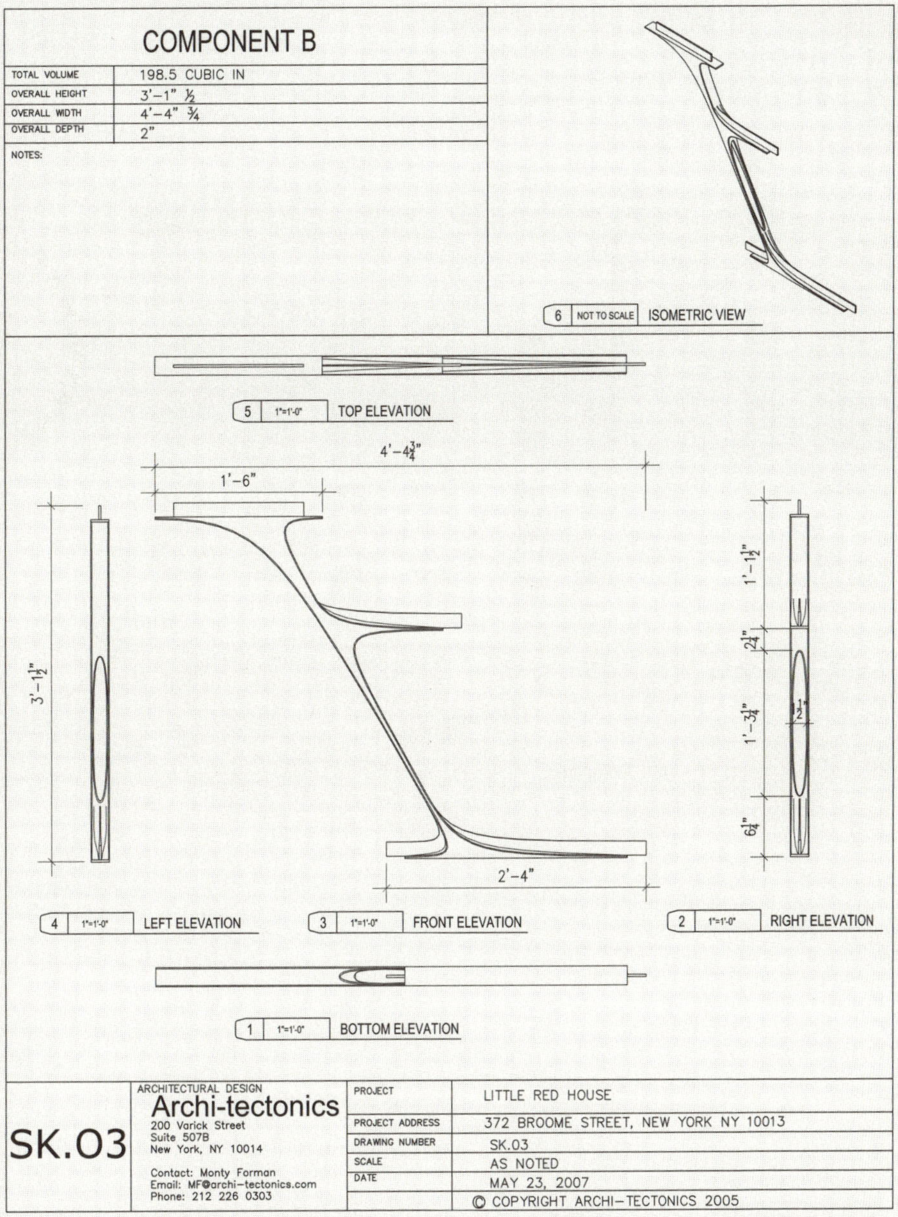

DIGITAL PROJECT IS A COMPUTER-AIDED DESIGN SOFTWARE APPLICATION BASED ON CATIA V5 AND DEVELOPED BY GEHRY TECHNOLOGIES

RAPID PROTOTYPING

A physical prototype was fabricated translating Digital Project files into advanced CNC- and 3D bending tools, enabling various test configurations and prototypes of the steel facade components and their precise fit. This also allowed the steel fabricators to provide instant feedback for fabrication, leading directly to adaptations of our design parameters. A final, full scale optimized prototype was then produced and tested on site for material properties and interfacing with the building facade.

RESIDENTIAL

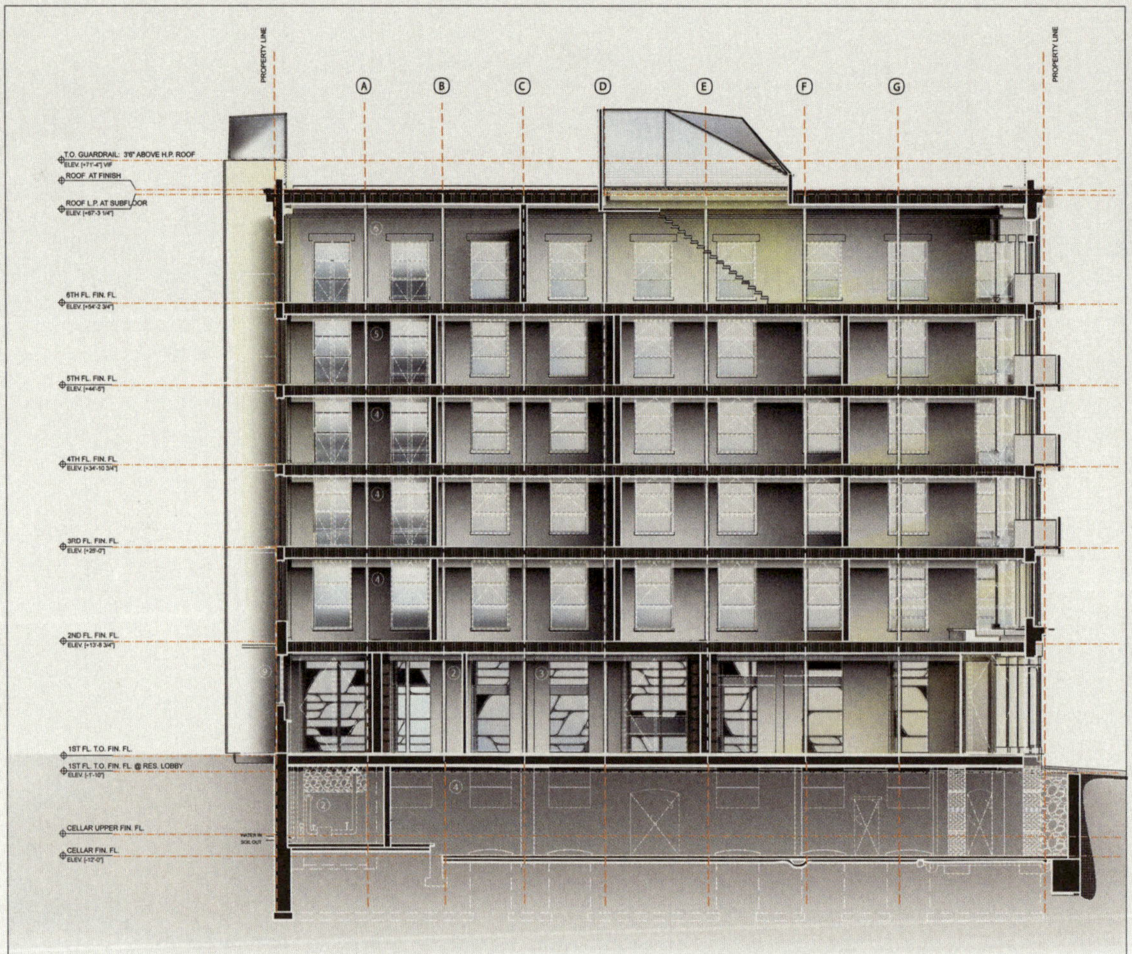

S1 3/16"=1'-0" NORTH-SOUTH SECTION

REPURPOSE & INHABIT

Innovative and ecologically intelligent building strategies were at the core of our design approach, lending the defunct Brewster Carriage manufacturing facility a new life converted into 24 spacious residential lofts. Upcycling was an important aspect of our energy balance but also a key factor

DEEP TEXTURES

to maintain the unique character of the building. We restored and strengthened cast iron columns, reused bricks or repurposed floor beams as hardwood planks for walls and window sills, giving the space a rugged, industrial atmosphere.

CAST IRON / STEEL STAIRS

For the two duplex penthouses we custom-designed patterned steel stair railings that lead to crystalline bulkheads giving access to extensive roof terraces and green roofs. In a file-to-factory manufacturing process, the digital patterns were sent to PDLAB in Toronto, an exquisite laboratory of ideas and custom fabrication, who manufactured the railings. The railings have an intricate laser cut pattern, which alludes to the rich history of the carriage manufacturing building.

AN.98

UPCYCLING

AN.99

GREEN ROOF / SYSTEMS

After reuse and recycling, the next step focused on the creation of a high-performance building through the interaction of a number of co-dependent systems. The challenge was to find ways for these systems to work within the limitations of the pre-existing structure. The roof was given new life as a green

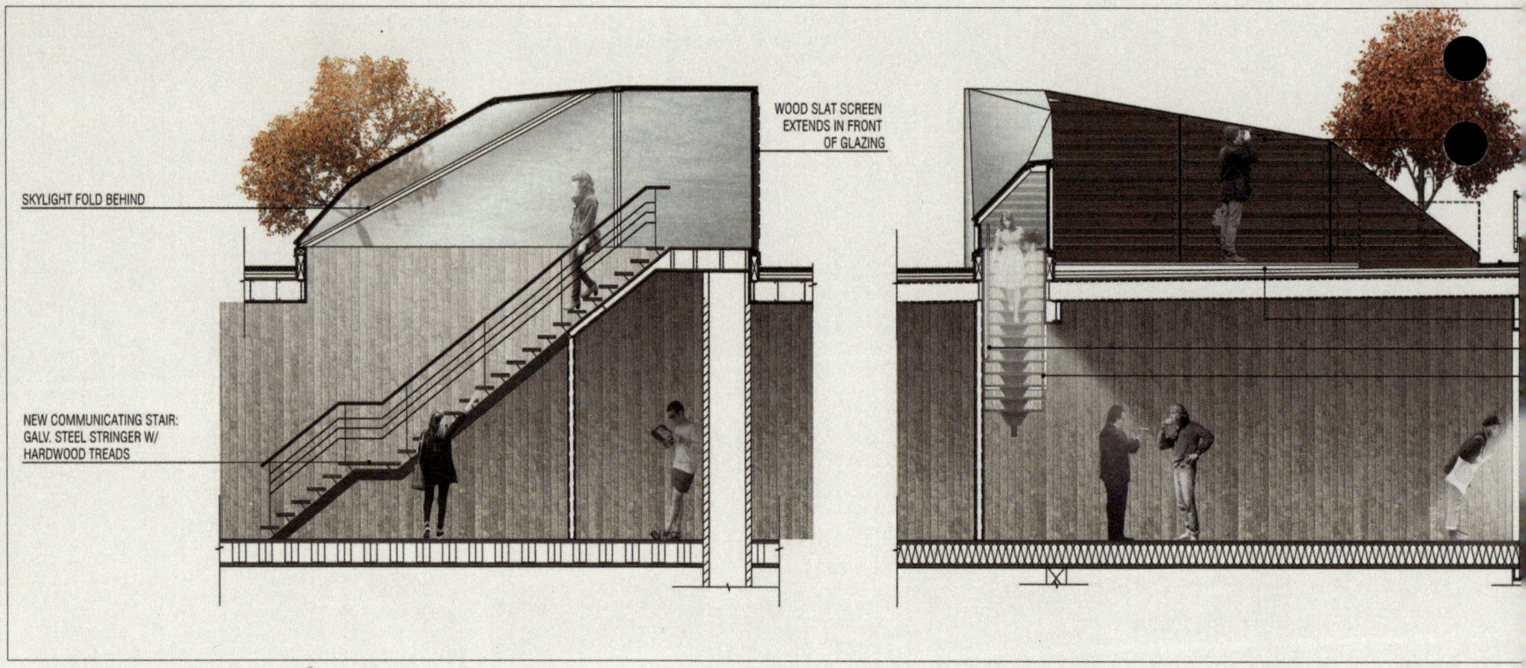

SECTION THROUGH DUPLEX PENTHOUSE GLASS BULKHEAD

system, providing a rainwater buffer, purifying the air, reducing the ambient temperature, regulating the indoor temperature, saving energy, and encouraging biodiversity in the city. The added structural load of the green roof in this residentially framed building became possible due to the use of an innovative lightweight soil engineered from recycled PVC. The roof also features solar evacuated tubes, the evacuated tube design was originally developed in the 1980s and has proven to be extremely robust. It is a vacuum tube solar hot-water heating panel, which heats approximately 1 liter water per hour (depending on geographical and weather factors), has over a 90% energy conversion efficiency, and provides residents with approximately 75percent of their domestic hot water needs.

AN.101-102

AN.103

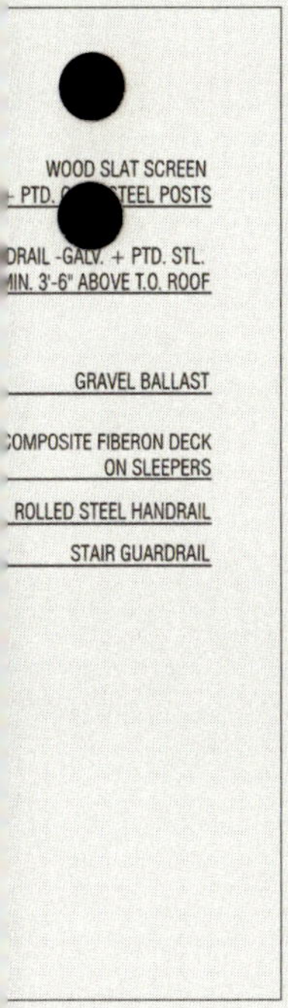

MODEL STUDIES GLASS BULKHEAD

CRYSTALLINE BULKHEADS

The transition of the penthouses to the roof warranted the introduction of fragmented light catchers; spacious crystalline glass bulkheads bringing natural light deep into the lofts below and also allowing access to the roof terraces. Inspired by quasi-crystalline structures, originating from similar parameters but not repeating, the fragmented glass plane volumes are unique for each penthouse; similar but not the same. Their tapered, tilted glass planes refract light, and at night act as urban lanterns, reminiscent of the building's illustrious past.

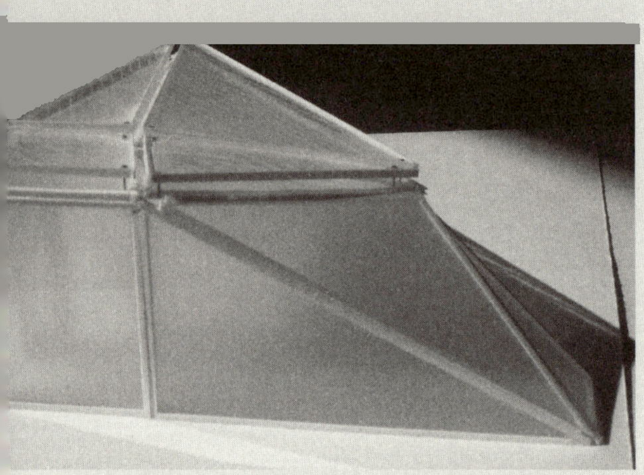

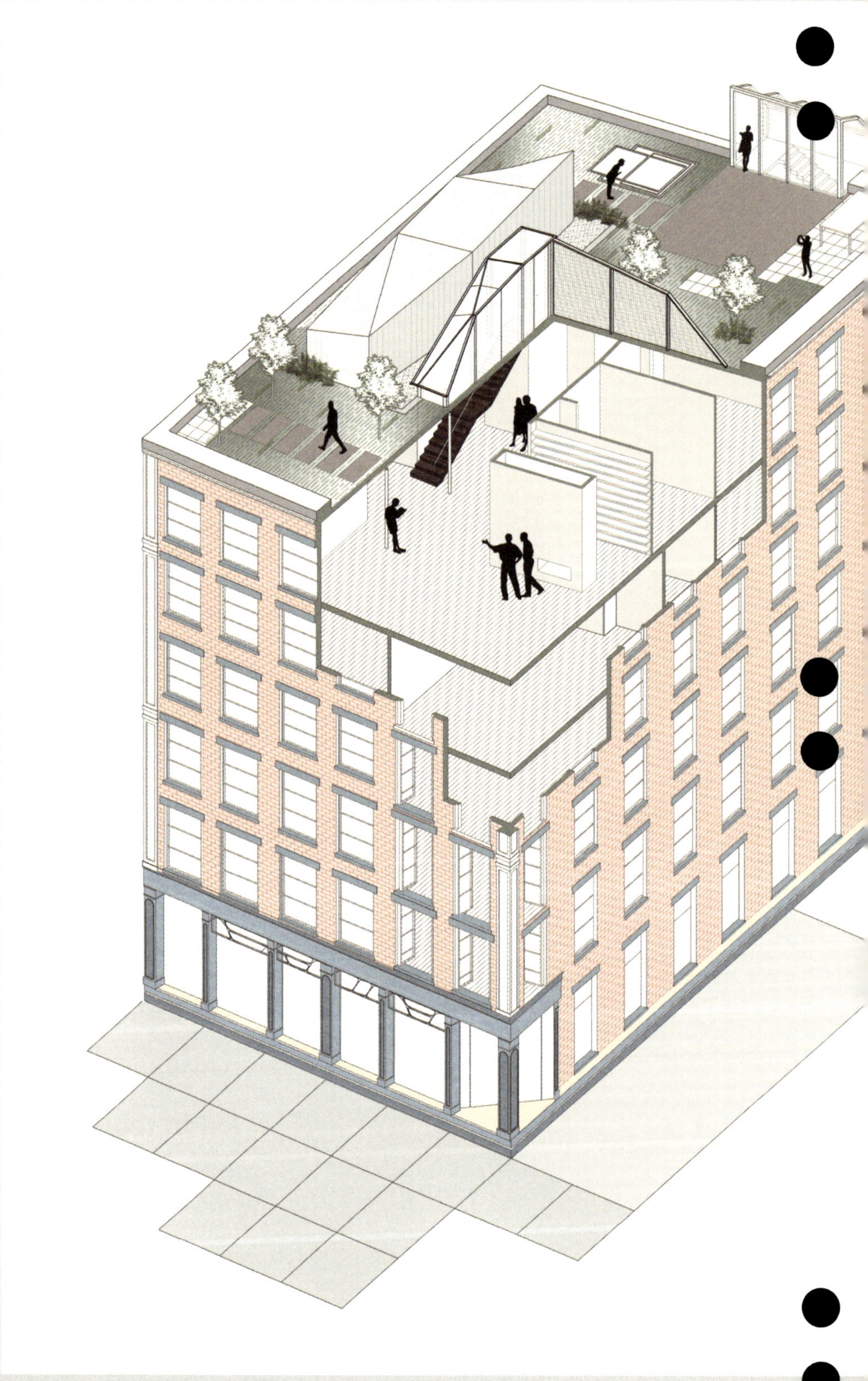

ISOMETRIC DUPLEX PENTHOUSE

AN.106-107

AN.108

RESTAURANT

THE VAULT

The Brewster Restaurant is located in the most mysterious space of the former carriage manufacturing building, the carefully restored cellar with its characteristic brick barrel vaults. This space exhibits distinctly the coexistence of early industrial details and archaic load bearing brick structures, supporting the surrounding sidewalks. Their shape

AN.110

ENTRANCE ON THE GROUND FLOOR WITH COFFEE SHOP

AN.111-113

is the simplest kind of vault, the barrel- or tunnel vault, semicircular in shape, beautifully lit from above by vault lights. Cast glass lenses, remnants of Soho's industrial past and originally installed to allow sunlight into the basements of factories before the introduction of electricity, bathe the vaults in an ethereal light, while raw wood beams and gigantic old steel elevator doors add visual heft and texture to the space.

The discovery and restoration of these industrial treasures also inspired us to reconsider the very notion of craftsmanship within the realm of digital design and FTF manufacturing. As these new tools at our disposal now allow us to optimize design through

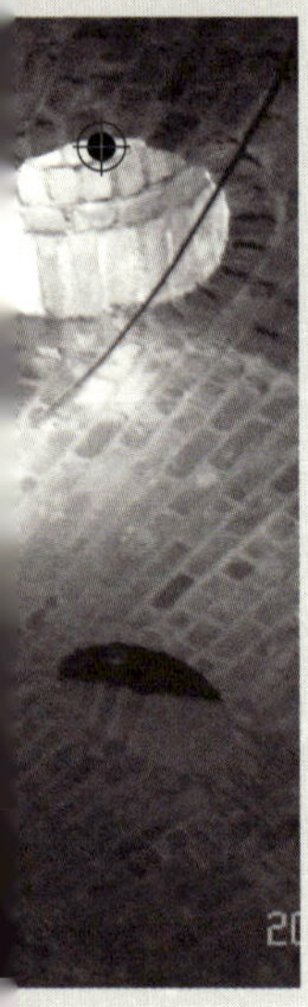

AN.114

PERFORATED SIDEWALKS AND BRICK VAULT

AN.115

instant material feedback, we employ an evolutionary design process more akin to Digital Craft than traditional industrial production which was focused on standardization and repetition.

To amplify the vault geometry, we focused on the design of the seams, joints, and folds of the spatial perimeter, the in-between space occupied by cast iron, steel, and glass in the historic structure. Seeking to create a truly authentic, forward-looking equivalent of these elements, rather than a nostalgic representation, we generated parametrically designed and digitally manufactured components, furnitures, and armatures, the Anomalies tracing the spatial void.

Elaborately detailed seating booths augment the curved vault details in bent steel frames lined with wood veneers and leather, and chandeliers elegantly integrated into its structure.

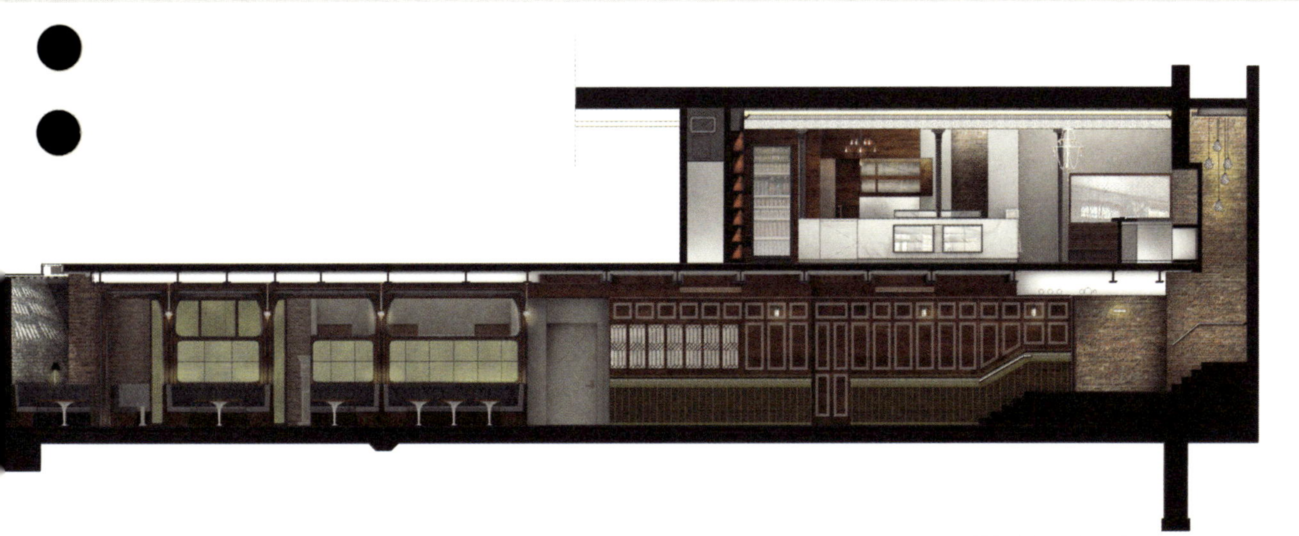

SECTION CUT

BREWSTER CARRIAGE HOUSE
AN.119-120

NEW YORK
AN.121

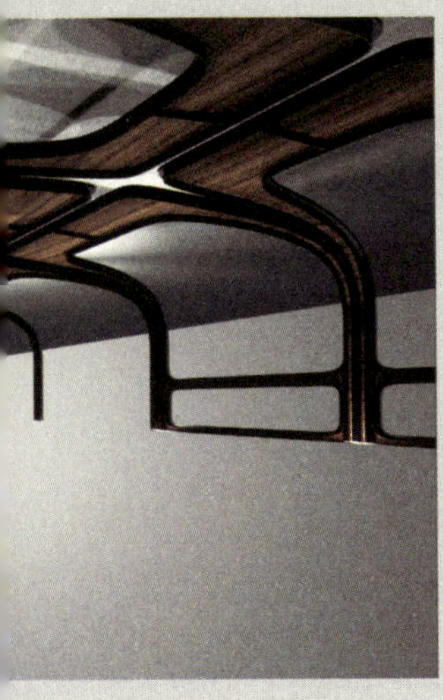

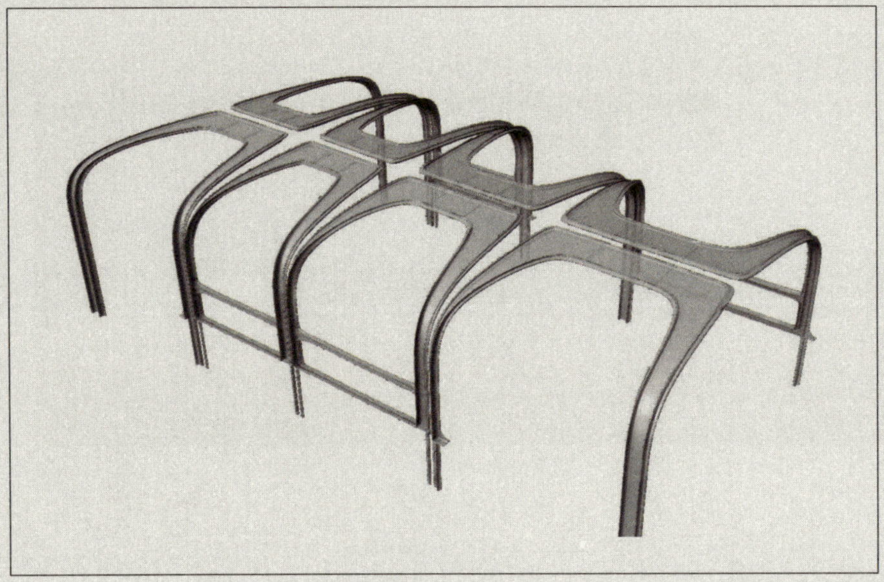

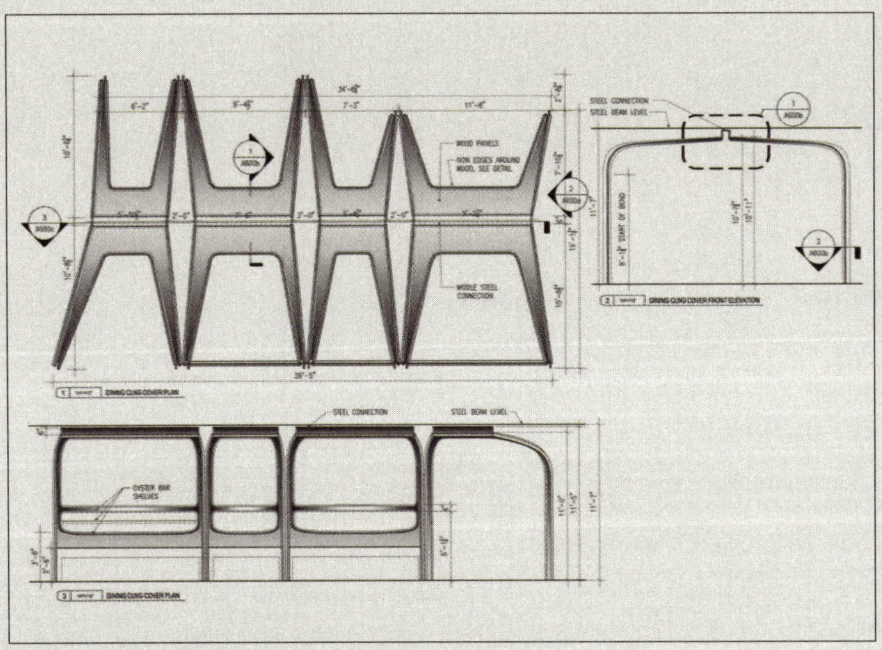

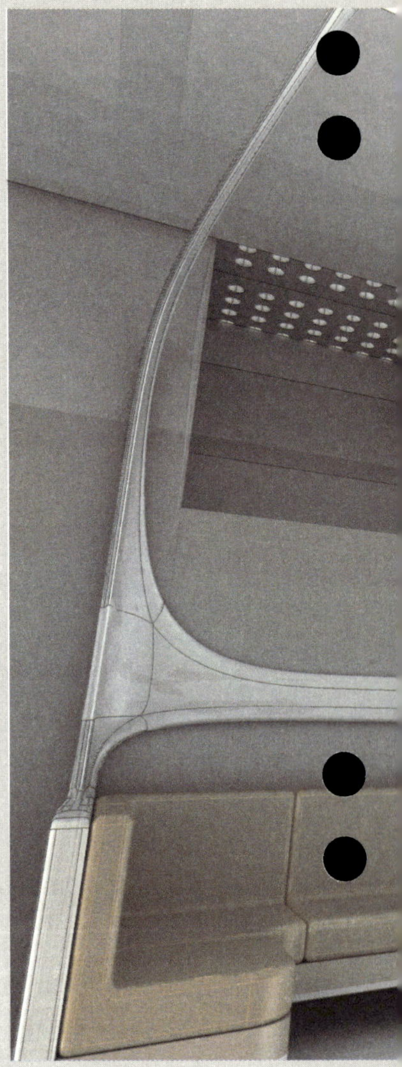

SKELETAL VAULT

Assembled into a framework of ribs and elaborate joints, the resulting space is faintly organic and machine-like but subtle and elegant, reverberating in the brick vault arches. The main dining space is defined most dominantly by this steel skeleton vault, an independent spatial body that creates cadence and intimacy in the dining area. The detailing of the vault merges the main space and the booth structure to create an integral whole. Its elaborate detailing emanates a warm, inviting atmosphere, at once futuristic and reminiscent of times past. While the design evokes what the client had once termed "a forgotten and simpler time before modern economies of scale and corporate amalgamation, a time of craft

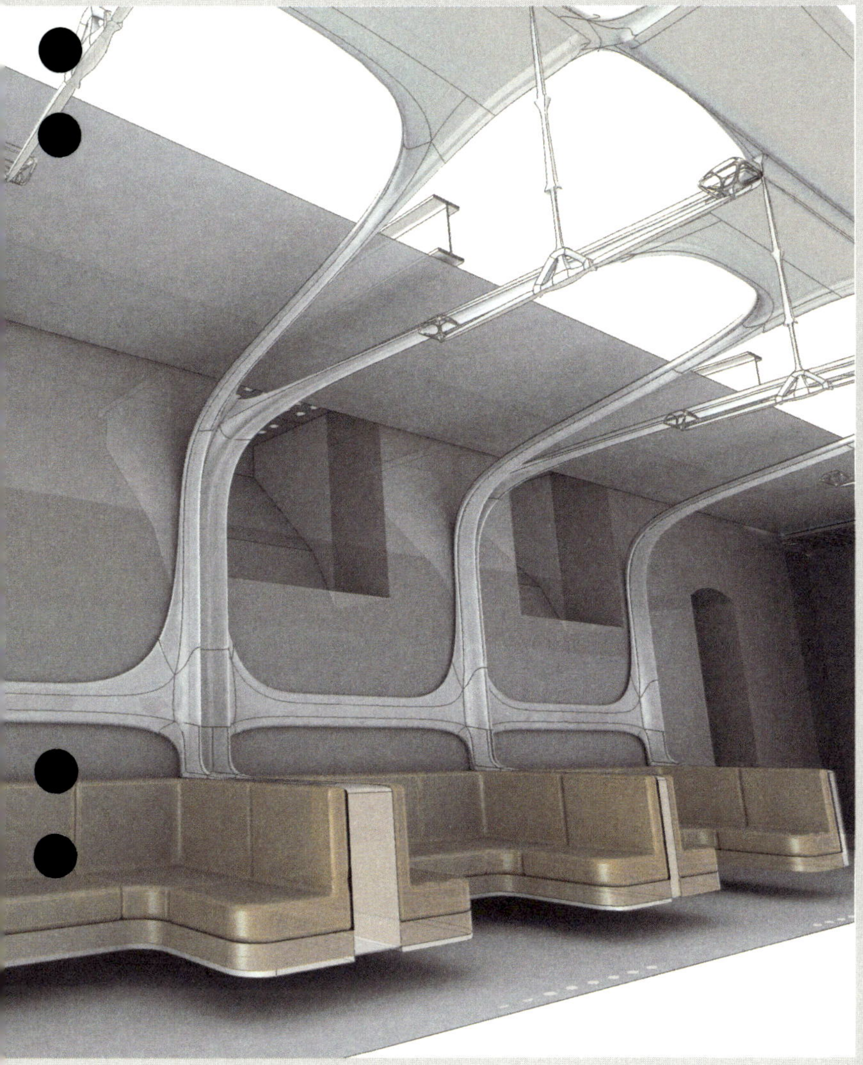

INTEGRATED LIGHTING AND SEATS IN STEEL VAULT

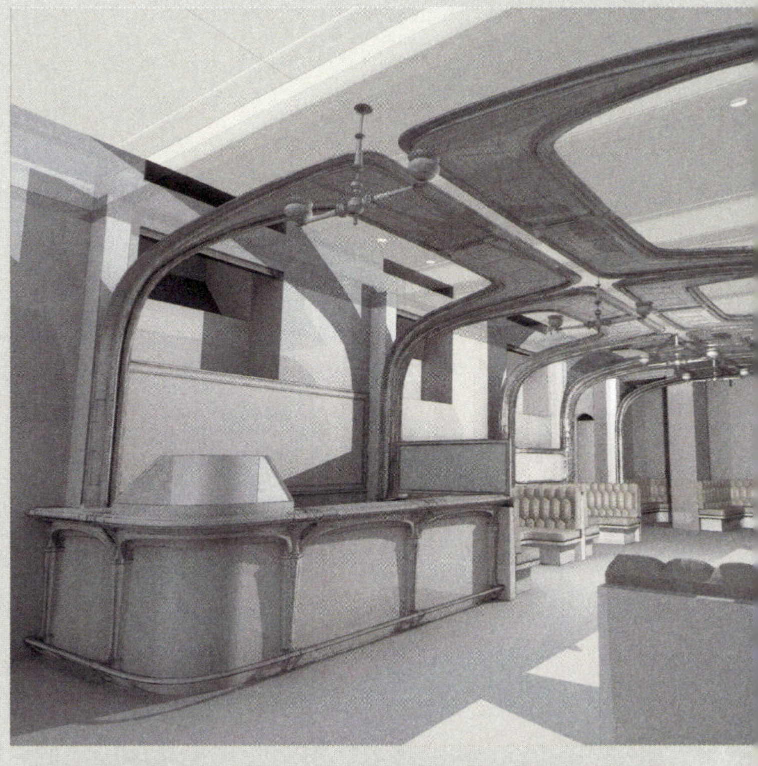

and the hand made," it employs only genuine design innovation and methodology. A view of the past fueled by potentiality rather than a sense of loss.

AN.124

AN.125-126

BAR DETAILS

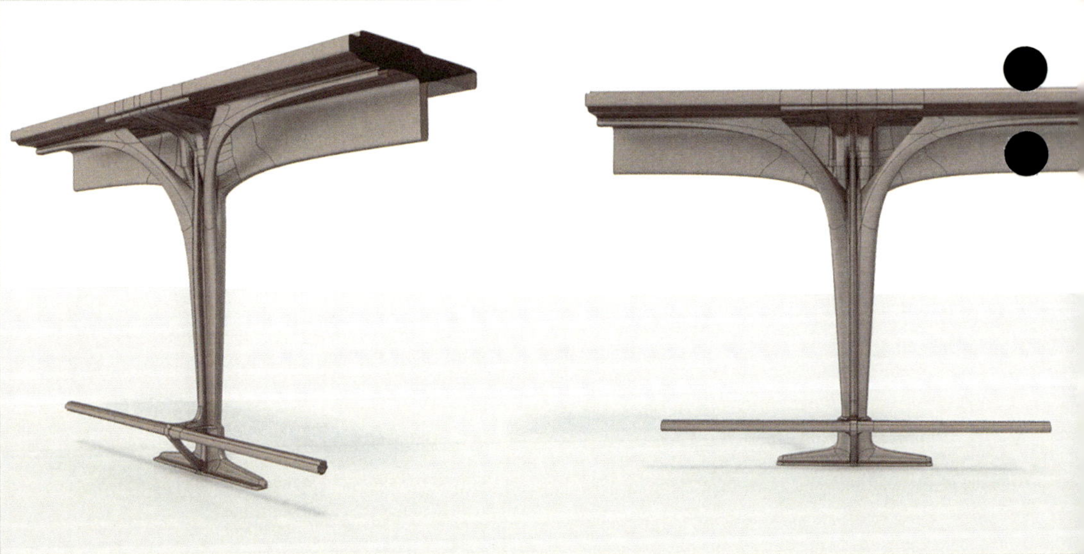

CAST OBJECTS

The bar—the main object one encounters when descending in the restaurant—was carefully designed. Having studied the elegant curved steel frame of the Brewster carriage, we created bar surfaces that are intricately detailed with deep crevasses and reveals. The back bar is similarly designed and beautifully lit by glass droplets overhead. The vault lights or deadlights embedded in the sidewalk let filtered light fall down on the bottles below. The client stated: "The space Brewster once occupied, shall be interpreted to be as true to these standards of originality and lost historical detail as possible."

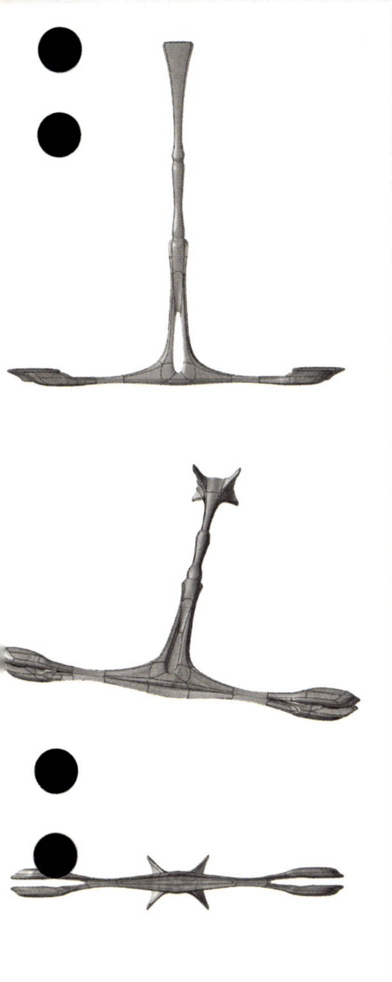

CUSTOM-DESIGNED CHANDELIER

BOOTH DETAILS

AN.129-130

BOOTH LIGHTING

AN.131

PROTOTYPE

PROTOTYPE

BREWSTER

the
RRIAGE HOUSE

GABRIEL
at the
BREWSTER

GABRIEL SCOTT
EST. 2012
at the
BREWSTER CARRIAGE HOUSE
Monday – Friday 10 - 6
Weekend by appointment

AN.71

AN.72-73

AN.74

AN.75

AN.76

AN.77

AN.78

AN.79-80

AN.81-83

Digital Project is a computer-aided design software application developed by Gehry Technologies, based on the french airplane software CATIA V5. Archi-Tectonics got to be one of the first offices to test it out in practice.

AN.84-86

AN.87

AN.88

NURBS in Rhino are Non-Uniform Rational B-Splines, mathematical representations of 3D geometry that can accurately describe any shape from a simple 2D line, circle, arc, or curve to the most complex 3D organic free-form surface or solid. (www.rhino3d.com/features/nurbs)

AN.89

AN.90

AN.91

Dennis Shelden, CTO and co-founder of Gehry Technologies, works with Gehry Partners and other leading architectural firms in the practical application of BIM technology to complex architectural projects. The software "brings advanced aerospace technologies to the architecture and building industries." (https://sap.mit.edu/article/standard/new-faculty-dennis-shelden)

AN.92-93

AN.94

AN.95

"In modern art, the term "found object" (a translation of the French "objet trouvé") is used to describe an object, found by an artist, which, with minimal modification, is then presented as a work of art. The idea is that the artist believes that the discovered object possesses a certain aesthetic quality—stemming from its appearance, social or personal history—and therefore displays it for the appreciation of others." (http://www.visual-arts-cork.com/definitions/found-objects.htm)

AN.96

AN.97

AN.98

"Upcycling, also known as creative reuse, is the process of transforming by-products, waste materials, useless, or unwanted products into new materials or products of better quality and environmental value. Upcycling has shown significant growth across the United States. For example, the number of online products tagged with the word "upcycled" increased from about 7,900 in January 2010, to 263,685 on April 2013, an additional increase of 879%." (https://en.wikipedia.org/wiki/Upcycling)

AN.99

AN.100

AN.101-104

AN.105

AN.106-108

"In the summer, green roofs retain up to 90% of the precipitation that falls on them and up to 40%in the winter." (https://greenroofs.org/about-green-roofs)

AN.109

AN.110

AN.111

AN.112

AN.113

AN.114

AN.115

AN.116-117

AN.118

AN.119-120

The restaurant space is defined by a skeletal vault that holds booths and custom chandeliers.

AN.121

AN.122

AN.123

A 3D print of the skeleton vault

AN.124

AN.125-126

AN.127

The custom designed chandelier, a branched ornamental light fixture

AN.128

AN.129-130

AN.131

AN.132-133

Patterns are embedded into the wood surface.

AN.134-135

AN.136-138

After we initially designed John Legend's apartment on 4th Street, he and his family then moved into the gut renovated Brewster Carriage House second floor loft that we designed. Recently, Legend and his family moved to the penthouse of the building.

COMMUNAL SINK

BLACK [K]NIGHT / TASHAN

The owner of the famed "Tiffin" Food Concept in Philadelphia, Munish Narula, was ready for a new step in his career. Together with Chef Silva, he developed the concept of "Indian tapas" for his new venture, the restaurant and lounge TASHAN in Philadelphia, a city known for its exquisite food culture. He asked Archi-Tectonics to develop a spatial concept for him.

Our concept in the design of the large 5,000-square foot restaurant space was to create several different dining experiences and a warm and relaxed

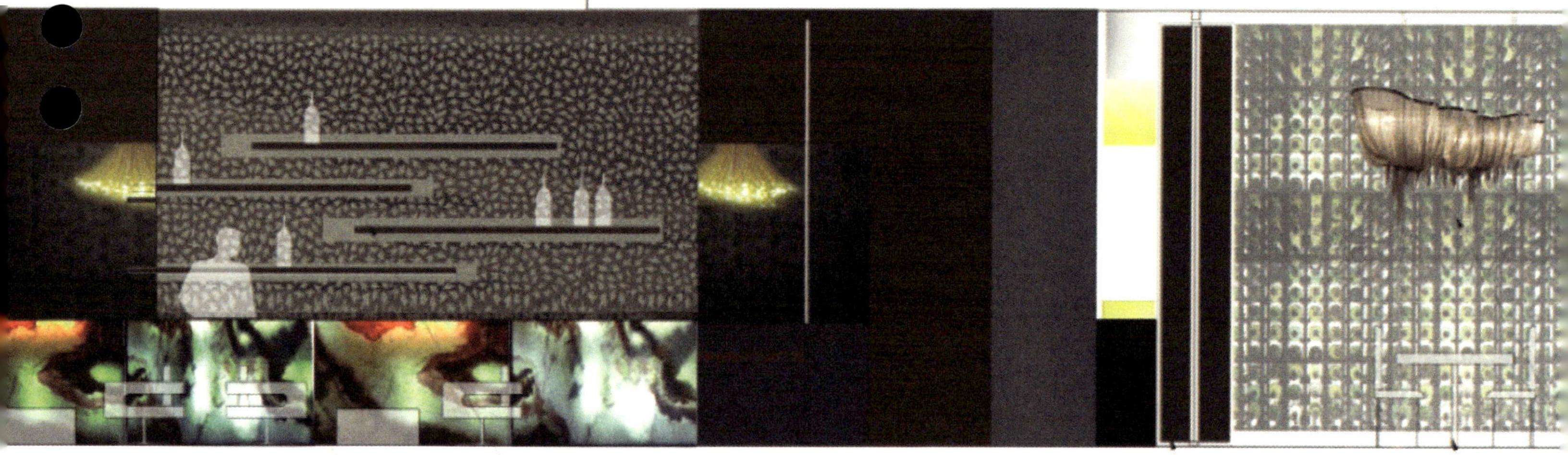

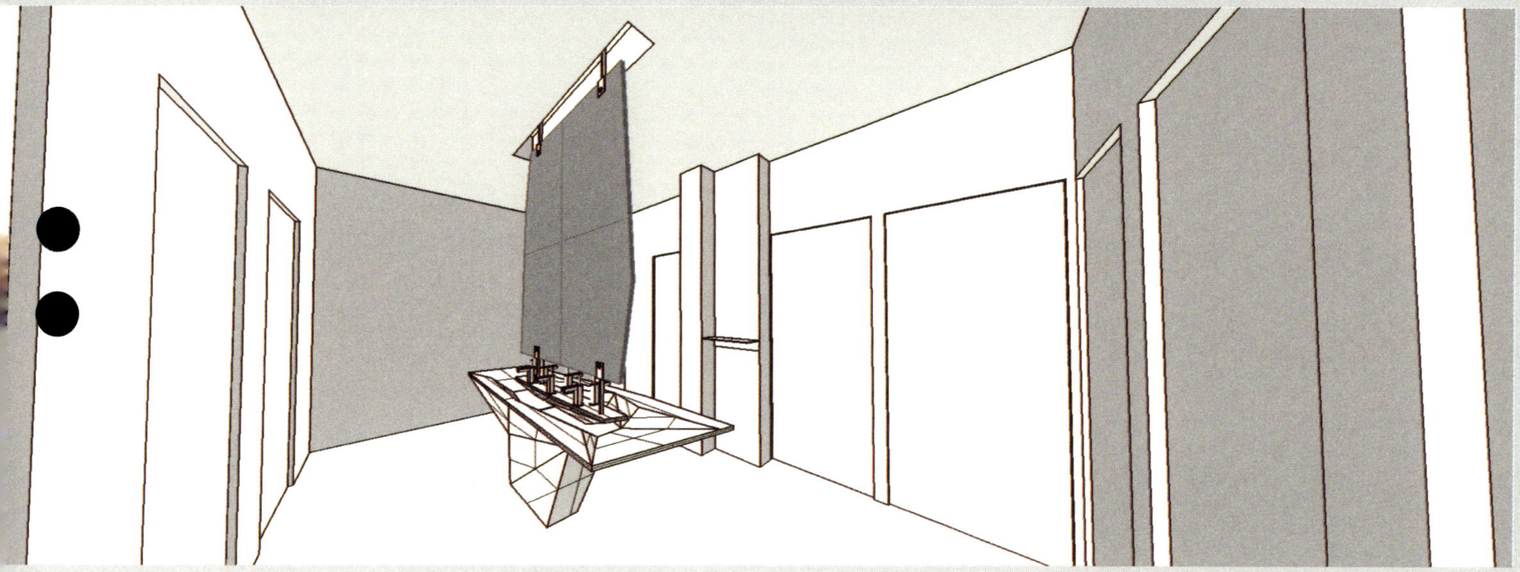

atmosphere. This was achieved by creating several distinct areas with different "speeds," starting with a relaxed bar lounge, followed by a more formal dining area, beautiful private booths, a secret wine room with select private dining, and a communal dining table close to the chef and the open kitchen. Although not meant to look Indian per se, the mix of modern lounge and dining furniture with antique Indian cultural artefacts created a playful and timeless contrast; the antiques created strange objects in an otherwise contemporary space. The dining furniture was custom-designed by Mexican designer Héctor Esrawe, and it was combined with innovative custom-fabricated components such as the bar, leather panel doors, and wood wall screens that accented and enhanced the overall atmosphere. Of course, this relaxed atmosphere extended to the most private space; a black communal bathroom with an enormous shared sink became an integral part of this dining experience.

AN.143-144

SECTION CUT

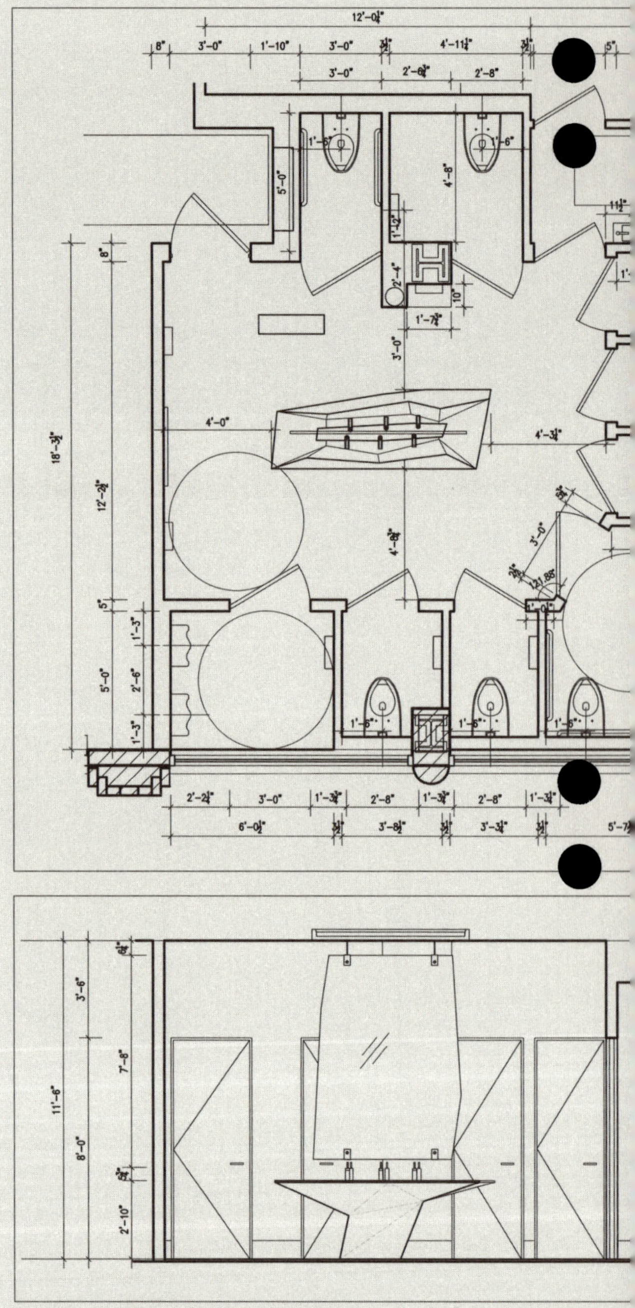

COMMUNAL BATHROOM FLOORPLAN
AND SECTION

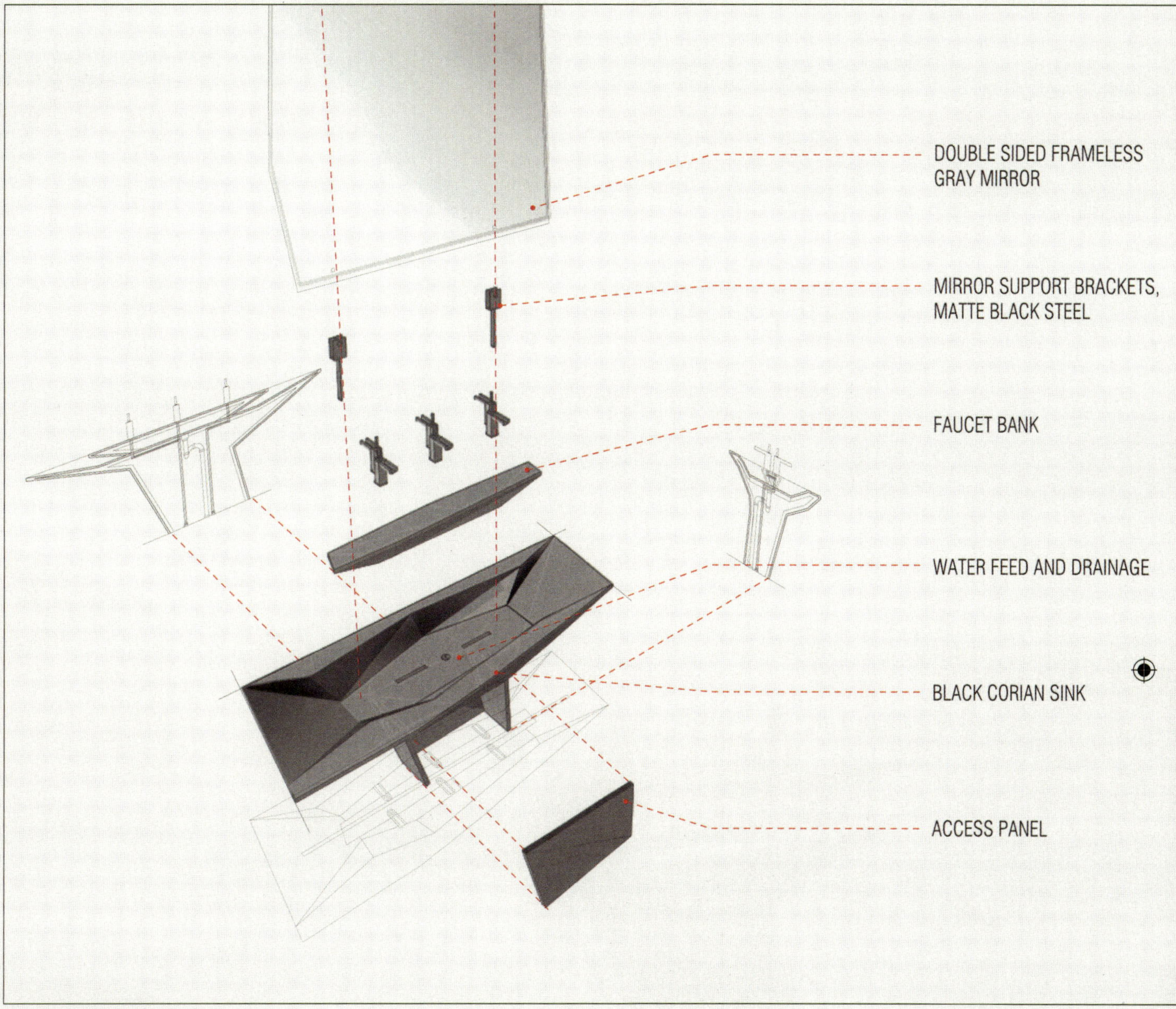

BLACK [K]NIGHT / BLACK SOLID

At the heart of tapas dining is the notion of community and sharing. We incorporated this not only into the design of the dining space, but especially in private spaces such as the communal bathroom. Not wanting to artificially separate diners into groups, one first enters a communal space around which private powder rooms are lined up. This spacious center space holds a large black custom-designed sink; the "Black Knight," which offers space for eight people to wash their hands simultaneously, while sharing some dialogue as well. In the separate powder rooms with black glass bead walls diners experience a moment of respite with mirrors, candles, and dimmed lighting.

SECTION CUT

UNIBODY

The extra large communal sink was designed as a unibody that hovers in space supported by just one section of its futuristic shape. The term Unibody comes from car design, something we are inspired by and aim to learn from while designing details.

A Unibody is achieved when the frame is the main supporting structure of a motor vehicle to which all other components are attached, comparable to the skeleton of an organism. This is also known as body-on-frame.

In the sink's case a structural, boatlike wood frame carries the whole structure clad with matte black Corian, seamlessly wrapping its sharp lines. Its sinks are made from the same black Corian and seamlessly integrated.

A delicate mirror is suspended above it from the ceiling, but it does not touch the sink. Its eight faucets can be used in unison, washing hands while admiring other people's hands. Discussions ensue...

777 South Broad Street is a LEED Certified Building.

As Owner and Developer, 777 South Broad █████ is committed to lessening the harmful impact buildings have on our natural environment As a means of measuring our efforts towards sustainable development and operations, █████ designed █████ Street to meet requirements of the US Green Building Council's (USGBC) Leadership in Energy and Environmental Design (LEED) Rating System. LEED is a credit-based rating system which identifies five environmental categories:

- Sustainable Sites,
- Water Efficiency,
- Energy and Atmosphere,
- Materials and Resources, and
- Indoor Environmental Quality.

The requirements of LEED serve to ensure:

- a lessened impact on the local ecosystem;
- reduced use of natural water resources, and reduced burden on municipal water supply and wastewater systems;
- improved energy efficiency through reduced amounts of energy consumed, and the use of more benign forms of energy;
- conservation of natural material resources, minimized pollution related to the harvesting, production, and transportation of materials; and
- better air quality for building occupants.

II. Implementation.
Each retail space has been designed to meet the Prerequisites and Credits of LEED. Following is a list of Credits that █████ has already achieved for the retail areas. The list includes a description of the requirements relevant to each Credit as well as guidelines for maintaining the Credit. These requirements have been met in the base building design; as they are incorporated into the fit-out of each retail space, they provide a solid foundation for pursuing █████ for Commercial Interiors. See Section III of these Guidelines for more information regarding LEED-C1.

ASSOCIATED FABRICATION

PROTOTYPE AS FINAL OBJECT

Associated Fabrication, our experienced manufacturer in Brooklyn, took the project to its extreme and engineered and fabricated this unibody as a solid black shape, where matte black Corian is clad on a smart 3D grid frame. Simple, light, and functional, this Corian solid not only performs perfectly but also touches the ground ever so lightly

As the body of the large sink hovers on only one vertical support, it also holds all of its structural system and its plumbing needs. With this precarious balance, it took some testing to get this right and stable. The close collaboration with the fabricators was instrumental in engineering the sink's structure and invisible connections for the ultimate seamless and fast installation in the space.

AN.154-155

AN.156

PREFABRICATION

AN.157

AN.158

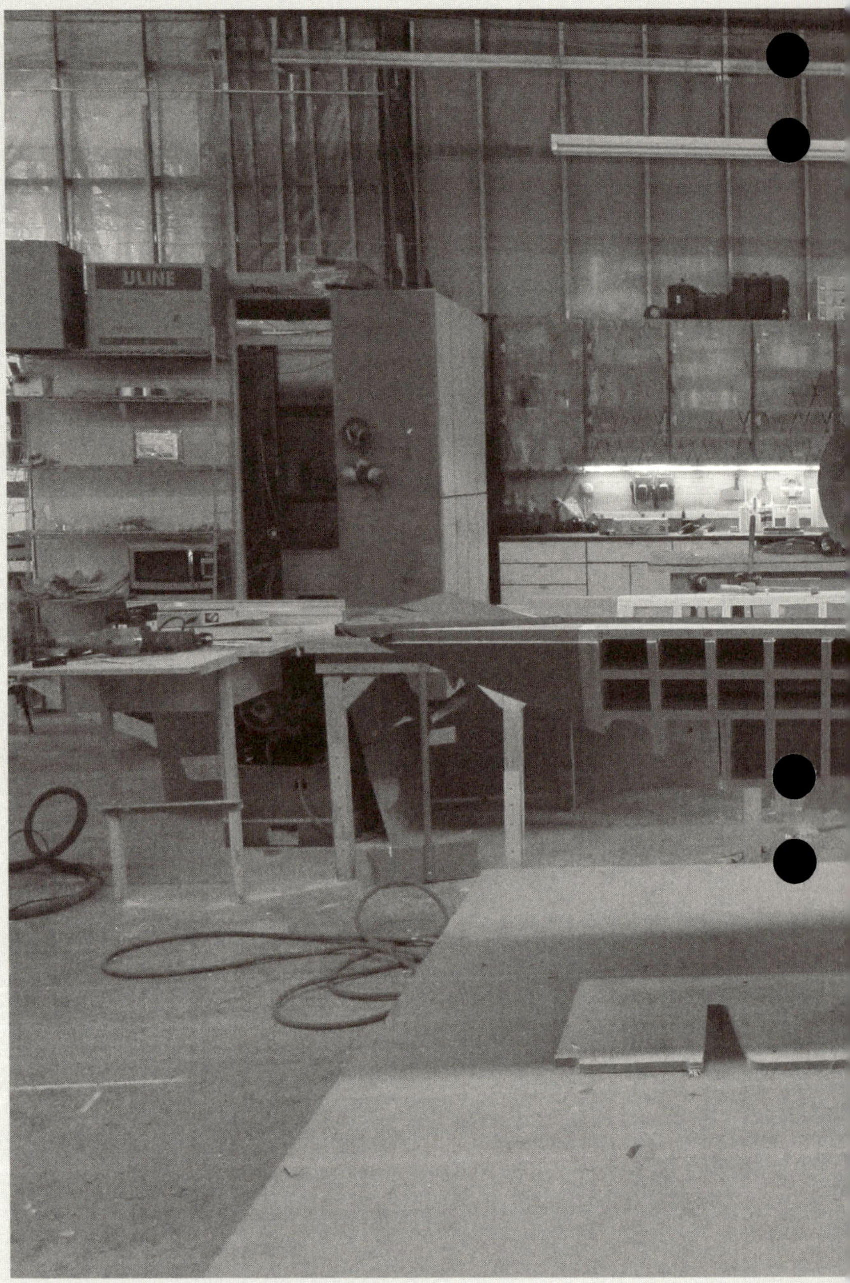

AN.159

SINK AS UNIBODY AND MONOCOQUE

AN.139

The term *tapas* means "warmth, heat, fire." The meaning of the word evolves in ancient Indian literature. The earliest discussions of *tapas*, and compound words from the root *tap* relate to the heat necessary for biological birth. Vedic scholars used mother nature's example to explain and extend this concept to hatching of knowledge and spiritual rebirth." (https://en.wikipedia.org/wiki/Tapas_(Indian_religions))

AN.140

AN.141-142

AN.143-144

AN.145

Sink as a unibody construction, meaning the body and frame have been integrated into one another.

AN.146

A section cut is used on a drawing to show an area or hidden part of an object by cutting away or removing some of that object. Here it is used to reveal the sink's inner workings, the hidden plumbing lines connected to the building's infrastructure.

AN.147-149

AN.150

AN.151

AN.152-153

The choice was made to create the sink like a solid 3D grid structure to help form its complex shape as a monocoque.

AN.154-155

Corian is a solid surface material that is non-porous, seamless, and has low VOC, with a minimum of 20% recycled content. (www.corian.com)

AN.156

AN.157

AN.158

In car design, computer-aided design software allows automakers to mold the shells of cars like clay to achieve precise contours. Unibody construction involves manufacturing the frame and body of the vehicle as a single piece. Here this principle was used for the sink configuration as a single object.

AN.159

AN.160-164

The New Materiality

Manuel DeLanda

In the last few decades an entirely new conception of the material world has emerged. Gone is the Aristotelian view that matter is an inert receptacle for forms that come from the outside (transcendent essences), as well as the Newtonian view in which an obedient materiality simply follows general laws and owes all its powers to those transcendent laws. In place of these passive notions, we can now conceptualize an active matter endowed with its own tendencies and capacities, engaged in its own divergent, open-ended evolution, animated from within by immanent patterns of being and becoming. What made this new vision possible was a series of changes to older concepts. Some were improved or refined, like the concept of causality, while others were radically transformed, like the idea of an eternal and immutable law which mutated into that of a distribution of singularities. Let's discuss these conceptual changes, starting with causality, the production of an event by another event.

The old conception of causality was inherently linear. The formula for linear causality is "Same Cause, Same Effect, Always." From this formula, naive forms of determinism follow: if every cause always has the same effect, we should be able to follow the chain all the way to a first cause. And vice versa, once that first cause occurs everything else is given: there is no novelty in the universe. But the different assumptions built into this formula can be challenged to produce different forms of nonlinear causality. The word "same," for example, can be challenged in two ways because it may be interpreted as referring both to the intensity of the cause ("same intensity of cause, same intensity of effect") as well as to the very identity of the cause. Let's begin with the simplest nonlinearity, the one challenging sameness of intensity. As an example, we can use Hooke's law capturing a regularity in the way solid bodies respond to loads, like a strip of metal on which a given weight has been attached. Hooke's law may be presented in graphic form as a plot of load versus deformation, a plot that has the form of a straight line. This linear pattern captures the fact that if we double the amount of weight supported by the metal its deformation will also double. More generally, Hooke's law states that a material under a given load will stretch or contract by a given amount which is always proportional to the load.

While some materials, like mild steel and other industrially homogenized metals, do indeed exhibit this kind of proportional effect, many others do not. Organic tissue, for example, displays a J-shaped curve when load is plotted against deformation. A gentle tug of one's lip, for instance, causes a considerable extension but after that, pulling it harder causes little additional extension. In other words, a cause of low intensity produces a relatively high intensity effect up to a point after which increasing the intensity of the cause produces only a low intensity effect. Other materials, like the rubber in a balloon, display a S-shaped curve, representing a more complex relation between intensities: at first increasing the intensity of the cause (blowing harder) produces almost no effect at all, as the balloon refuses to bulge; as the intensity of the air pressure increases, however, a point is reached at which the rubber balloon suddenly yields and rapidly increases in size, but only up to a second point at which it again stops responding to the load.

The fact that the J-shaped and S-shaped curves are only two of several possible departures from strict proportionality implies that the terms "linear" and "nonlinear" are not a simple dichotomy. Rather, nonlinear patterns represent a variety of possibilities of which the linear case is but a limiting case. A stronger form of nonlinear causality is exemplified by cases that challenge the very identity of causes and effects in the formula "Same Cause, Same Effect, Always." When an external stimulus acts on an organism, like a simple bacterium, the stimulus acts in many cases as a mere catalyst. A biological creature is defined internally by many complex series of events, some of which close on themselves forming a causal loop (like a metabolic cycle) exhibiting its own internal states of stability. A switch from one stable state to another can be triggered by a variety of stimuli. Thus, in such a system different causes can lead to the same effect. For similar reasons two different components of a biological entity, each with a different set of internal states, may react completely different to external stimulation. That is, the same cause can lead to different effects depending on the part of the organism it acts upon, like a hormone that stimulates growth if applied to the tips of a plant but inhibits it if applied to the roots.

Conceptually, the switch from linear to nonlinear causality involves taking into account not only an entity's capacity to affect (a load's ability to push or pull) but also another entity's capacity to be affected (a particular material's disposition to be pushed or pulled.) Whereas in Hooke's law only the load's capacity to affect is considered, once we switch to organic tissue or rubber, the different capacities of these materials to be affected need to be included.

And in the case of catalysis, the internal states of an organism define capacities to be affected that can be triggered by stimuli with very different capacities to affect. Thus, an important conceptual move in the direction of an active materiality is the characterization of material systems not just by their properties but also by their capacities. Let's illustrate this with a simple example. A knife is partly defined by its properties, such as having a certain shape or weight, as well as being in a certain state, like the state of being sharp. A sharp knife, on the other hand, has the capacity to cut things, a capacity that can be exercised by interacting with entities that have the capacity to be cut: cheese or bread, but not a solid piece of titanium. Philosophically, there is an important distinction between properties and capacities. Properties are always actual, since at any given point in time the knife is either sharp or it is not. But the causal capacity to cut is not necessarily actual if the knife is not currently being used. This implies that capacities can be real without being actual. The technical term for this ontological condition is "virtual." This double life of material systems, always actual and virtual, is an important component of the new materiality.

Another component of the new conception is a material semiotics. At the end of the nineteenth century a classification of signs was introduced that included three categories: symbols, signs that stand for their referent by a conventional relation; icons (e.g. drawings, diagrams, maps) that stand for what they represent by a relation of similarity (or isomorphism); and finally, indices or traces, signs that indicate what they stand for by having a causal relation to it. The classic example of an index is the relation between fire and smoke (the presence of smoke indicates that of fire) but other examples include fingerprints and footprints, tree rings, symptoms of disease, and facial expressions. When a metallurgist or a carpenter is working on a piece of metal or wood, they are constantly checking for indications that the operations they are performing are having the desired effect: if the carpenter is sanding a surface he or she will touch it looking for any sign that the surface is not smooth, and when a blacksmith is hammering the edge of a sword, he or she will be checking the edge for signs of rigidity. More generally, working with materials will typically involve the detection of natural signs that express the potentialities of a given material submitted to a particular operation. Had these "natural signs" become part of twentieth century semiotic theory, which came to be dominated by symbols alone, the separation between meaning and causality would not seem as tenuous as it does today.

But the main source of confusion in this regard is that the word "meaning" is used in multiple ways. When someone asks, in the midst of a conversation, "What do you mean?" this is normally a request for the dictionary definition of a word, or its signification. But if a distraught friend comes to us for advice and utters the sentence, "My life has no meaning," it would be foolish to take that as a request for semantic content. Rather, what our troubled friend is trying to say is, "My life feels unimportant, irrelevant; it feels like I do not make a difference to anyone." In this case, the word "meaning" is used to denote significance. That the two words are entirely different can be seen from the fact that something without signification is termed "nonsensical," whereas something without significance is termed "trivial." Now, imagine our master carpenter or metallurgist trying to teach an apprentice to practice the craft. Words may be used as part of the teaching, but the skills needed are better taught by example and learned by doing. When the student asks, for example, "Does it make a difference if I sand with the grain as opposed to against the grain?," the teacher will respond "Yes, following the direction of the fibers as you sand is significant." And when the student asks, "Does it make a difference if I allow the molten metal to cool down slowly or fast?," the teacher will say, "Yes, annealing will yield a ductile metal while quenching yields a rigid metal, so the two operations are significantly different." In this example we are using words that have signification but it is quite simple to imagine the training taking place in silence with the teacher guiding the disciple to notice the natural signs expressing the effect of different causal interventions, and to understand the significance of these effects for the final product.

In conclusion, the new materiality refers not only to an active matter with its own powers, capable of giving birth to form without the need for eternal essences, but also to a matter that is expressive as it emits a variety of natural signs that indicate its causal powers. Human beings are required to interpret and use those signs, but not as disembodied thinkers using only symbols but as embodied tinkerers, using bodily skills to causally intervene on that active matter, teasing out forms and assigning significance to them. We need to consider both the new materiality capacity to be affected and our own capacities to affect it, to enter into a partnership with it when giving birth to new forms.

S.03 SMART SKIN

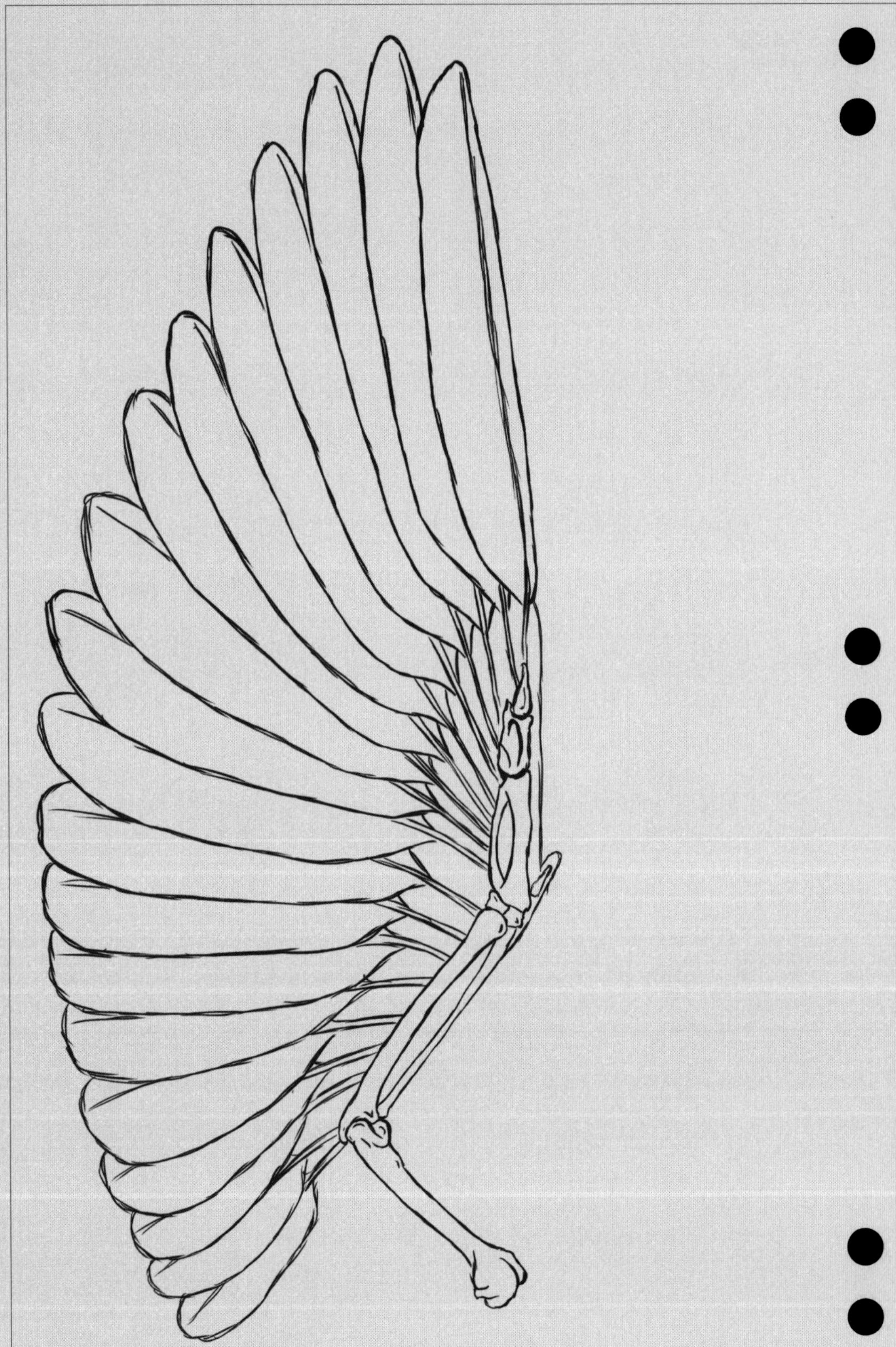

Historically, building skins have been compared to human bodies with live attributes such as "sweating" (condensating), "breathing" (ventilating), and "glaring" (reflecting). The traditional protective mass of the building skin has increasingly been taken over by monitoring systems, similar to our nervous system and brains, transforming skins into connective membranes rather than separative devices. Simultaneously, the standardization of the glass wall into a curtain wall system is allowing for faster installation of high efficiency building skins.

Bionic science, the construction of artificial systems that have some of the characteristics of living systems, has studied the body's skeleton, the spinal cord and its signal transmission to optimize the structural systems and routes of energy transfer in tall slender buildings. In this context, the human brain—intelligent controller of the body—has two major functions: reacting to stimuli and commanding other organs. The human skin, on the other hand, with its complex permeable capacities has a significant role in communicating between the exterior microclimate and the endoclimate of the body. This can be directly translated into essential smart building features giving a facade agency, such as self-healing membranes, as well as performative behaviors like energy absorption, repelling or retaining, and active adaptable permeability.

FEATHERING

Layering adds to the transformative capacity and efficiency of a facade as a climate adaptor. Feathering was the inspiration for the 512 GW Townhouse. The transformational behavioral aspects of the wing, relative to its change in performance, results in feathers of different shapes and textures. Similarly, the building's facade trellis panels transform when they fold outwards. The slats on the panels spread out like feathers and thus reduce friction in their scissor movement. As they slide horizontally the panels also adapt as a whole, gradually adjusting their climatic performance and levels of interior privacy. When the panels are open, the slats feather out and intersect, while closed they align into one smooth surface, shading the interior spaces behind a lattice screen.

Humans have often imitated the bird wing in an attempt to fly (an ornithopter, from Greek *ornithos* "bird" and *pteron* "wing," is an aircraft that flies by flapping its wings), most famously in Leonardo da Vinci's flying machines. The facade of 512 GW is not looking at biological mimicry of the bird wing, but rather at its operational intelligence. Bird species developed distinct wing configurations over the course of millions of years through evolution, adapting to specific environments and developing specializations required for different forms of flight: to glide, flap, or hover. These evolutionary improvements are informative when studying adaptable behavioral aspects of architectural components and the spaces they impact.

TRANS-FORM

Digital and cross-platform design has not only revolutionized the architectural production process, it has led to a reconceptualization of how architectural form is conceived. Complex geometries, facilitated by file-to-factory design methodologies, allow for mass customization rather than mass standardization, which made the curtain wall system successful. Digital fabrication has facilitated faster and higher-precision production and has brought back a return of freeform patterning and imbedded ornamentation. Often referred to as digital craft, these patterns are no longer applied on building surfaces, but rather are integrated directly into the surface, creating new (digital) aesthetics, exciting material hybrids, and intense tactile experiences. This changes the way architecture is designed, manufactured, and assembled, and allows architects to create smart environments that are at once haptic, adaptable, and responsive to changing circumstances and environments.

497 GW

INFLECTION

FOLDING [SUR]FACES

In the 497 GW project, located on the edge of Soho, a new 11-story structure folds over a renovated six-story warehouse. The New York City building code is here reinterpreted; the horizontal plane of the traditional urban fabric is questioned by the insertion of a diagonally folded surface that bifurcates the facade plane. It integrates the strict building setback codes into the new folded vertical landscape of the west facing glass facade. The crease between old and new as mediation and the glass inflections as spatial device

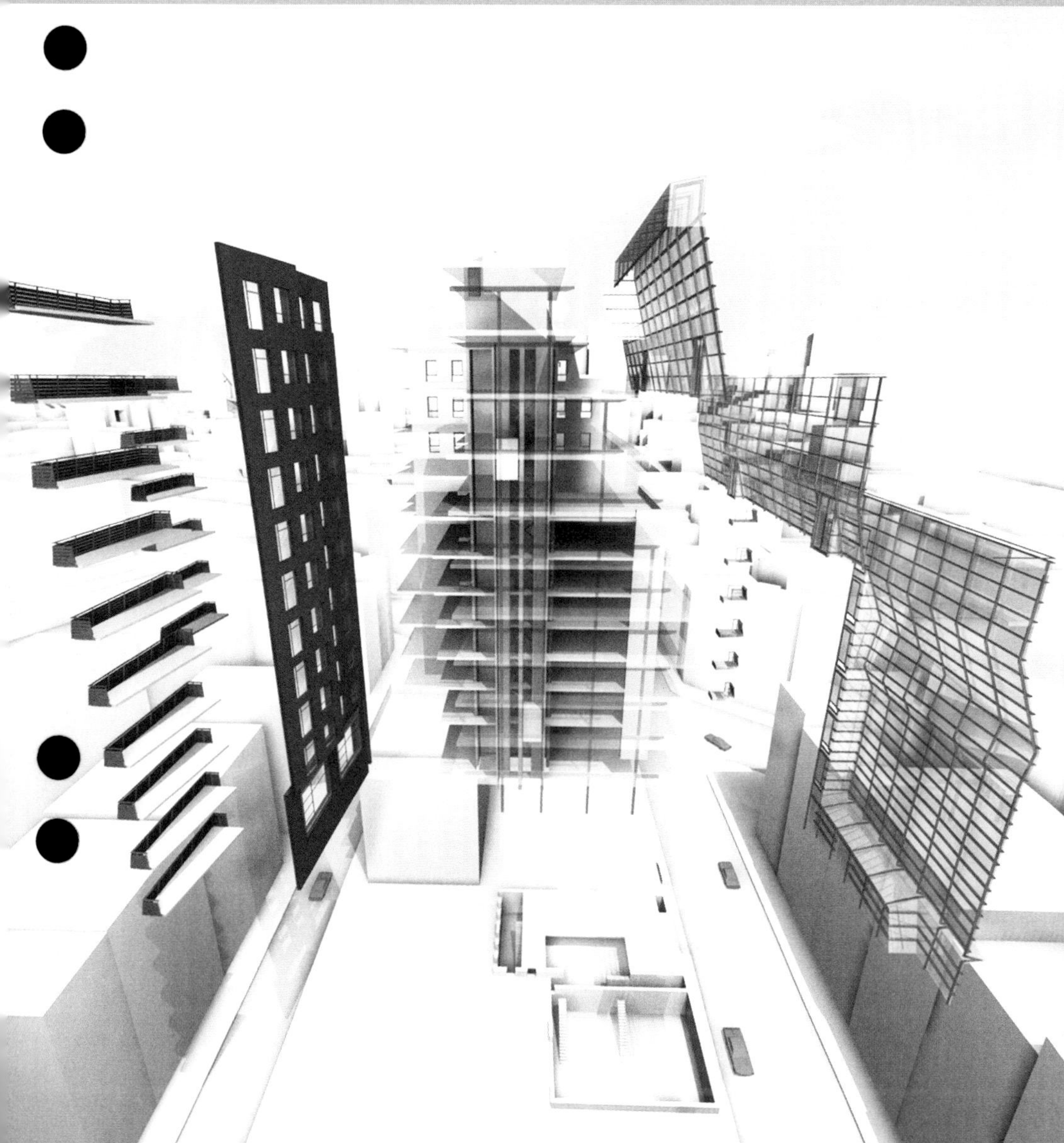

allow for slippage between interior urbanism and urban privacy. The crystalline facets of the facade allow for it to move away from a separative two-dimensional membrane into a three-dimensional glass zone, or object, to be occupied and inhabited. Herbert Muschamp, famed architecture critic wrote in *The New York Times*: "Dubbeldam's folds are philosophically as well as visually grounded... [She] crystallizes urban complexity within the discrete architectural object."

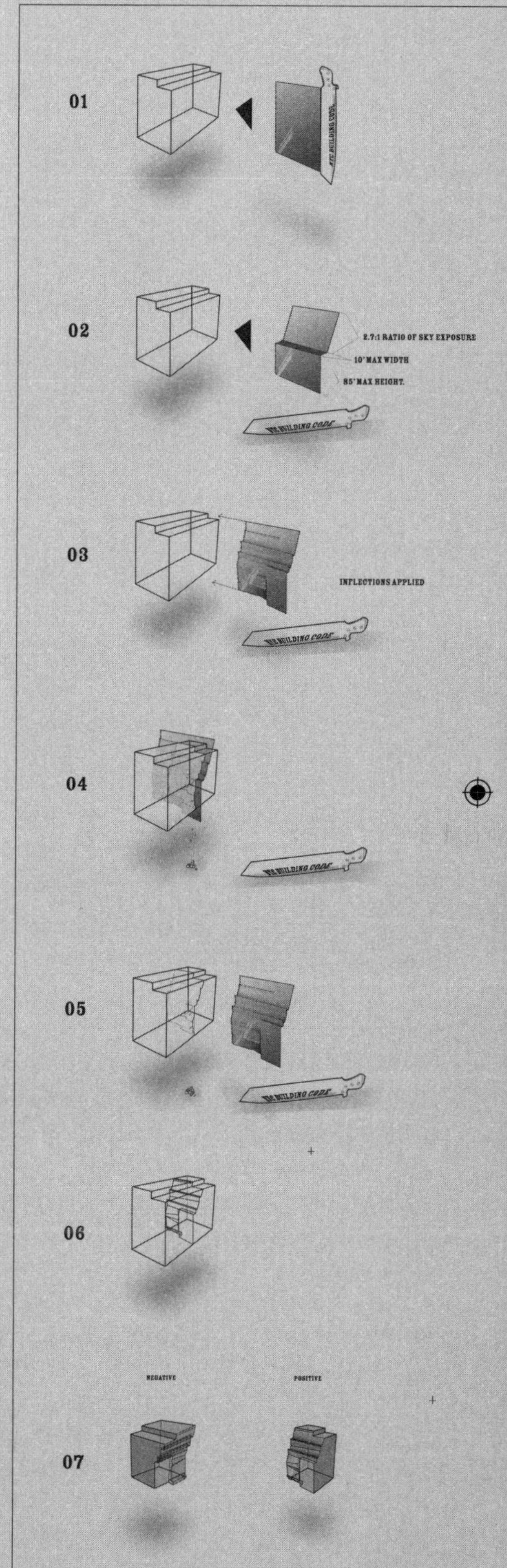

DECODING THE BUILDING CODE

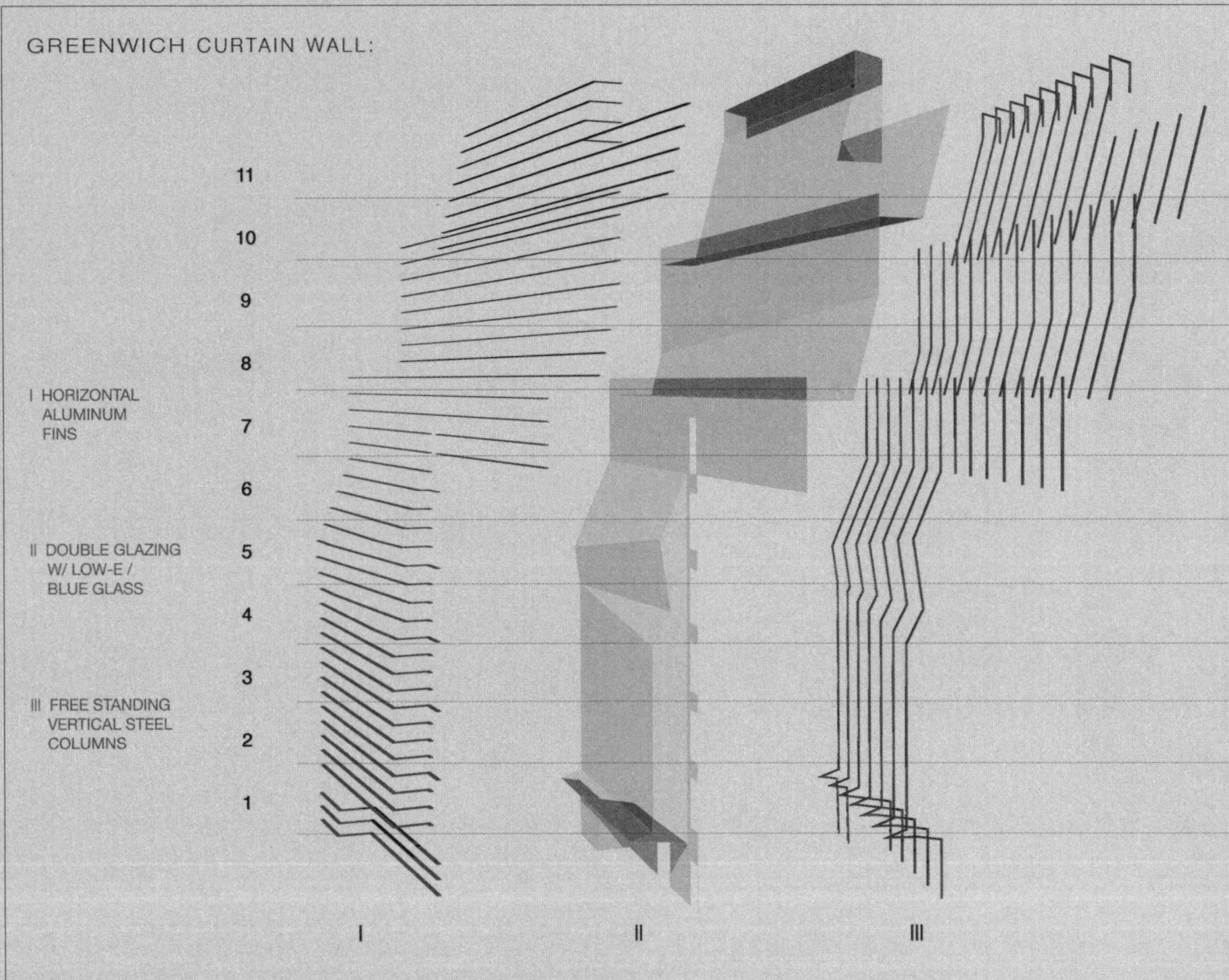

BUILDING CODE RE-INTERPRETED / INFLECTION

For the new eleven-story glass extension we studied the New York City building code, and used "inflection" as the mathematical tool to negotiate the zoning requirement's allowable 85 foot high straight facade plane with the prescribed tilted setback plane for the higher floors, in a ratio of 2.7:1. This inflection—the change of curvature from convex to concave over a point or line—resonates through the facade as bending in the glass, resulting in a set of folded oblique planes that collapse skyviews on streetviews and negotiates the urban streetscape with interior private spaces.

Architecture is by nature a slow profession. Only through avant-garde movements and technological inventions has architecture challenged notions such as traditional craftsmanship, proportional systems, and aesthetics. A generative architecture expresses itself as a recording of the performative behavioral processes, a registration of surface deformations. The relation of the skin-body, animate body, investigates the close relationship between material intelligence and resulting spatial volumes.

3D GLASS AS SOLID

INFLECTIONS AND REFLECTIONS

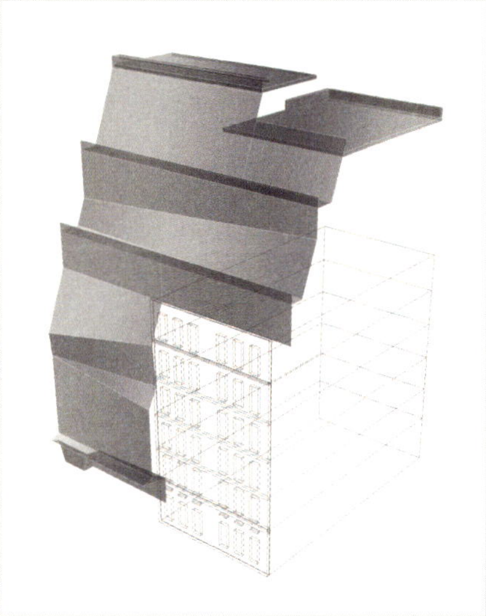

DECODING THE BUILDING CODE

SS.10

SS.11-12

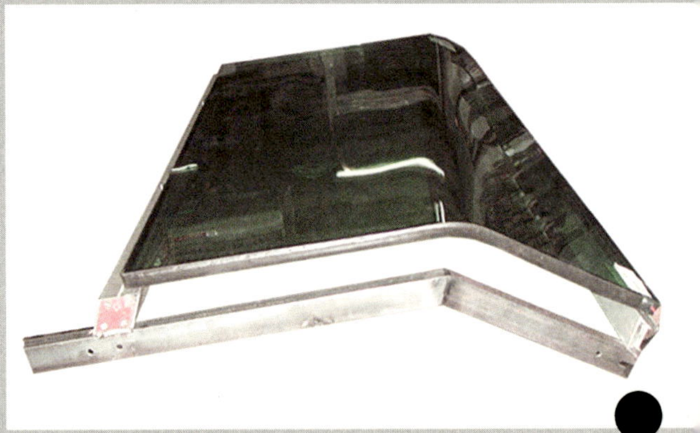

SEPARATION OF MULLIONS

GLASSINESS

At the curtain wall's ends the glassy effect takes over; mullions disappear, and the glass is simply suspended on stainless steel pins from the thin steel (S6) mullions and glued at its mitered corners. At the ground floor the curtain wall folds out as a glass plane (canopy) over the entrance area, lobby, retail, and art gallery. At the top of the curtain wall the glass planes fold over and down to the roof, ending the facade as a 3D voluminous glass bulkhead. The 497 GW building transforms structural innovation into a poetic reading of glass waves.

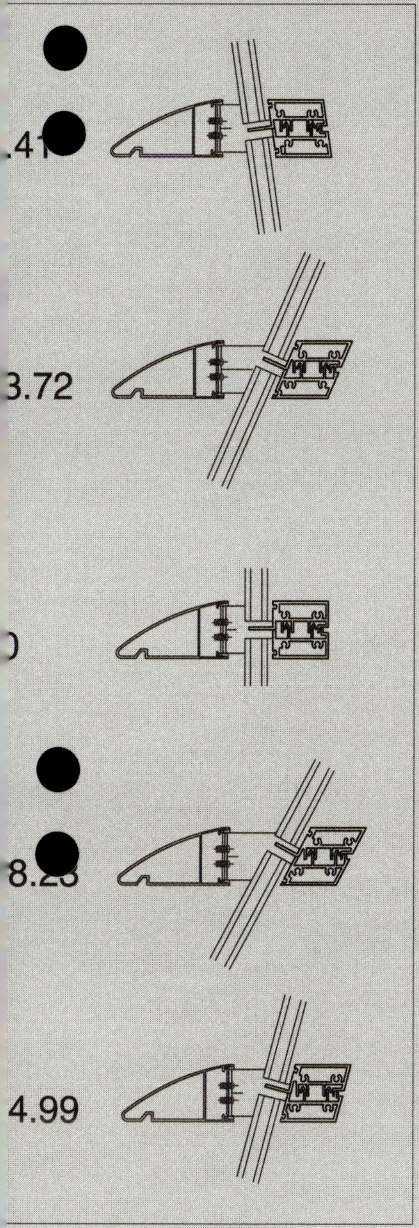

CUSTOM MULLIONS

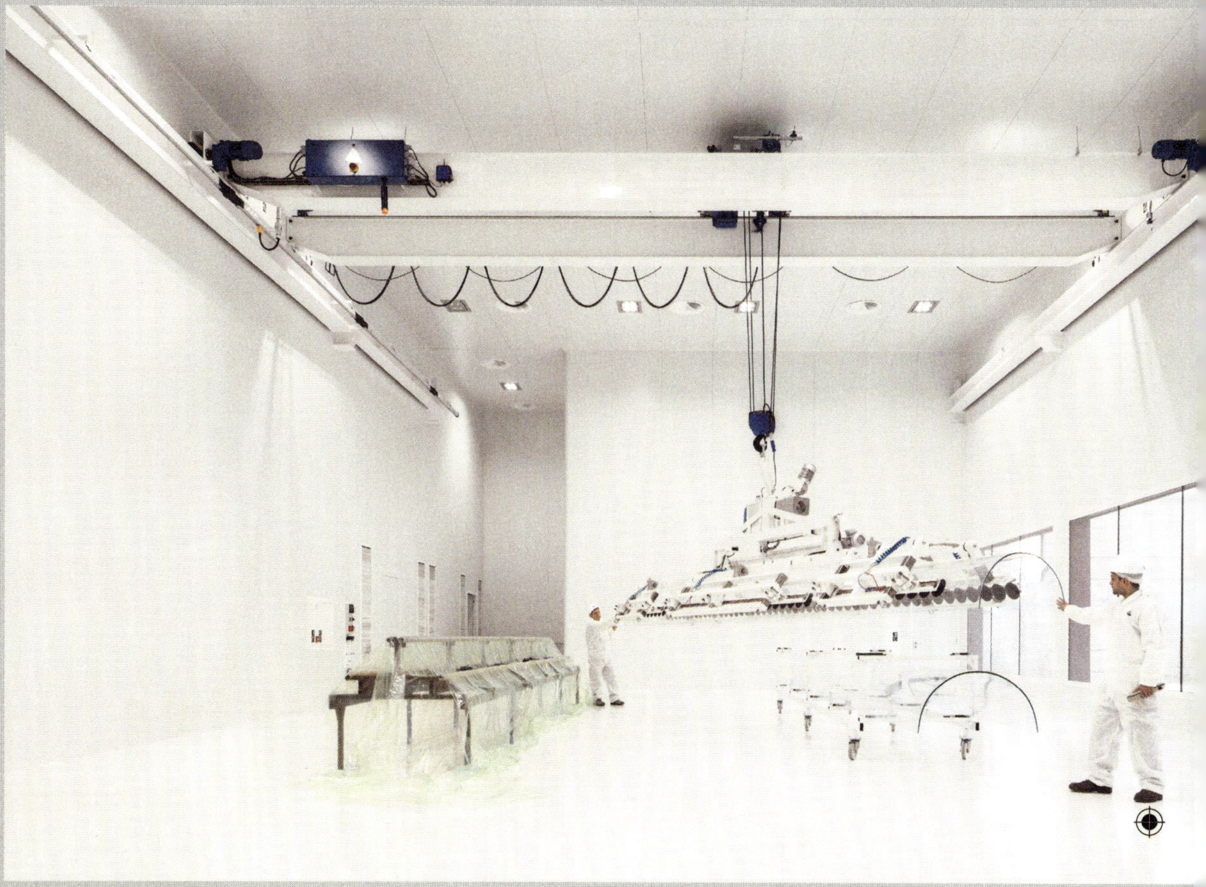

CRICURSA FACTORY

SEPARATION OF MULLIONS

A fully custom curtain wall was created from thin steel verticals connected to a suspended structure of glass planes and horizontal aluminum fins. Mullions were separated: welded steel vertical mullions provide a strong base to stabilize folds, and aluminum horizontals provide thermal breaks at the joints of the glass panels, which are suspended off the verticals with spacers, thus creating a facade of horizontal bands rather than a facade grid. The solar 1-inch insulated glass units are assembled as a unitized system. For environmental efficiency, we added a low-E coating of metallic oxide, which blocks ultra-violet radiation in the summer and provides passive solar energy in the winter.

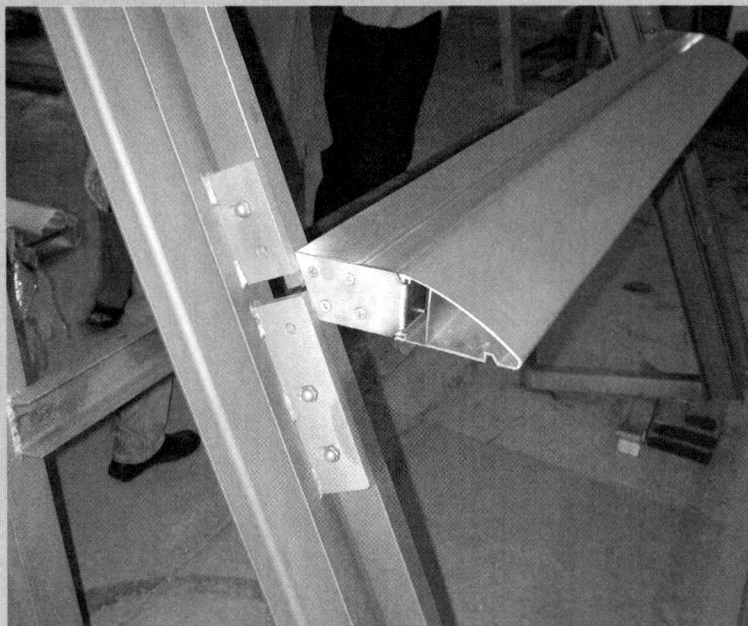

CUSTOM MULLION PROTOTYPES

INNOVATION / RESISTANCE

Trying to price this facade design with its folded surfaces proved quite a challenge. Although we sold it to the curtain wall companies as a standard curtain wall with only a 10 percent anomaly in the form of glass folds, the companies still came up with excessive, unattainable quotes. We had two choices: not build a folded curtain wall, or simply not call it a standard curtain wall. We decided to go custom.

Considering this now a "custom-designed" glass facade, we hired a curtain wall professional, and with the help of William Logan from Vidaris, we

SS.18

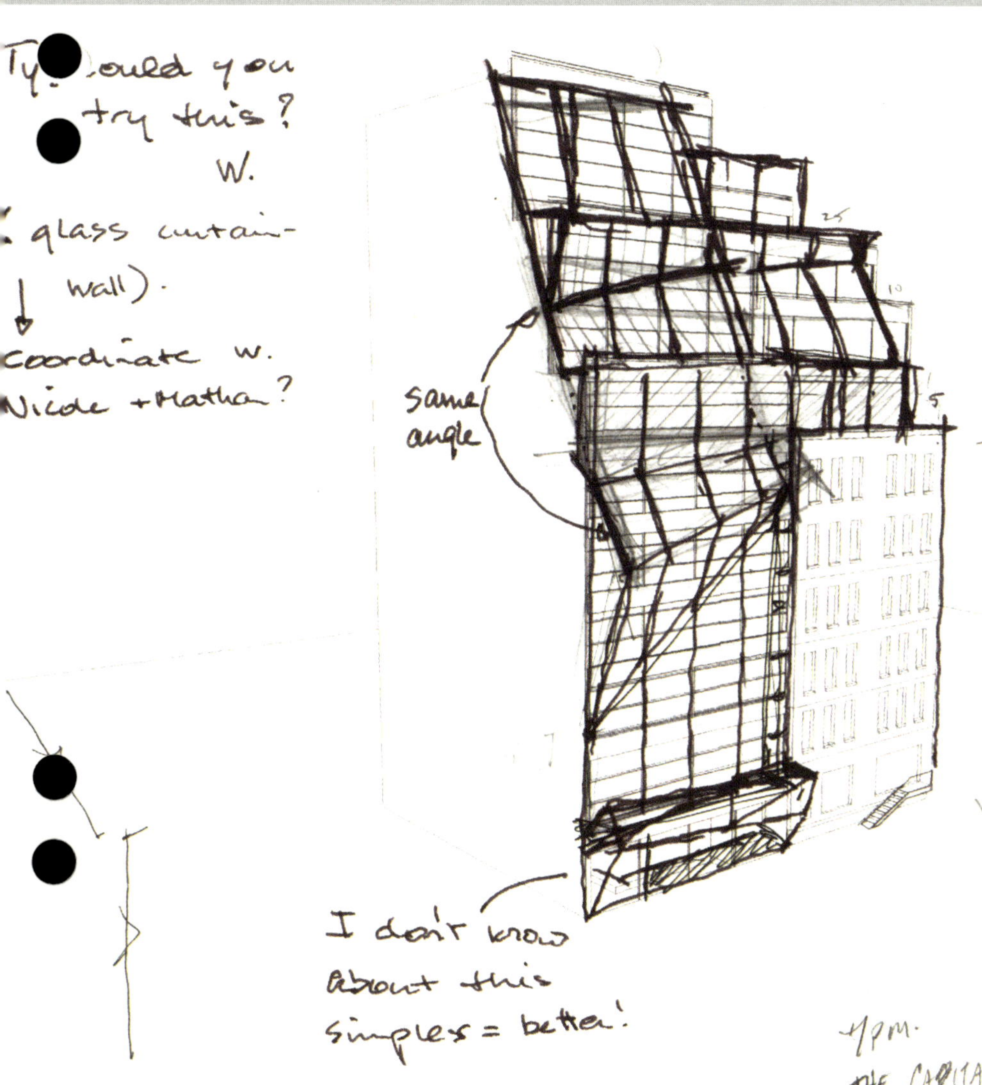

SS.19

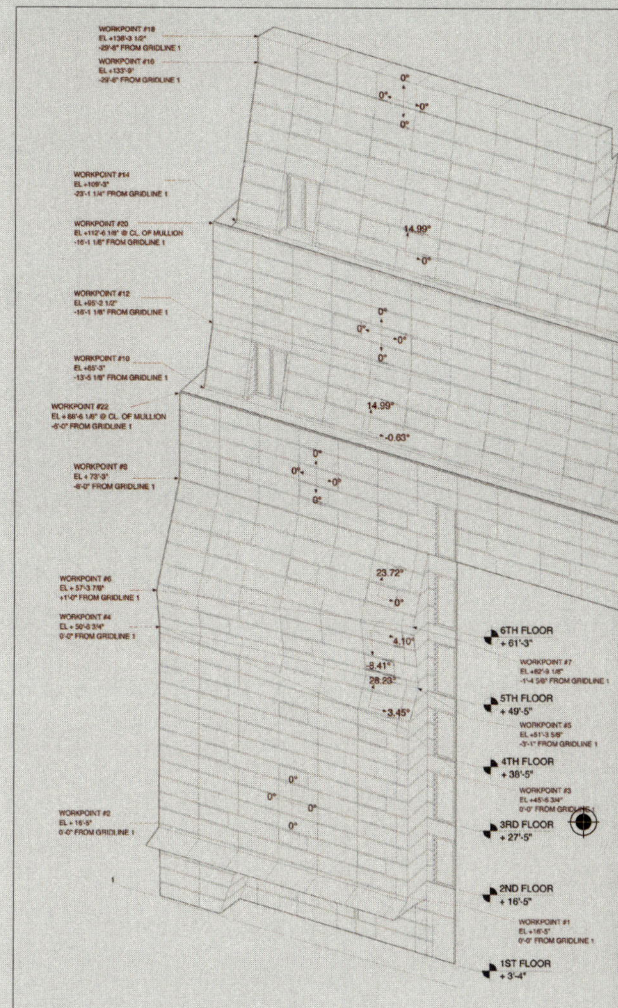

A FIRST PARAMETRIC MODEL

developed our "dream facade," an optimization of the standard system, we developed a customized facade of ultra-thin folded steel verticals (S6 profile) that carry suspended structurally glazed units on steel pins. The welded steel mullions facilitated and reinforced the glass folds, and provided the required mathematical precision for the folded geometry of the facade. Structurally glazed facade units demand a high-level precision with ⅟₁₆-inch of tolerance. Lastly, we decided to actually have the glass bent.

In 1999, 497 GW was one of the first parametrically designed facades, where a 3D computer model was distributed electronically to the different manufacturers with only X,Y,Z coordinates, no measurements were provided. In order to prevent mistakes as different cultures, countries, and companies were involved, FTF manufacturing allows a safeguarding of innovation, precision, cost reduction, and provides highquality.

SS.20-21

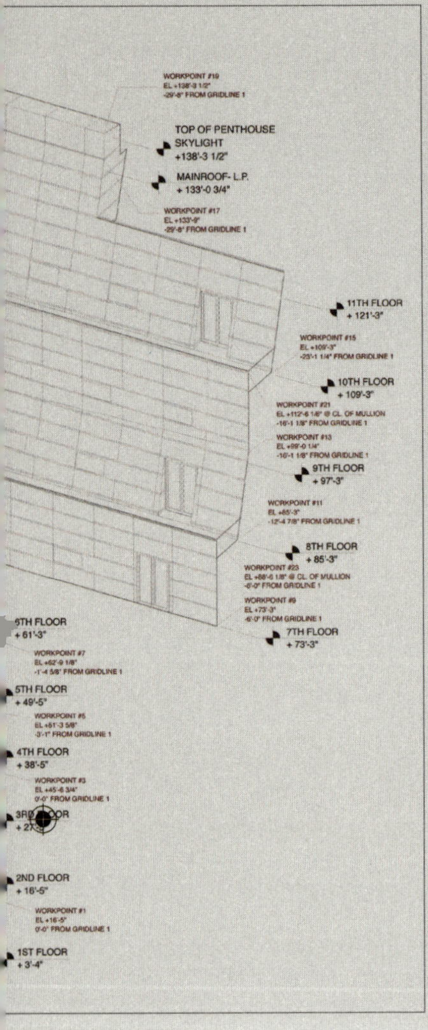

PARAMETRIC STUDY

SS.22

BENT ANNEALED DOUBLE GLAZING

VIF VERSUS VIC

The computer model is universal. For this facade, we worked with expert manufacturers: Cricursa from Spain for the bent double glazing units; United Aluminum from Hong Kong for the custom extruded mullions, following the angles of the bent glass; and United Aluminum in Brooklyn to custom weld the steel mullions (S6) and install it all. Even the site installation drawings for the general contractor were to fit the 3D model, so rather than VIF (verify in field), we asked for VIC (verify in computer), making this one of the first fully parametric construction processes.

This digital coordination allowed for pre-fabrication of the facade during construction, rather than measuring the site once complete, and a fast enclosure of the building. The facade was installed in merely three weeks. The complex three sub-profile glass construction—with its smooth, clean transitions between adjacent panels of glass—required the

INSTALLATION UNIFIED SYSTEM

CRICURSA
SPAIN

skills and precision of automotive glazing technology. Our curtain wall consultant worked directly with the design team to structurally optimize the cascading facade in order to produce nearly unobstructed views. The resulting folded, structurally glazed facade is bolted to thin lattice work of steel mullions, offering residents panoramic views of the city.

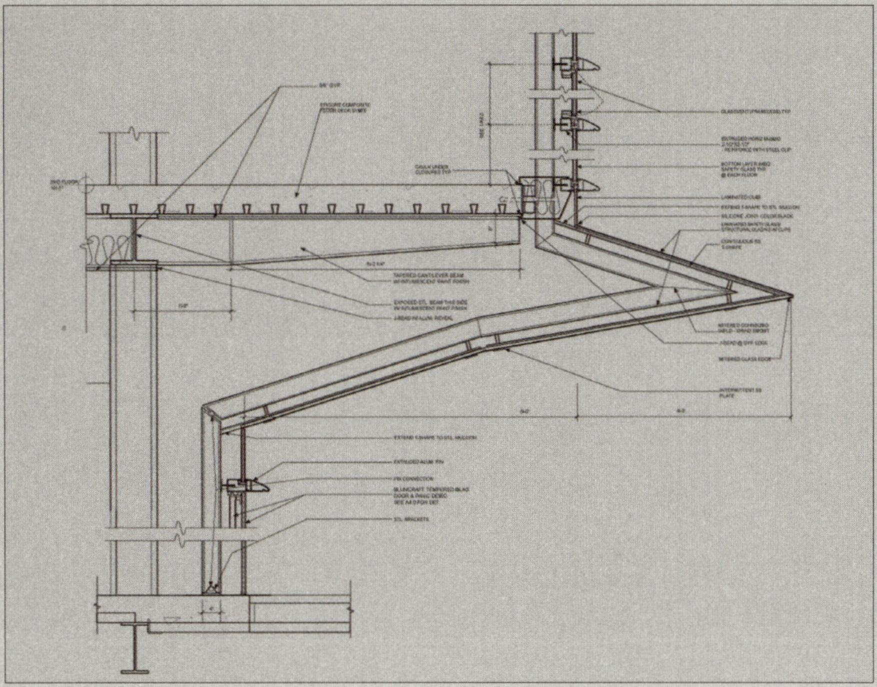

3D GLASS AWNING

GLASS HORIZON

The predominance of structural glass continues on the roof, where large, frameless glass bulkheads refract light down with their crystalline shapes. Stainless "spider connections" hold the glass tightly in place. To strengthen the top of the building for wind load, rather than making the mullions heavier, we added steel cables to reinforce the mullions, inspired by boat design, for example. Our curtain wall consultant is a sailor himself, and his knowledge combined with our daring facade engineer made this ultra-light solution possible. The frameless glass bulkhead creates a glass horizon with an invisible edge reflecting the sky.

SS.28-29

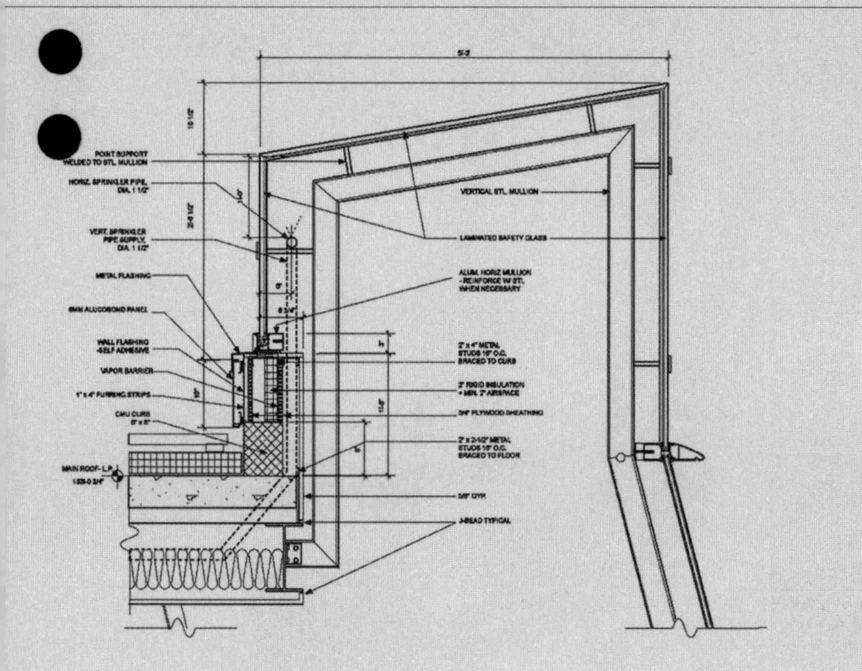

SS.30

GLASS BULKHEAD

SS.31-32

LOFT 8B

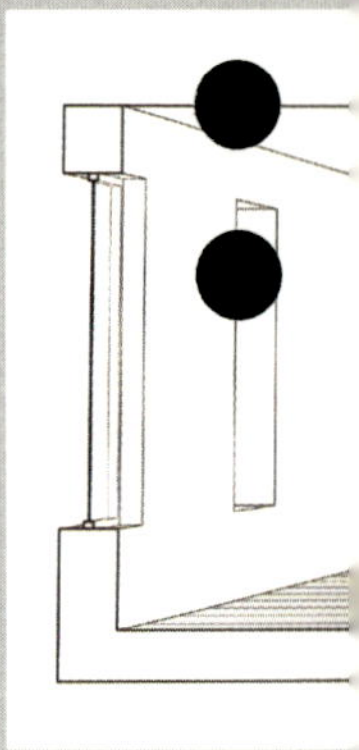

"A pliant system is easily bent with other elements and in so doing results in multiplication. Its multiplicity means that it is both one and many; it appears to be singular, and yet is replete with finer programmatic elements fostered through connections and affiliations with other elements."
– Greg Lynn

A PLIANT SYSTEM

The 3,200-square-foot Schein loft is located on the eighth floor of the 497 GW glass and concrete extension, cantilevering over the existing brick warehouse with a glass setback. Its slanted curtain wall is regulated by solar sensors: electric shades react instantly to sun strength, lowering to keep the space cool. The interior is organized around a simple folded bog oak spine that solidifies the glass folds of the facade into the folded spine geometry, continuing deep into the loft. The spine reorganizes

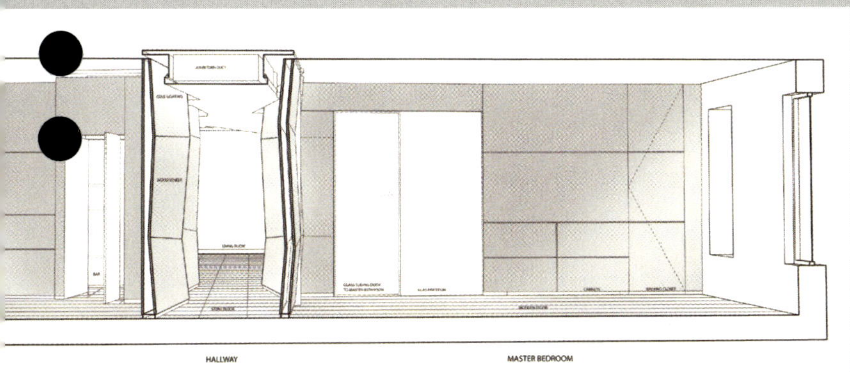

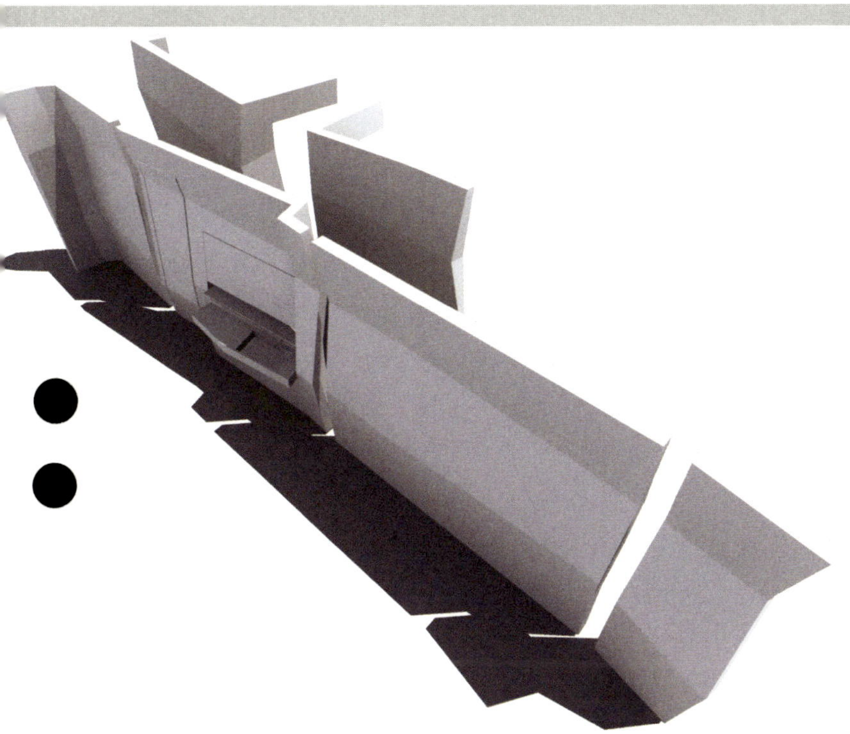

AXONOMETRIC

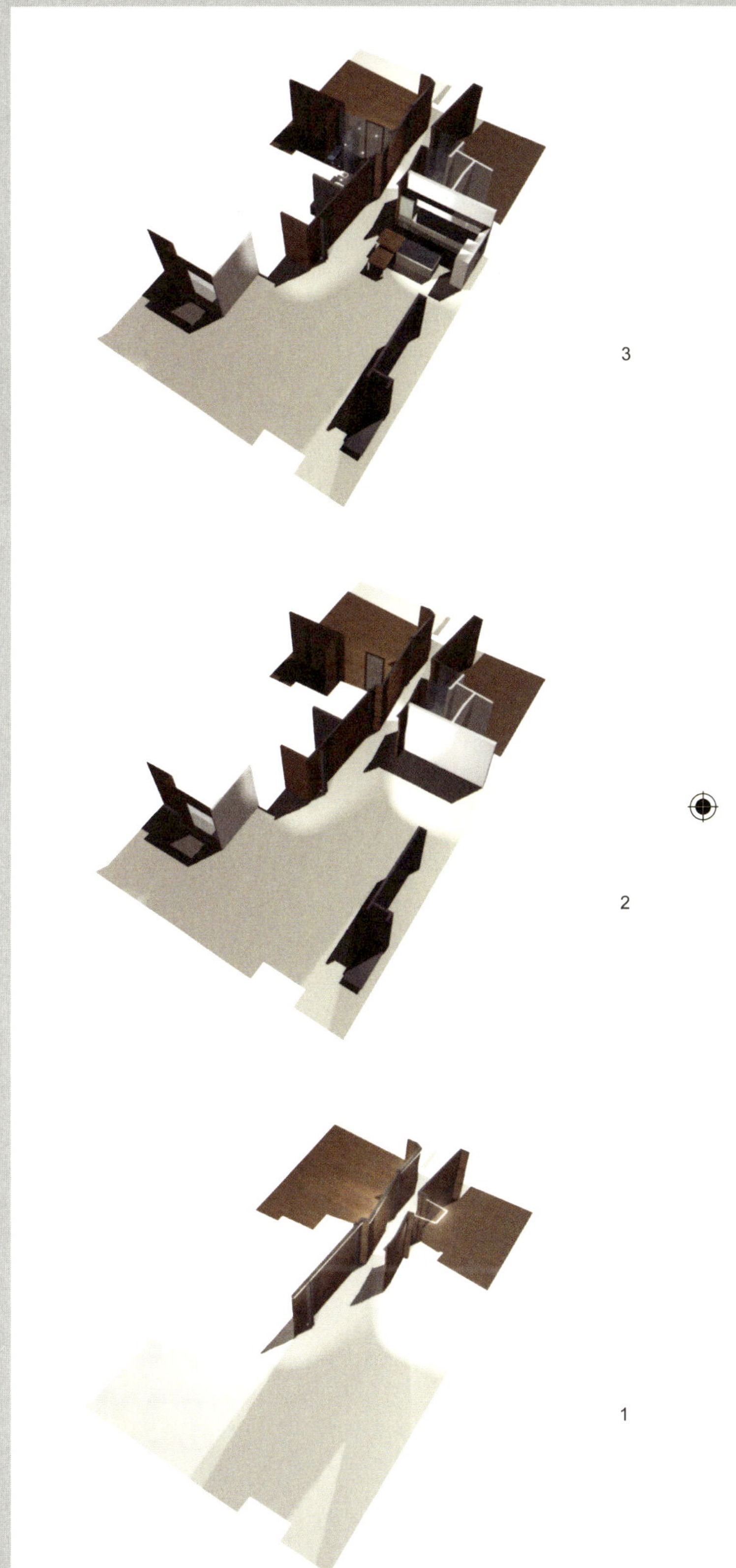

the interior spaces as a series of overlapping zones rather than enclosed rooms, tracing soft boundaries and creating spatial connectivity. The strange texture of bog oak gives the spine both a modern geometrically intricate pattern, as well as a sense of ancient mystery. Not to be fooled by its sensory surface, the spine also doubles as an infrastructure for central air, recessed light, and sound, held by a freely suspended ceiling plane.

BOG OAK

BOG OAK

What happens when an oak tree soaks in a swamp for thousands of years? It turns a deep black as acidic water is absorbed into its fibers. A natural material, recycled bog oak is a wood that is naturally stained by tannins in a blond and black pattern, after having been buried airtight in peat bogs for an extended period of time. The log of a bog oak is very strong and resistant, and its natural pattern fascinating. For the loft, we asked the general contractor to source bog oak in America's deep south, where this ancient European method has been cultivated. The bog oak planks were then sliced into a thin veneer, which was installed on site. The millworker carefully laid out the veneer pattern following the spine wall's folds. The result was a soft textured wall and its delicate preciousness made us ask the installer to keep it as natural as he could, and just protect it. He ended up treating the veneer with a silicon spray.

SS.39

SS.40

IN-FOLDING

The spine's walls flank all private zones, the primary bedroom with bathroom suite, the music room, a darkroom, and guest bedroom are all organized along this smooth axis. Within the folds one finds translucent doors to give access to private areas, and folded sections of the wall function as pivoting doors. The spine travels from the living quarters on the west window wall, to the private areas on the east facade, allowing light to travel throughout. The main bedroom with the en suite blue glass bathroom has a spa-like and escapist quality. The bathroom has a custom-designed backlit blue resin sink, an overflow bath, and the blue glass tiles with low recessed lights.

SS.02

SS.03

SS.04

Building code regulations are written, rewritten, and interpreted by a legion of builders, manufacturers, architects, engineers, fire marshals and inspectors. To complicate matters, there is no common language—there is no uniform building code in the United States. Apart from that, the "new" New York City code of 2014 has a mere 90 updates.(https://bct.eco.umass.edu/publications/articles/decoding-the-building-code/)

SS.05

SS.06

SS.07

SS.08-09

SS.10

SS.11-12

Separation of mullions for bent double glazing

SS.13

SS.14

SS.15

A standard curtain wall system, as per Kawneer's definition, is "a stick-frame assembly with weather performance achieved by drainage and ventilation of the glazing rebates. Drainage and ventilation is achieved via the mullion or via each individual transom on zone drained." (www.kawneer.com)

SS.16-17

SS.18

Original concept design sketch by Winka [made in train]

SS.19

Parametric design is a process based on algorithmic thinking that enables the expression of parameters and rules that, together, define, encode and clarify the relationship between design intent and design response. (https://en.wikipedia.org/wiki/Parametric_design)

SS.20

SS.21

"Curved annealed glass is manufactured by slowly heating flat glass up to the softening temperature, around 550°C, when the glass starts slumping due to gravity on the customized mould" (www.cricursa.com)

SS.22

SS.23-24

SS.25

Section through the structurally glazed entrance awning

SS.26-27

SS.28

"Rigging" is derived from Anglo-Saxon wrigan or wringing, "to clothe". Stainless steel rigging hardware was used to improve the structure's efficiency and cohesiveness, to withstand the enormous windload on the buildings bulkheads. The system of ropes, cables and chains Square-rigs tensions the bulkhead in place. (https://en.wikipedia.org/wiki/Rigging)

SS.29

The wind load increases around the bulkhead of the building, rather then enlarging the elegant S6 steel profiles, we decided to use stainless steel tension cables to stiffen the frame, like the cables commonly used for sailboat rigging.

SS.30

SS.31

SS.32

SS.33-34

From Greg Lynn's "Architectural Curvilinearity: The Folded, The Pliant and The Supple," Constructing a New Agenda: Architectural Theory 1993-2009. By Krista Sykes. (New York: Princeton Architectural, 2010), 32-61.

SS.35

SS.36

SS.37

Bog oak is wood that has been buried for many years in boglands, and through the lack of oxygen and the acidic and anaerobic bog conditions, the wood has been preserved from the natural process of decay, and colored by the tannins naturally present in the acidic water. (https://en.wikipedia.org/wiki/Bog-wood)

SS.38

SS.39

Infolding is the process of folding inward in of an outer layer so as to form a pocket in the surface. (https://www.thefreedictionary.com/infolding)

SS.40

SS.41-51

SS.52

3D section cut through new addition with bent glass facade and east facing balconies

V33

OPTIMIZATION VERSUS VARIATION

In the early nineteenth century, Tribeca was developed as a residential neighborhood close to the city's center in Lower Manhattan. Its street grid was laid out at right angles off of Greenwich Street and on a diagonal off of Broadway, creating blocks of different lengths and irregular open spaces. After the Civil War, shipping hubs moved from the East River to the North River, now the Hudson River. With a newly thriving industrial waterfront, the residential

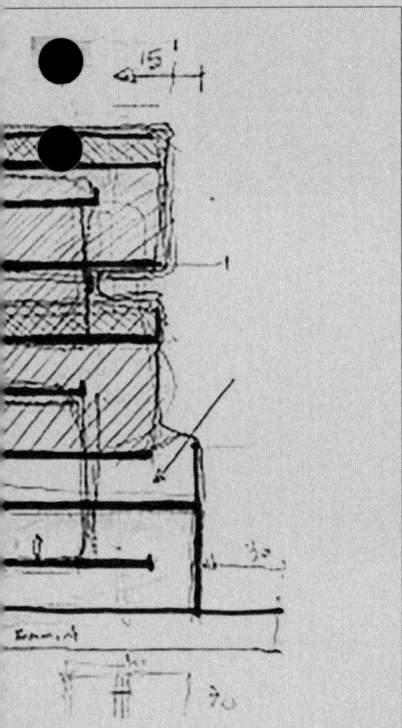

SKETCH BY
WINKA DUBBELDAM

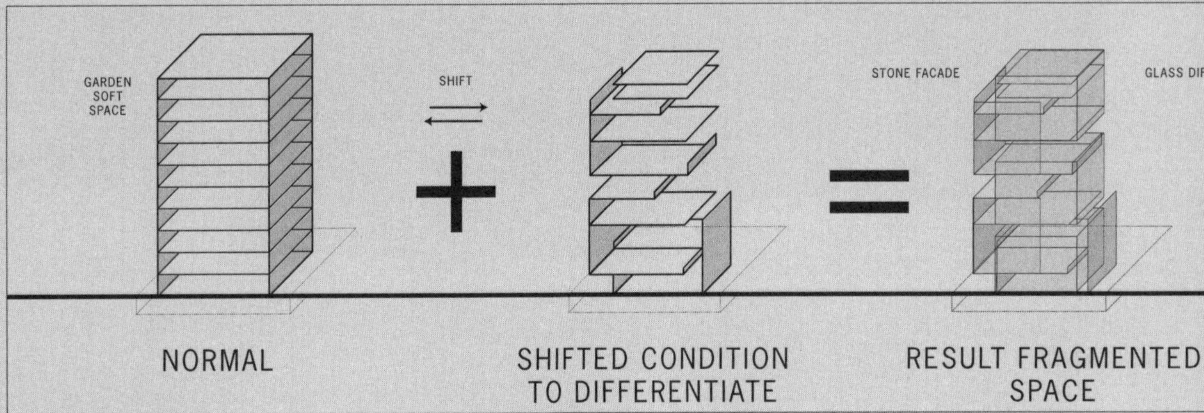

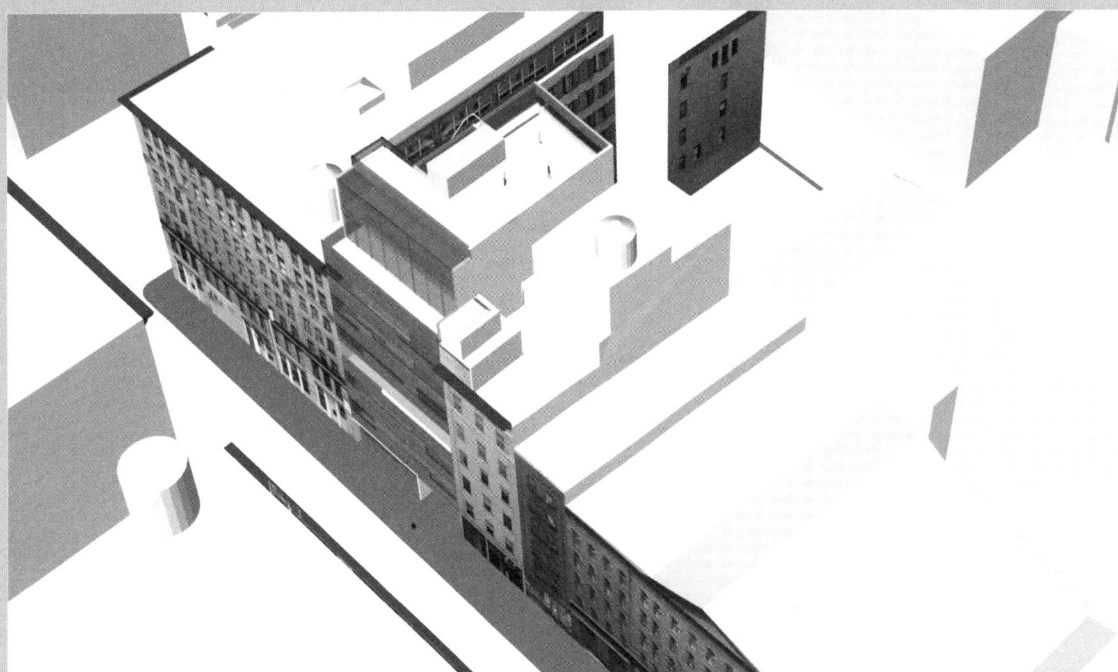

neighborhood was poised for change. Around 1812, Washington Market was established near the current site of the World Trade Center. It grew considerably over the following decades, and by the middle of the century it had become the city's major source for consumables. The growth of the market was, no doubt, fueled by the shipping industry on the river nearby, facilitating the transfer of goods.

V33 TRIBECA

In Tribeca's landmark district, the conceptual choice for the new V33 building was not to copy a historical building, but to focus on creating a new building matching the material quality and proportional systems of the area's landmarks. Extreme ceiling heights, tripartite facade subdivisions, and solid natural materials were some of the common characteristics of the neighborhood. The building volumes were optimized: a north street facade

RENTIATION

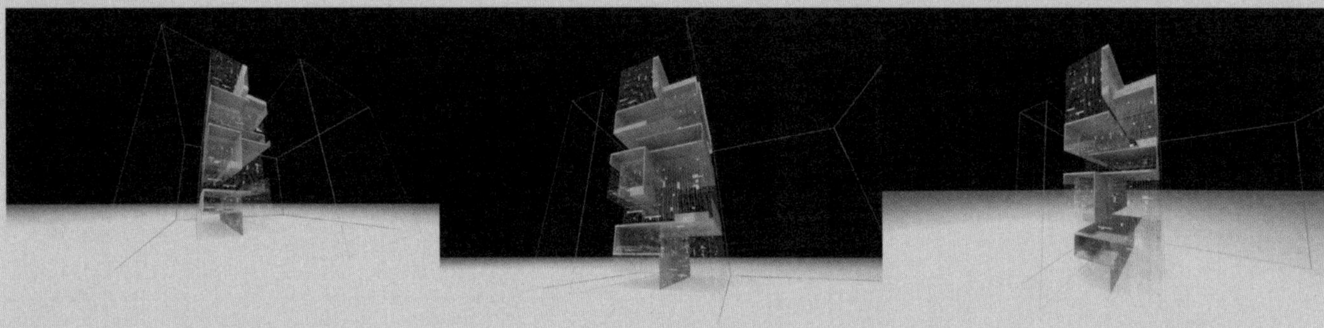

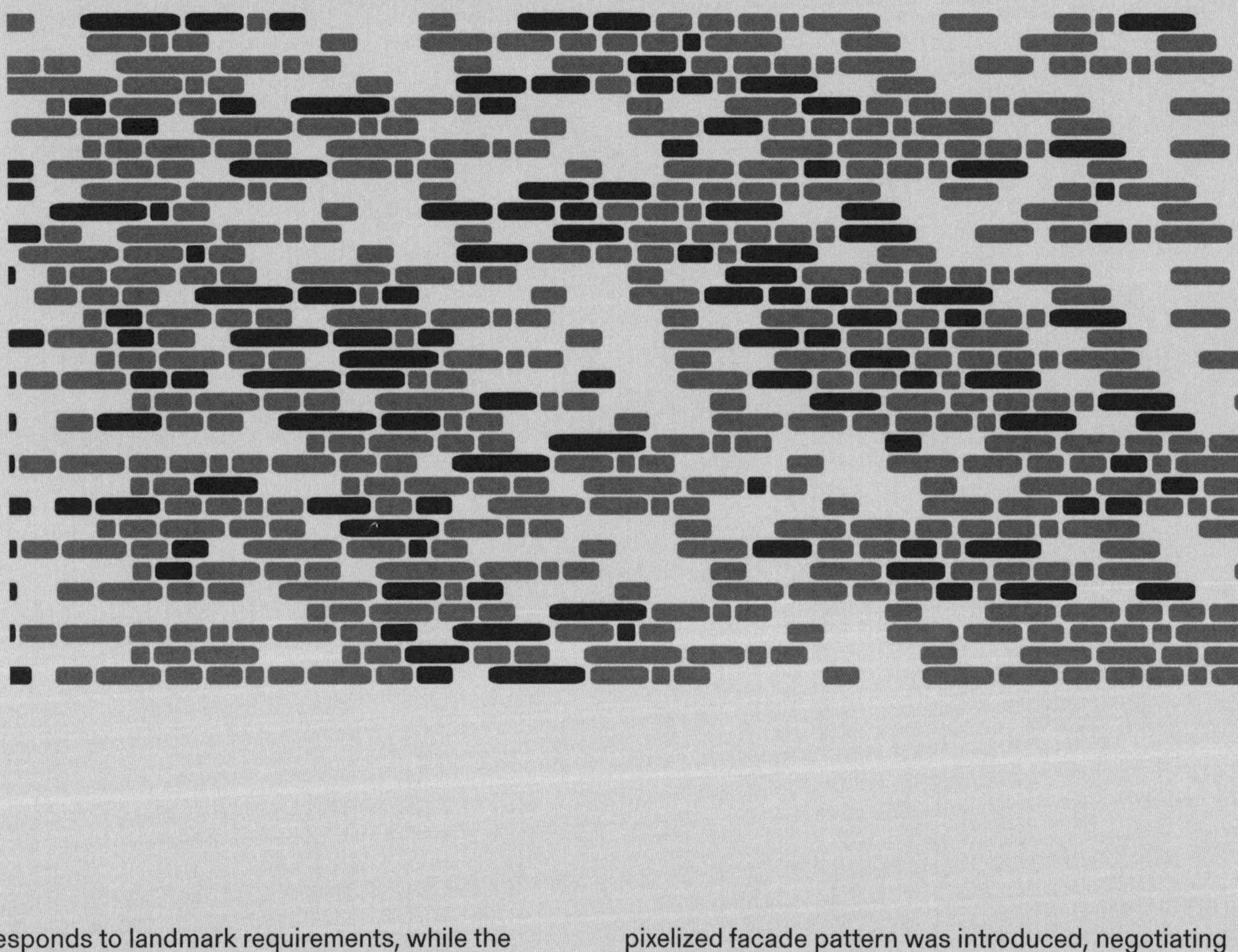

responds to landmark requirements, while the south garden facade is highly articulated with 12-foot-deep balconies and sunrooms. Double-height glazing brings in enough light, while also allowing for natural shade.

As the area's landmark buildings vary greatly in style and size, the decision was taken to extrapolate the differentiation further; a three-dimensional pixelized facade pattern was introduced, negotiating the facade rhythms of the two neighboring buildings. The resulting computational pattern is comprised of translucent stone and glass, creating a range of facade reflections, translucencies, and spatial conditions throughout the course of a day. During the day the facade's translucent stone has an interior glow effect; at night, the facade's stone glows towards

SS.59

FACADE PIXELATION

SS.60

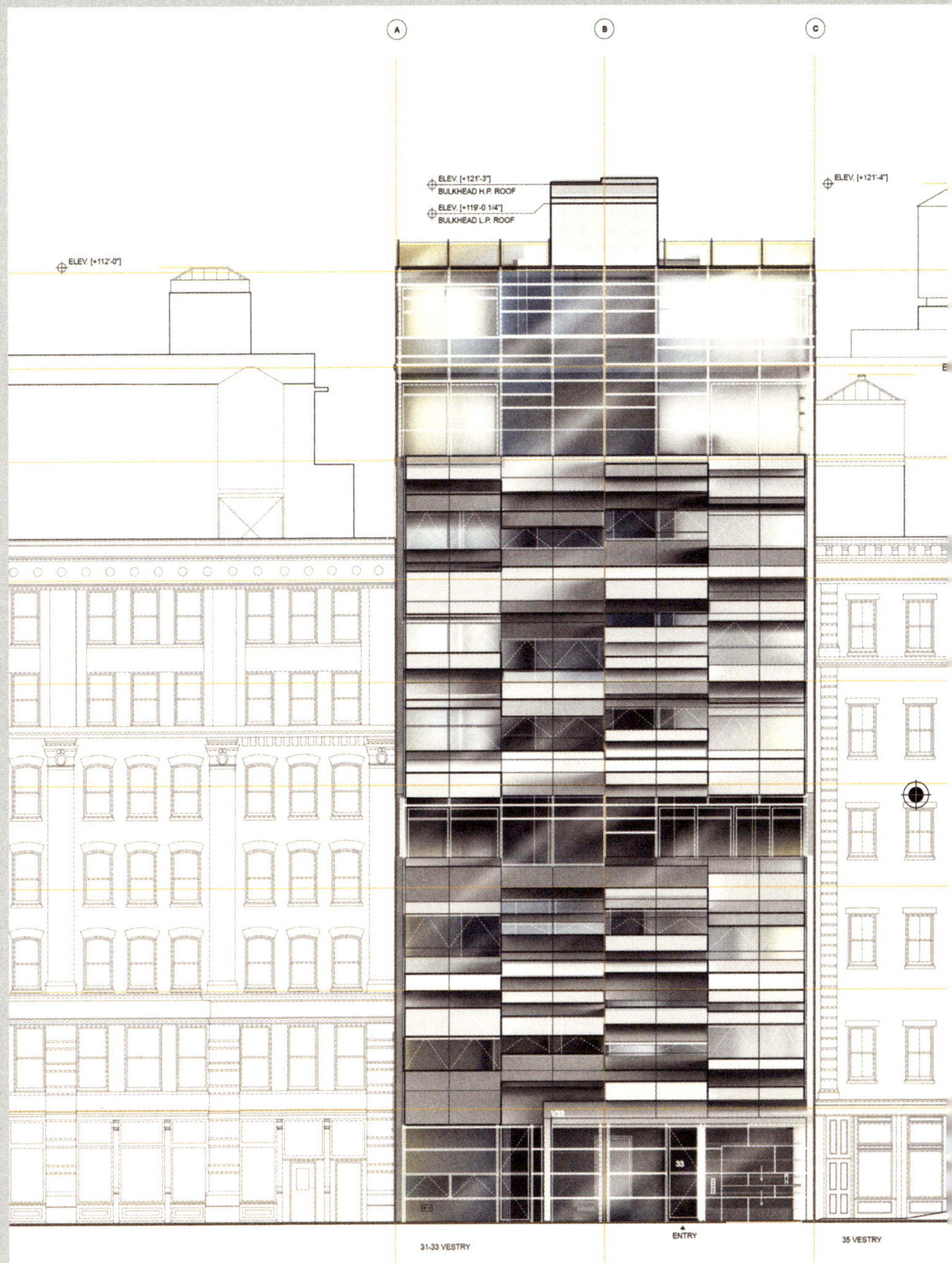

the streetscape. V33's facade thus meets historically contextual demands while introducing aesthetic, technological, and material innovations. The facade's translucent stone is engineered by curtain wall manufacturer Archiglaze, located in Italy with a branch in the United States.

TRIPLEXES, DUPLEXES, AND FULL FLOOR LOFTS

SS.63

RENDER BY THE SEVENTH ART

AZUL LAGOA QUARRY PORTUGAL

QUARRY VISIT PORTUGAL

The facade's translucent stone was selected to match landmark buildings in Tribeca. The best matching stone was Azul Lagoa stone, which was sourced from a Portuguese quarry. A personal visit to the quarry was needed to guarantee that the stone corresponded with the requirements. It turned out to be quite the challenge; in these solid blocks of gray marble it was difficult to detect the stone's interior veining. The only way to approximate knowing what the color and pattern were going to be, was by spraying a tiny bit of water on the large marble blocks with a plant spray bottle. Several of the 7-by-7-by-7-foot marble blocks were chosen and marked with a "W," indicating "Winka's choice." The Azul Lagoa stone blocks were then machine-cut in ultra-thin slices and transported to Italy to be laminated on glass.

Rochas Metamórficas / Metamorphic Rocks
CALCÁRIO CRISTALINO/ CRYSTALLINE LIMESTONE

CARACTERÍSTICAS FÍSICO-MECÂNICAS
PHYSICO-MECHANICAL PROPERTIES

Resistência mecânica à compressão Compression breaking load	Kg/cm²	863
Resistência mecânica à compressão após teste de gelividade Compression breaking load after freezing test	Kg/cm²	977
Resistência Mecânica à Flexão Bending Strength	Kg/cm²	256
Massa Volúmica Aparente Volumetric Weight	Kg/m³	2 703
Absorção de água à P.At.N Water absorption at N.P. conditions	%	0.10
Porosidade aberta Apparent porosity	%	0.28
Coeficiente de dilatação linear térmica Thermal Linear expansion coefficient	$X10^{-6}$ per° C	14.8
Resistência ao desgaste Abrasion Test	mm	2.0
Resistência ao Choque: altura mínima de queda Impact test: minimum fall height	cm	55

ANÁLISE QUÍMICA
CHEMICAL ANALYSIS

SiO_2	0.36%
Al_2O_3	0.69
Fe_2O_3 (Total)	0.11
MnO	vest.
CaO	53.89
MgO	0.99
Na_2O	0.04
K_2O	0.06
TiO_2	0.00
P.R.	43.47
CO_2	43.37

TOP: MARBLE BLOCKS WERE CHOSEN AND MARKED WITH A "W," INDICATING "WINKA'S CHOICE."
MIDDLE: VISIT TO SELECT AZUL LAGOA STONE WITH ARCHIGLAZE IN QUARRY IN PORTUGAL

SS.67

SS.68

THIN-CUT TRANSLUCENT STONE

CURTAIN WALL ASSEMBLY

In fabricating the curtain wall, Archiglaze utilized a vacuum process to laminate stone and glass materials with differing chemical qualities. The engineered result dramatically decreases the stone's thickness while simultaneously creating strength and flexibility. The translucent stone facade is light in weight and extremely translucent.

TRANSLUCENT AZUL LAGOA

PROTOTYPING

The facade's protoype was built in Archiglaze's factory in Florence, Italy. The sliced Azul Lagoa from Portugal was laminated on glass or aluminum honeycomb panels through an extreme heating and pressure process. By double-glazing it, adding another layer of glass, a highly insulated unit was created, with the untreated stone layer always located on the exterior of the building. The facade pixelation was further detailed using an ultra-thin German mullion system. The Schüco curtain wall bridges the divide between aesthetic and slimline requirements with a narrow stile mullion system that allows high visibility. The system with 50-millimeter face width is designed as a flush-fitted all-glass look with the efficient production of the structural glazing insulating glass with a two-part stainless-steel spacer. This translucent natural stone surface was one of the first installed exteriors in New York City.

SS.70-71

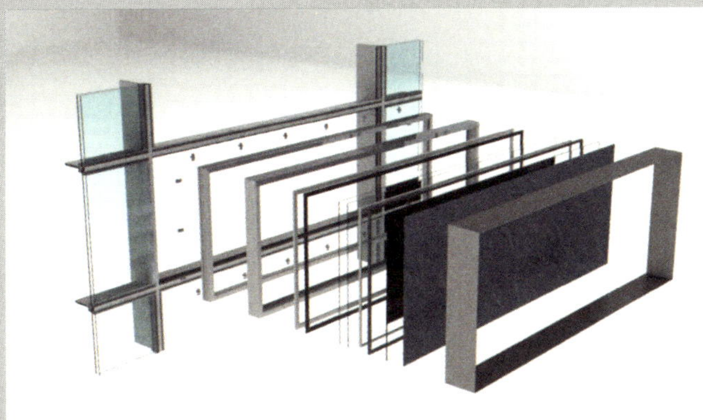

SS.72

SCHÜCO FACADE SYSTEMS FWS (FACADE WALL SYSTEM)

SS.73

SS.74

CURTAIN WALL INSTALLATION

The on-site installation of the 3D pixelated curtain wall was also done by Archiglaze. The engineered system dramatically decreased the stone's thickness while simultaneously creating strength and flexibility, and made for a translucent stone facade that is lightweight and extremely translucent. The thin slimline mullion frame further expressed the translucency.

Archiglaze: "Due to the pixelation and the asymmetric inward and outward movement of the facade volumes and lines of the project, the connection system between the projected panels and the curtain wall profiles required complex calculations and design. Above are the 3D modeling drawings of the details of the pressure locks and

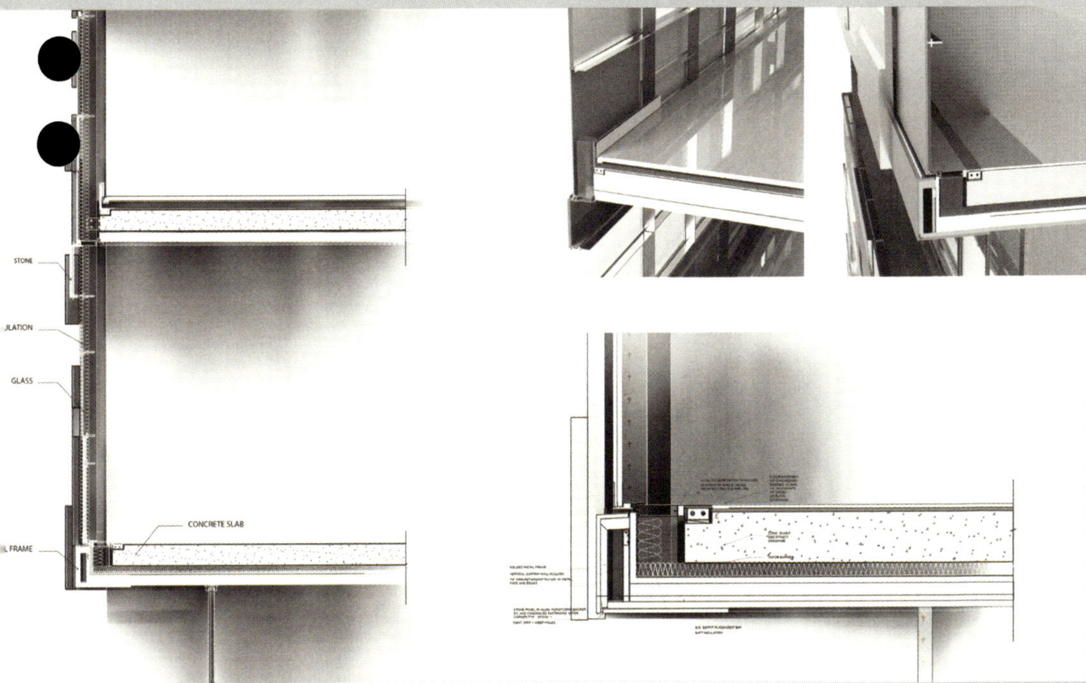

CONSTRUCTION DETAILS

the projected panel main frame. The connection was provided through a pressure lock firmly inserted into the mullion profile and with two nail-wings working inside an engraving made continuously in the Schüco window profile."

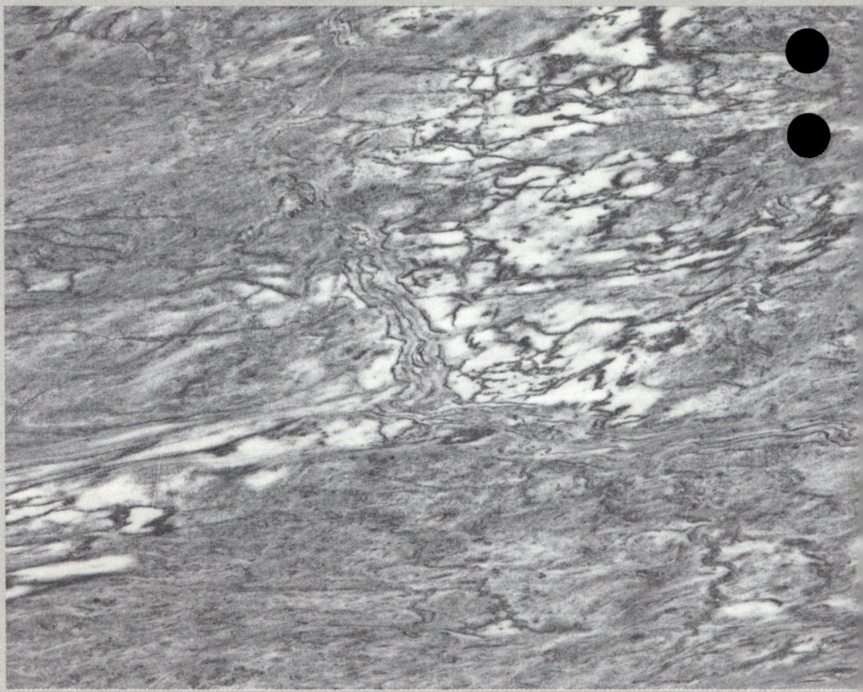

3D PIXELATED TRANSLUCENT STONE PANELS

URBAN VILLAS

The V33 condo has only seven custom-designed units, each resembling more of a villa type with their large cantilevering terraces and sunrooms. The units are a generous size (between 3,500 and 5,000 square feet), have large outdoor spaces (terraces and gardens), and, sometimes, have multiple floors, in addition to the building's private parking with a car elevator. The double- and triple-height poured-in-place concrete units allow for large cantilevers and all stairs are simple concrete steps suspended from the concrete walls. The concrete stair and elevator core run straight up and stabilize the building. As each unit at least occupies a full floor, they have a lot in common; such as the benefit of both north and south facade exposure, and level changes to indicate change in use, rather than too many walls. Facing north, natural light filters through the translucent stone facade, and, facing south, sunrooms absorb light from double height terraces, and have natural shading from the large cantilevers. The exclusive, upper-most duplex penthouse has a private rooftop terrace on multiple levels, and a private swimming pool.

SS.80

SEE PG.325

SS.81

SS.82

TRANSLUCENT AZUL LAGOA, LAMINATED ON GLASS

AZIZ ANSARI

SCHOOLHOUSE

SS.53

SS.54

SS.55

"In the simplest case, an optimization problem consists of maximizing or minimizing a real function by systematically choosing input values from within an allowed set and computing the value of the function. The generalization of optimization theory and techniques to other formulations constitutes a large area of applied mathematics. More generally, optimization includes finding "best available" values of some objective function given a defined domain (or input), including a variety of different types of objective functions and different types of domains." (https://en.wikipedia.org/wiki/Mathematical_optimization)

SS.56

"Originally referred to as the "Lower West Side," there are differing accounts as to where the name "Tribeca" came from. It originated in the 1970s, after a Special Lower Manhattan Mixed Use District was adopted for the area south of Canal Street, between Broadway and West Street. A realtor, advertising real estate within the new district, referred to it as Tribeca, which stood for the Triangle Below Canal.... The architectural development, which spanned roughly 50 years from 1860 to 1910, encompasses a balance of utilitarian and decorative forms in a range of popular styles of the period." (www.6tocelebrate.org)

SS.57-58

"In computer graphics, pixelation is caused by displaying a bitmap or a section of a bitmap at such a large size that individual pixels, small single-colored square display elements that comprise the bitmap, are visible. Such an image is said to be pixelated." (https://en.wikipedia.org/wiki/Pixelation)

SS.59

SS.60

SS.61

SS.62

V33 Branding:

"The Seventh Art challenges conventions of brand development and marketing by bringing a global perspective to the branding process and mixing its expertise in architecture, urban design, fashion and lifestyle."

SS.63

SS.64-66

SS.67

SS.68

SS.69

Translucent stone panels are a thin natural stone veneer permanently bonded to a glass substrate, allowing significantly improved light transmission and large sizes. Here produced as double glazing to withstand the North American climate.

SS.70

The Schüco FWS 50 SG system used here is a super narrow stile mullion system that allows high visibility with a custom titanium anodized finish. (www.schueco.com)

SS.71

SS.72

SS.73

SS.74

SS.75

SS.76-77

SS.78

Azul Lagoa is a marble from Portugal with a blue-grey tone, medium grain and a distinct vein. It also has some white shaded zones and a relatively high degree of hardness. Some variations occur in characteristics such as color and vein intensity.

It is hard enough to be sliced very thin and to have a translucent quality.

SS.79

The facade pixelation transforms the normative view "out" into a fragmented set of random landmark building pixels, a scramble of the neighborhood.

SS.80

SS.81

SS.82

SS.83-92

SS.93

512 GW

1+1=3

Located west of Soho in Manhattan, 512 GW was originally planned as a simple extension to a 1900s townhouse for one family. Adding the tall extension to the small 19-by-40-foot building converted this townhouse into an eight-story vertically stacked tower of rooms with interlocking volumes responding to the city's setback rules. Interior and exterior spaces alternate and intersect to maximize spatial variety, while strategic cuts allow light to enter deep into the building section and create curated views towards the surrounding neighborhood. As the extension grew and finally equaled the original structure, the decision was taken to completely transform it into an "object

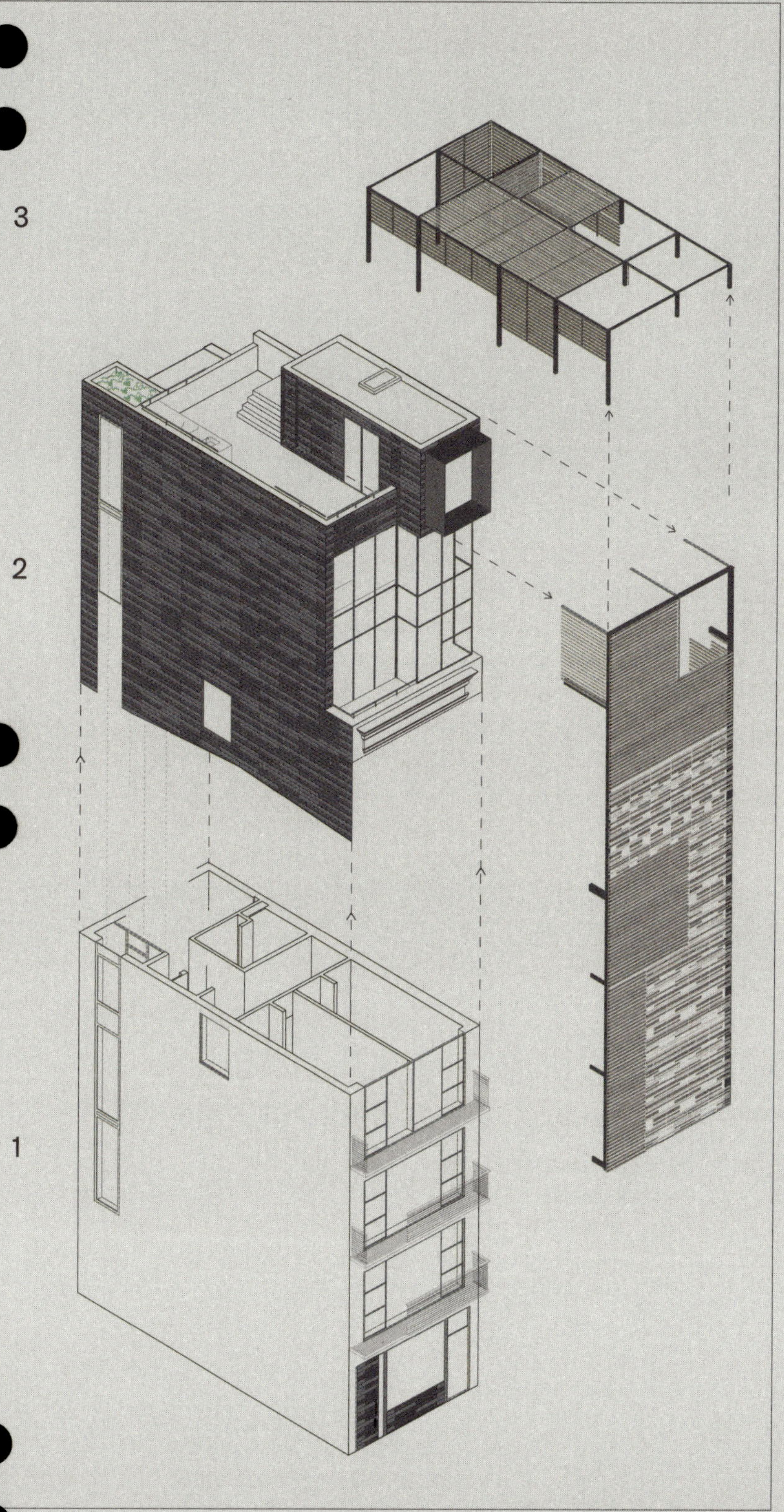

CLIMATE SKIN

in object" formation. We wrapped the entirety of the structure and its exterior spaces in a third unifying structure—a climate skin. This extra-large volume of multiple patterns and densities is made from a steel frame with a lattice of fixed and folding panels clad with Trespa™ slats. The townhouse was recognized by the 2020 *Rethinking The Future* Global Architecture and Design Awards, focused on innovation and sustainability, which celebrated its smart climate facade that "adapts to environmental conditions and significantly reduces heating and cooling costs."

SS.96

SS.97

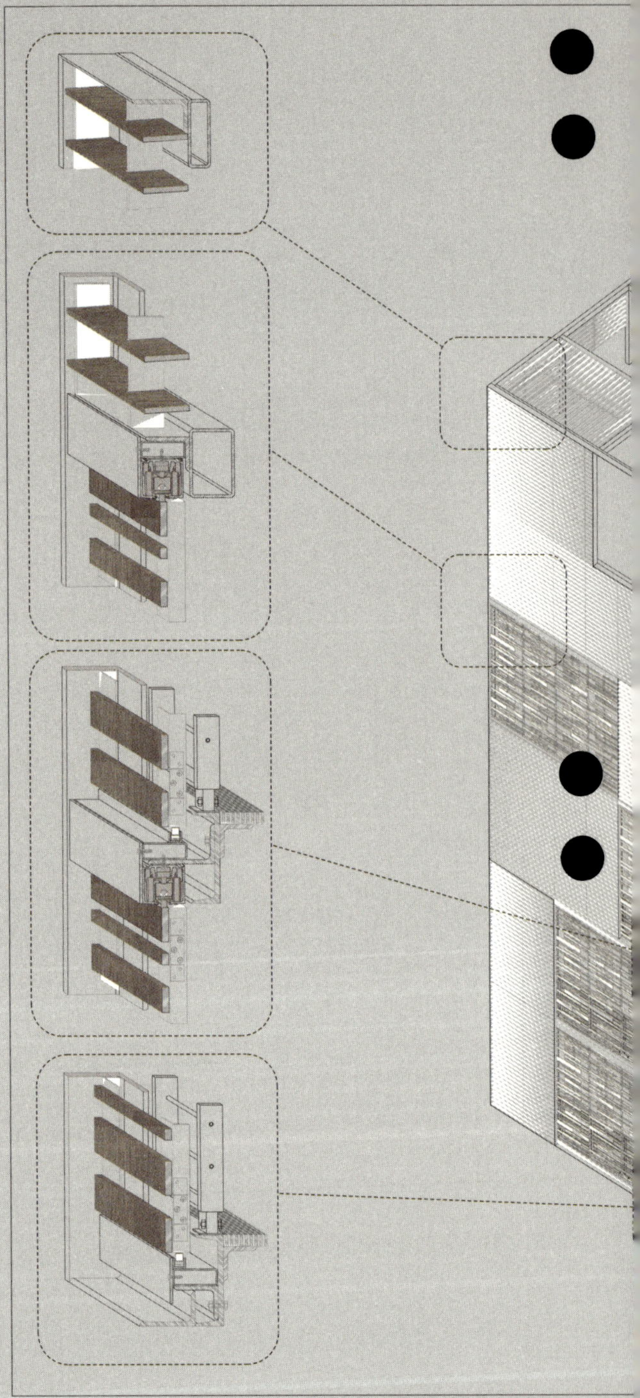

FACADE LAYERING: COMPOSITE MORPHOLOGIES

The trellis's volume is larger than the building structure itself; it also wraps the private exterior balconies and terraces that extend over the street and over the roof. New balconies are the memory of what used to be the fire escape—it was removed, but its landings remain. Plants and vines grow over the trellis, further creating shading and variable levels of privacy for this single-family townhouse.

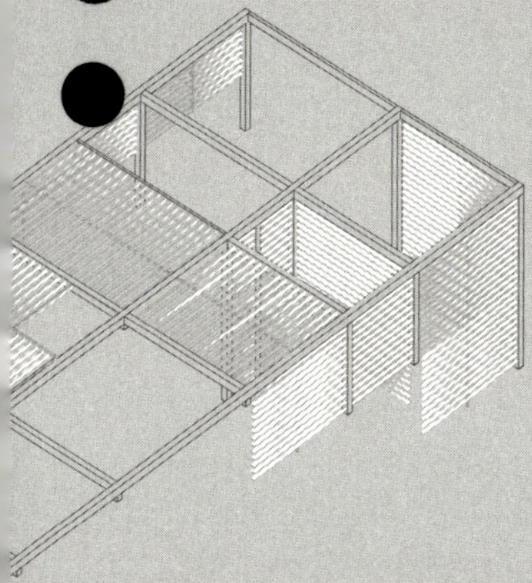

Extensive prototyping assisted us in creating a precise optimized pattern for the trellis and further developed the intricate movement of the trellis panels. The facade transforms the townhouse completely as panels open and close: when closed, it forms one smooth surface; when open, fins fold out of the facade like feathers of a birdwing.

SS.101-102

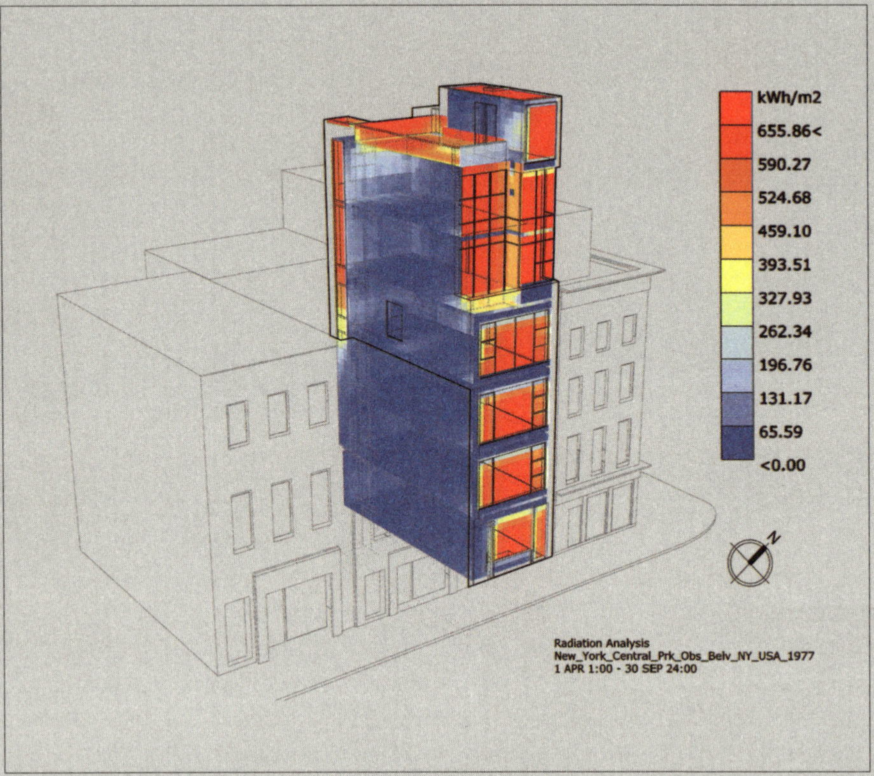

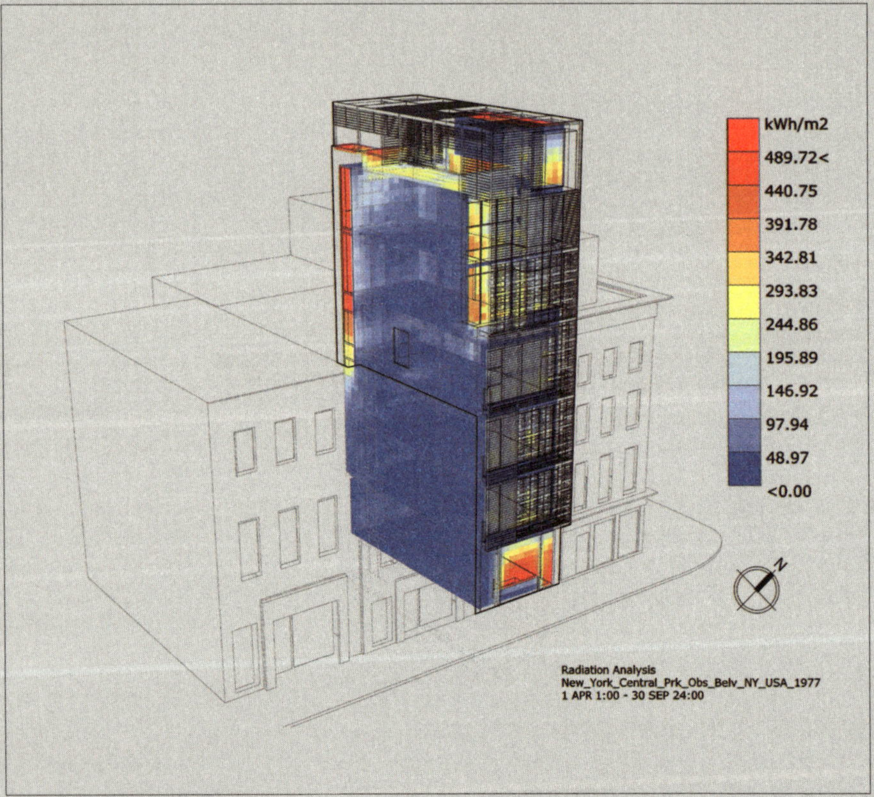

SUMMER: PASSIVE COOLING

SS.103

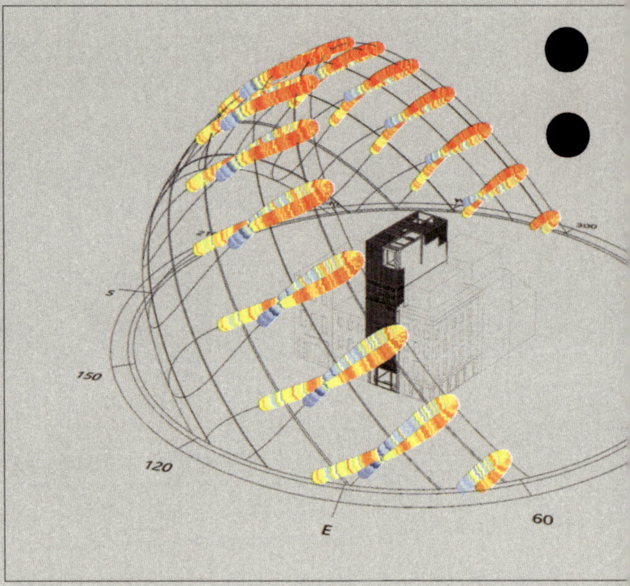

SUN EXPOSURE

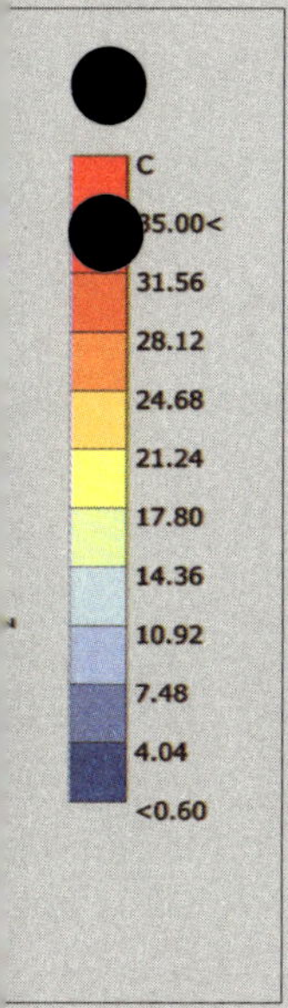

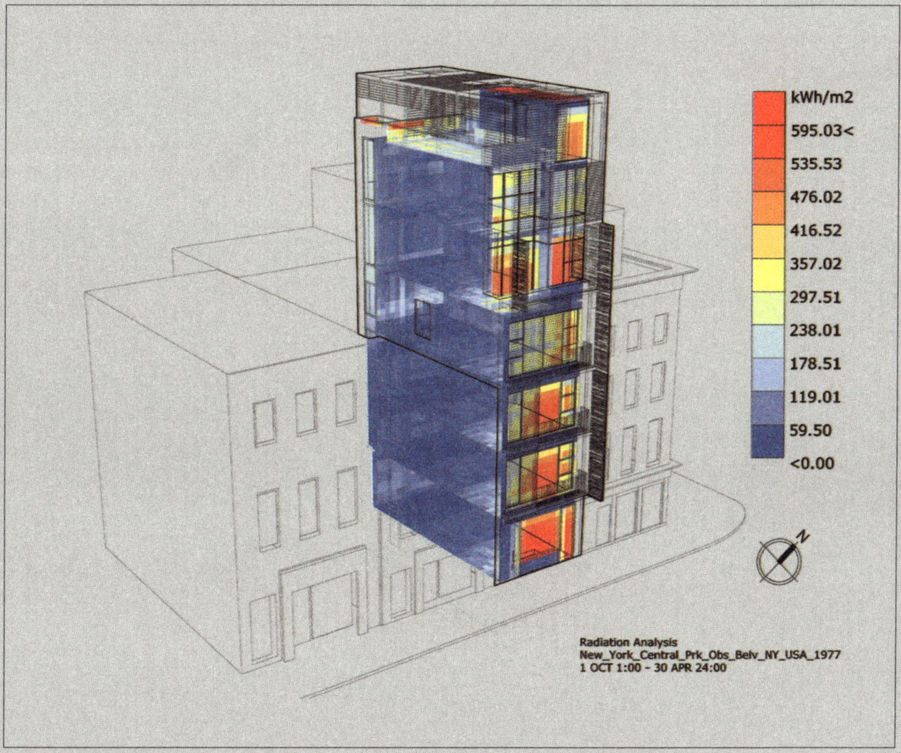

WINTER: PASSIVE HEATING

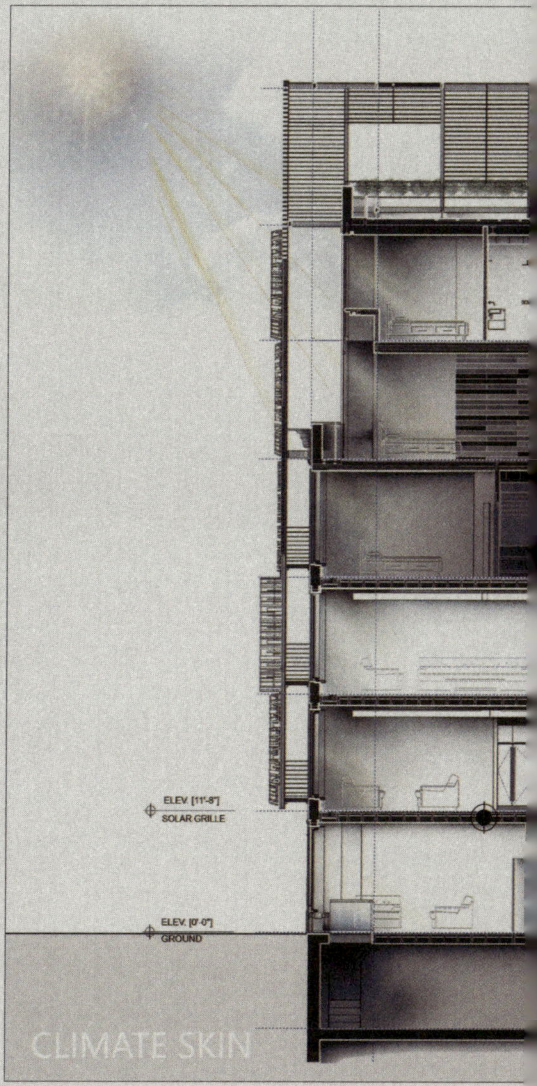

FACADE LAYERING: CLIMATE CONTROL

The existing townhouse was doubled in size and transformed into a new smart object. By adding a trellis volume much larger than the building itself (a trellis or screen is not bound by building codes), we created a new interstitial exterior space, thus blurring the distinction between interior and exterior. This "smart climate control envelope" serves as an adaptable perimeter to the building, creating a microclimate that provides passive solar energy in the winter and shading in the summer to help stabilize the house's environment. The effect of the climate trellis was studied in Ladybug and Honeybee, open source environmental plugins for Grasshopper. The model indicated and calculated that interior radiation is reduced by 45 percent during warmer months, significantly lowering the need for air conditioning, while still allowing indirect and natural light to enter through the horizontal slats. When the operable trellis is opened during colder months, interior radiation is 25 percent higher compared to having the trellis closed, allowing for passive solar energy and reducing the need for heating.

SS.106-108

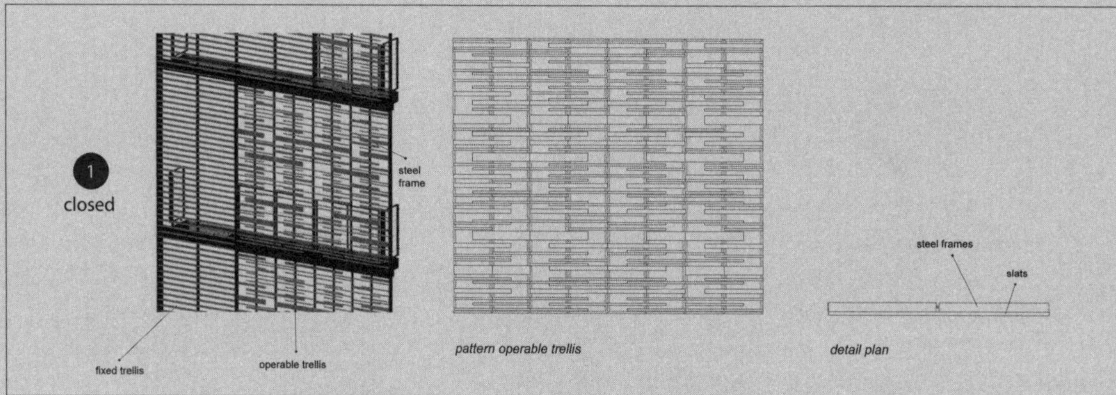
1
closed
steel
frame
fixed trellis
operable trellis
pattern operable trellis
steel frames
slats
detail plan

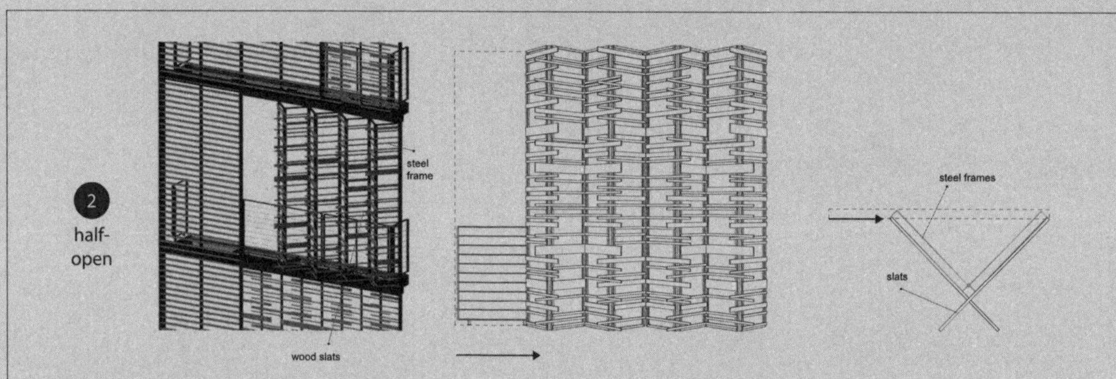
2
half-
open
steel
frame
wood slats
steel frames
slats

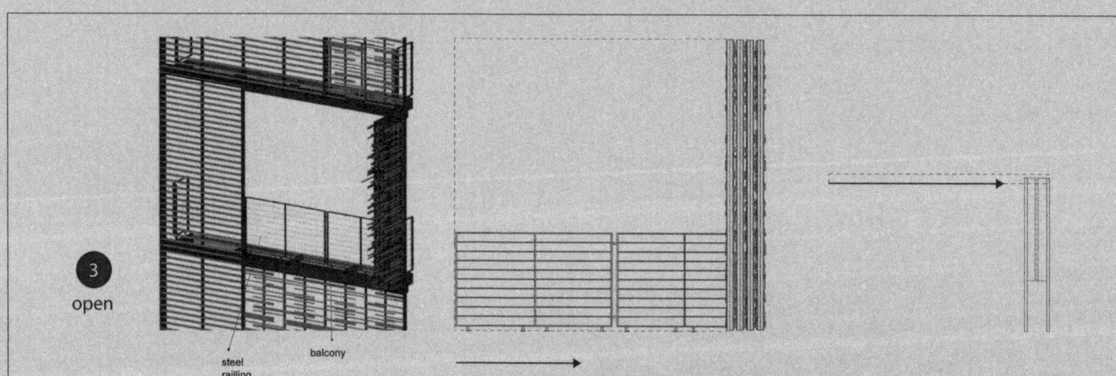
3
open
steel
railling
balcony

SS.109

SS.110

SS.111

TRANSFORMATION AS BLADES MOVE OPEN AND CLOSED.

PROTOBODY

The prototyping phase tested the material transformation of the protobody. Like an intricate bird wing, the trellis changes character and configuration at different seasons and at different times of the day. For a bird wing morphology may differ. The shape of the wing is defined by two important parameters: the aspect ratio and wing loading. For the townhouse the climate skin's panels open and close to adjust the effect of the climate inside. Folding open they transform; the slats intersect and fold out like feathers. When closed they are smooth and flat like the wing. The climate skin is equipped with two different system of slats: the fixed horizontal slats, which provide stable shading and optimal view; and the folding panels, which regulate the climate. The climate skin serves as both a filter and an amplifier between the privacy of the house and the public streetscape.

SS.112

SS.113

EXTERIOR BALCONIES CANTILEVER OVER THE SIDEWALK, MEDIATED BY TRELLIS

BODY WITHIN BODY

We developed a "body within body" concept. A heavy body (the building volume) and a light body (the transformable trellis lattice) create the space between as the resultant occupiable zone. The trellis escapes the city's restrictions; the new stacked addition with setbacks as defined by building code is wrapped by a much larger climate skin composed of a varying trellis object that is free of any code. The trellis has agency; it visually unifies the existing and new structures, and differentiates itself as the climate skin, the "third building."

Jane Bennett writes, "organic and inorganic bodies, natural and cultural objects [...] all are affective. I am here drawing on a Spinozist notion of affect, which refers broadly to the capacity of any body for activity and responsiveness."[1] Bennett equates *affect* with *materiality*, or *thing*-power, similar to DeLanda's notion of material realism. This virtual, multi-patterned climate skin encases the building, transforming and protecting it, while also creating new spaces in its folds. Bennett states, "bodies enhance their power in or as a heterogeneous assemblage."[2]

SS.114

SS.115-116

SS.117

SS.118

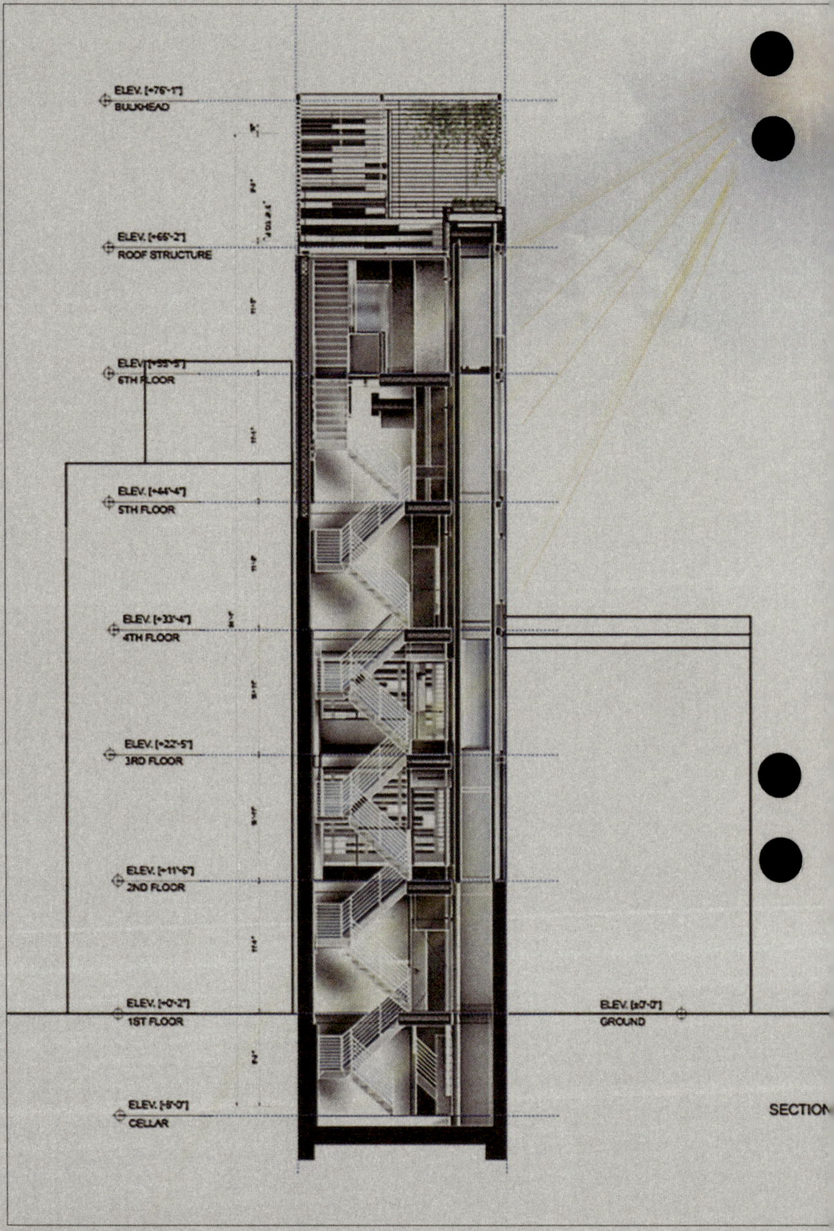

THE STAIR AND ELEVATOR CORE GETS SOUTH EXPOSURE THROUGH LARGE CUTS IN THE BRICK WALLS

CUTS / VERTICALITY

Several extensive vertical cuts operate as connective voids in the townhouse. A double-height void between the kitchen and dining room connects to the stairs with double-height windows overlooking the living spaces. A double-height facade void creates an atrium between the study and primary bedroom allowing for spatial interlacing, and long views through the urban streetscape. In the rear of the building, a dramatic south-facing continuous window slot lights the glass elevator, which in turn radiates light over the eight-story black steel staircase with a skylight above. This dramatic stair and elevator core is flanked by double-height spaces with huge glass windows, highlighting the sensation of extreme verticality, and transforms ascending and descending through the core into a dynamic spatial experience.

SS.121

SS.122-123

SS.124

MEDITATION ROOM

SS.125

ROOF TERRACE AS "ROOM"

ROOF "ROOM"

At the top of the building the brick and wood warehouse transforms in a glass and steel extension. Colors are lighter, light radiates in from all sides. At the top floor the stair core takes a sharp 90-degree turn and shoots up through the bulkhead, where one finds a meditation spot in a steel black box that penetrates the trellis and looks east over Spring Street. The roof terrace is transformed in a roof room with pantry and dining area, as it is wrapped in the vegetation-covered trellis volume, creating shade and privacy. The terrace floor and seating steps are clad in recycled Ipe wood and its dark gray concrete plank facade wraps the terrace before it cascades down the tall north facade.

SS.126

"NEW WEST SOHO TOWNHOUSE
TO FEATURE DOUBLE-SKIN DESIGN
BY WINKA DUBBELDAM"
Future New York
By Ondel Hylton, 2017

"A worn Hudson Square walk-up building at 512 Greenwich Street is getting the starchitect's treatment. Winka Dubbeldam's firm of Archi-Tectonics is making over a four-story loft building into a seven-story, single-family townhouse. The project is located along a lightly-trafficked section of Greenwich Street near Spring Street. The lot is behind Philip Johnson's Urban Glass House and across from Archi-Tectonics own project at 491 Greenwich Street. According to city records, an LLC purchased the building in 2015 for $3.7 million.

The revamp won't be any old ordinary conversion, rather, the existing load-bearing walls will be reinforced to allow the building to be extended by three stories, and a new glass elevator will be introduced. To visually unify the two parts, the exterior will be wrapped in a porous trellis system that will include some operable openings. The screen's overall intent is to provide a greater degree of privacy for the home's inhabitants while still allowing light to infiltrate spaces."[3]

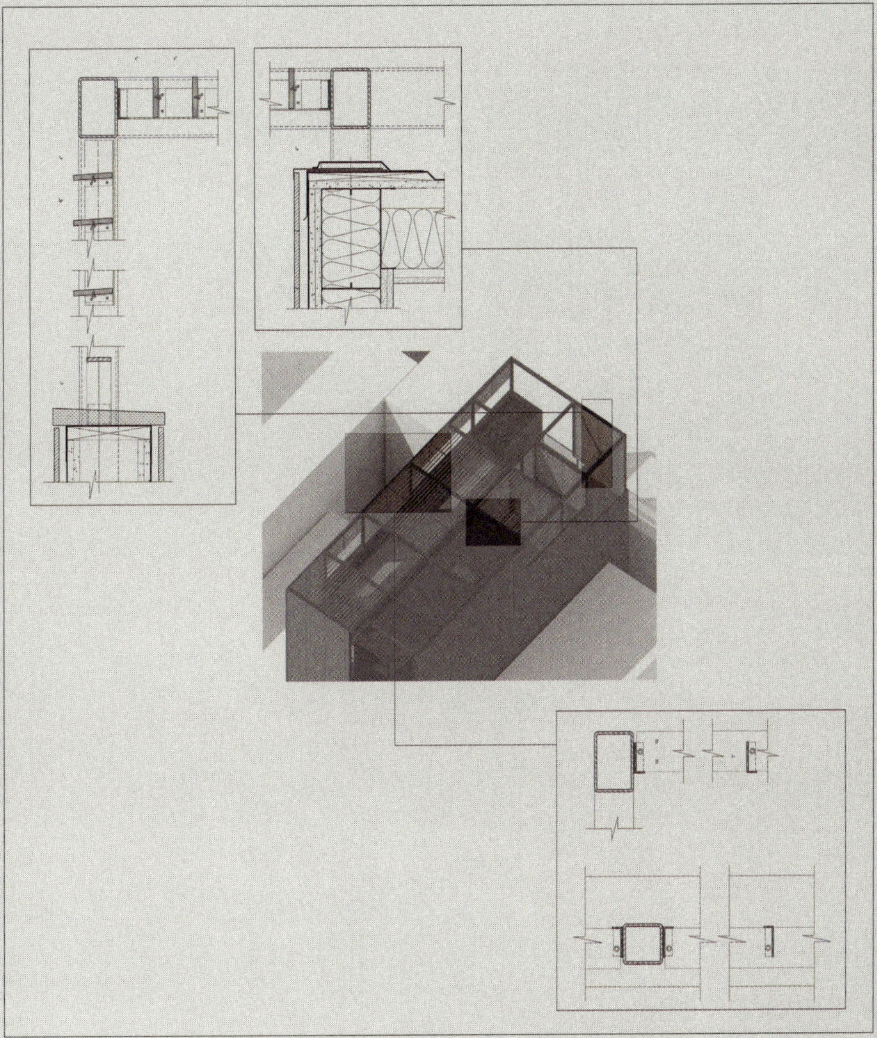

3D TRELLIS AS EXTRA-LARGE VOLUME WRAPS EXTERIOR SPACES ON THREE SIDES

BIKE
LANE
CLOSED

ANDY WARHOL
PETER LINDBERGH

PETER LINDBERGH

DISCOVER THE LYRICS THAT LIFT YOU
pandora
SOUND ON

SS.93

2020 *Rethinking The Future*: Global Architecture and Design Award: "This comprehensive renovation and addition to a converted former 4-story industrial building creates a comfortable, 8-story one family residence wrapped in a smart climate facade that adapts to environmental conditions and significantly reduces heating and cooling costs." (https://awards.re-thinkingthefuture.com/rtf-awards-2020-runner-ups/512townhouse-archi-tectonicsnyc-llc/)

SS.94

SS.95

"New York City's 1916 Zoning Resolution was the first citywide zoning code in the United States. Proposed after the bulky Equitable Building was erected in 1915, the resolution was a measure adopted primarily to stop massive buildings from preventing light and air from reaching the streets below. The resolution established limits in building massing at certain heights, usually interpreted as a series of setbacks and, while not imposing height limits, restricted towers to a percentage of the lot size." (https://en.wikipedia.org/wiki/1916_Zoning_Resolution)

SS.96

SS.97

"In 1784, Daniel Maseres invented the fire escape, which, being fastened to the window, would enable a person to descend to the street without injury. Part emergency exit, part makeshift patio, the fire escape has played an integral role in shaping the development of cities in the United States. The first rules were imposed in the early 1860s when the New York City Department of Buildings ordered the implementation of an additional form of egress on tenements with more than eight families above the first floor." (https://www.theatlantic.com/technology/archive/2018/02/how-the-fire-escape-became-an-ornament/554174/)

SS.98-99

SS.100

SS.101-104

"Ladybug Tools is a collection of free computer applications written in Python, that support environmental design and education, and that is parametric, open source and free. Honeybee supports detailed daylighting and thermodynamic modeling, and is a great tool during the design phase of the project." (https://www.ladybug.tools/honeybee.html)

SS.105

SS.106-108

TRESPA Meteon® panels are an extremely stable, and solid panel, based on thermosetting resins, homogeneously reinforced with wood based fibers and manufactured under high pressure and at high temperatures. It is temperature and fade resistant, and does not warp. (www.trespa.com)

SS.109

SS.110

SS.111

SS.112-113

Jane Bennett states: "An acknowledgement of something like this, of a kind of thing-power, may be at work in the 'agency-versus-structure' debate in the social sciences, according to which structures are described as powerful entities that work with and against human purposes. [...] The vital materialist must admit that different materialities, composed of different sets of protobodies, will express different powers." (Bennett, *Vibrant Matter*, 29-31.)

SS.114

SS.115-116

SS.117

SS.118

SS.119

SS.120

SS.121

SS.122-123

SS.124

SS.125

SS.126

SS.127

SS.128-129

SS.130-139

1 Jane Bennett, *Vibrant Matter: A Political Ecology of Things*, (Durham, N.C.: Duke University Press, 2010), xii.
2 Bennett, *Vibrant Matter*, 23.
3 https://www.cityrealty.com/nyc/market-insight/features/future-nyc/new-west-soho-townhouse-feature-double-skin-design-winka-dubbeldam/10841

Interview With Winka Dubbeldam

Zack Saunders, founder of ARCH[or]studio and *Arch2O* contributing editor, speaks to Winka Dubbeldam about projects throughout her career, the role of the architect today, and how her work has evolved since her early experiments with form, space, and the digital.

Seldom do architects operate in the two worlds of theory and practice as effortlessly and eloquently as does Winka Dubbeldam and her office Archi-Tectonics. From lectures and exhibitions presenting research into protobuildings and protocities to proposing architectural and urban design projects which can only be described as prototypes of a new way of inhabiting space, Archi-Tectonics' work effectively blurs the boundaries between theory and practice. Whether it is rethinking the basic components which comprise a building, incorporating technology into architecture in new ways, or inventing new protocols for inhabitants to contribute to the conceptual development of a city, the work consistently calls for a paradigmatic shift in architecture towards more inclusive, intelligent design methodologies.

As a practicing professional in the field today, how are you able to navigate the ever-changing landscape of what it means to be an architect?

When people say "architecture" they think of every building, but a building is not necessarily architecture. It's important to make that distinction. As a practicing architect I prefer to work with manufacturers directly, rather than designing a building and then relying on a contractor to price it. That means we first develop the most complex part of a building with a manufacturer and get their cost-estimate, then we choose the GC and provide them with different vendors they can work with. Otherwise, if you try to do anything innovative, the GC will just double the price for the building as a whole, and the risk is that it gets value-engineered out. So, we tend to take that research responsibility here in the office, and I see it really as a part of being an architect. It's also intellectually stimulating, it's really good for the office to speak with the manufacturers directly—we learn a lot from them and I feel this adds to the intelligence of the building itself. You can advance building innovation this way.

The rewriting and innovation of architectural design and its structures requires a revolutionary change in the thinking of how architecture is conceived. From the notion that a building is a composite of standardized elements such as columns, floors, and walls, we have to rethink a building being composed of mass-customized components. By making the components more integral and intelligent, human occupation is accommodated rather than allowed, interactive rather than passive. From a construction standpoint, smart components require a level of prefabrication, but not prefabrication as pure repetition, but rather mass-customized units defined by performance analysis. The component's intelligence, the "proto-body" refers more to car and plane design than to architectural design, is more system-based than mechanical assembly-based. This organic, systematic way of thinking is common ground for scientists and industrial designers, but is relatively new for architects. This design method will not only change the way architecture is conceived, manufactured, and assembled, but allows for an innovative approach to how architecture could innovate and develop in the next millennia.

How do you define intelligent architecture?

We develop intelligent architecture in two ways: we look at industrial design to develop new details and manufacturing and we collaborate with experts in R&D. We collaborated with the MIT Media

Lab to understand incorporating technology into architecture itself. With the robotic Q-Tower for instance, we took existing smart technologies, such as automated blinds reacting to sunlight, a virtual doorman systems, and smart delivery lockers, and designed a new interface that connects all these disparate control systems and allows for feedback between the inhabitant and the space itself. These sensor systems are not necessarily new, but the combining of these systems in one interface was new. We also designed a smart-delivery storage closet system that stores several storage boxes on a track in the basement, that can be called up to the apartment, similar to a robotic carpark.

The other way we develop an intelligent architecture is by looking at the design of cars and airplanes. There, windows are electric and self-cleaning, and seats are held in gaskets. But in buildings, we can hardly open our aluminum windows. It's interesting to me that people have such a short-term vision for something that is in essence a long-term investment, a building.

Could you tell me more about the 'Q-Tower' project?

The Q-Tower is a 24-unit tower located in Philadelphia's artistic Northern Liberties. The building has been developed as a "smart" robotic tower, with integrated systems reactive to its inhabitants. Our collaboration with Ted Selker of the Context Aware Computing Lab at MIT Media Lab was aimed toward integrating interactive systems in living environments, developing the tower as a "learning" system. The MIT Media Lab is recognized for its work in creating environments that use sensors and artificial intelligence to create feedback to inhabitants. Together we developed a system of interlaced sensor technologies facilitatings the interaction of the users with the tower as a unit: RFID controlled contactless fast-pass access, robotic storage, smart controls, sensors for lighting, sound, and air-conditioning, are all combined to increase ease of use and, of course, energy-efficiency.

Each living unit has been designed to be "special" to its inhabitant. Algorithmic rule sets allocate room type and variation based on programmatic relationships, transparency percentage, and transition parameters. Each potential transition is considered before the optimal window subset is chosen and the next decision tree is started. All trees are looping and linked, and are therefore affected by both past and future decisions. The result is an envelope that is able to respond fluidly to both the dynamic programmatic building conditions and to itself. A FTF method was developed so that single continuous metal sheets can be bent according to algorithmically generated geometries generated in parametric software. FTF allows for easy fabrication and large variation, translating into reasonable costs. Also, the building is climate sensitive, using geo-thermal energy, smart dimming, and thermostats, all on sensors.

That's something that has always fascinated me about architects, their ability to be highly rigorous and precise when necessary, while simultaneously possessing the ability to explore an idea or a set of ideas in a more exploratory and abstract, even artistic, sense.

I actually studied sculpture *and* architecture! When I started studying architecture I couldn't think "flat," and that's probably a big reason why I was a very early adaptor of 3D digital design. I was also lucky that as an architecture student I worked for the office BOA [Beware of Architects] in The Netherlands, that introduced computer designs to me. The fact that we were working with Rem Koolhaas to execute projects like the Netherlands Dance Theater in The Hague and other early projects of OMA prompted the need for such advanced technology. Personally, to get inspired I like to read theoretical and philosophical texts. This was also the reason why I moved to the United States: when studying in Holland there was no theoretical interest and I was intellectually bored, which was solved by a post-graduate year at Columbia University in New York City.

You were a part of two important exhibitions early on in your career: the Un-Private House *at the MoMA, where your Millbrook Residence sat alongside the likes of Elizabeth Diller's Slow House and Rem Koolhaas's Maison à Bordeaux, and your solo exhibit* From HardWare to SoftForm *which was quite experimental in its approach and content at the time. Could you speak on the relationship between your early digital and spatial explorations, and your later more commercial work as a practicing architect?*

Most of these installations represent our idea that we prefer to discuss larger issues when invited to exhibit. With the installation in the Frederieke Taylor Gallery *From HardWare to SoftForm*, we studied the tension between environment and dynamic shapes, and with the help of the MIT Media Lab, we created an interactive transformative holographic experience for visitors [MoMA bought the 3D model and the animation stills for their collection]. Max Protetch, invited us to join the 80 international architects studying the World Trade Center site after 9/11. When we were invited for the *A New World Trade Center* exhibit, it just seemed like the worst moment to limit our reaction to this awful event to just a tower design. For the longest time I didn't really want to participate. Finally, I agreed if we could submit a gaming interface rather then a tower design. Max trusted us even though we had to work right up opening day to finish. That same exhibit went on to the American Pavilion at the Venice Architecture Biennale, and the Library of Congress bought it for their collection; that is where our game is now.

But you're right, it was a period that was really about discovering, thinking, and developing; all of those projects fed into our 2006 Princeton Architectural Press monograph *AT-INDEX,* which positioned our work as the consequence of larger fields of research. The more recent installation for Downtown Bogotá, *My Ideal City*, in AEDES Berlin was in essence a bottom-up project. We decided to present the project as distinct "chunks" of scenarios, floating in the middle of the space and held by contributions by the people of Bogotá on the surrounding walls.

Being able to engage with the public in such a way, and then using that data to inform the design itself is, I'm sure, very challenging. Did this process change the way you think about the city, about architecture, and urban design?

Collaborating with PSFK really helped, and it gave us a sense of the trends, but we had to study enormous amounts of data to understand the dynamics of the city. Bogotá has 8 million people in the Capital District, and 75 percent of the overall population lives in cities. Latin America also has the fastest growing middle class. As in any research one has to have an assumption of the outcome and then check and test it against data. When my client launched the "My Ideal City" website we had around 4,500 followers the first weeks, that quickly increased to around 80,000 followers—it was amazing to see how quickly the interest in the project grew. Master plans in Colombia tend to fail; the short four-year presidential period is too short for large scale interventions, and corruption does the rest. A bottom-up proposal is strategic, inclusive, and a kind of architectural acupuncture. Specific interventions accelerate what is good and counteract what doesn't work, and eventually cause architectural, social, and economical growth. Some of these "acupunctures" are now implemented: such as providing micro-housing for the students of the 33 schools in downtown. Most important is the feedback of any intervention; for the micro-housing the feedback was reduction in travel, traffic, and pollution, and increase of retail and facilities downtown, creating social presence and hence a safer environment.

How do you select a project to pursue?

I don't think we select projects as much as they come to us; usually a client already knows the work and they see something that they appreciate, which gives us the opportunity to really work with the client in a meaningful way. I feel like I've studied too long and I value my work too much, so if I build a little less as a result, then I'm totally fine with that. I think that my drive is to do what I believe in, it's a slower approach, but it works in the long term. I don't feel the need to produce just for the sake of producing.

How do you respond when someone asks you "what do you do?"

We aim for each building to have an innovative intervention and we see that part as not only being technologically innovative, but as the aesthetic and conceptual driver for the building as a whole. For us, this idea of innovation is like the ripple effect when you toss a rock in the water, it transforms the water as a whole. Similarly, if we innovate a building system, the effect of that innovation will ripple through the building. Of course, we love the hyper-articulated and highly innovative parts. I've realized that it's very important that a building has identity and character. When we built 497 GW, we integrated an existing warehouse with a new glass and steel structure by decoding the building code in a way that transformed the curtain wall into a continuous folded glass system. When people started buying lofts though, they talked about the building like it was a pet, it was *their* building, they really took ownership of it. They were not just buying an apartment somewhere, they wanted to live in *that* building.

What's next for Winka Dubbeldam?

I feel like I'm in the middle ... I'm looking forward to the other half! I am interested in collaborative models and teamwork that leads to creating larger innovative models, such as Alta view [a healthy living community] or our design master plan for the eco park and stadiums for the Asian Games 2022. And maybe it is a bringing together a bit more of what you noticed as interactive and as a learning experience in the earlier installations, but then in the practice, let's say.

This interview was originally conducted by Zach Saunders for Arch2o.com in 2018.

The full interview, including images, can be found here: www.arch2o.com/interview-with-winka-dubbeldam/

PROJECT INDEX

PORTS 1961
P. 26-55

Year:
    Completed 2011
Location:
    Shanghai, China
Client:
    Ports 1961
Project Type:
    Flagship store
Size:
    2,750 sq ft
Design Team:
    Principal in charge:
    Winka Dubbeldam;
    Project Leader: David Barr;
    Team: Thomas Barry,
    Hiroyuki Miki, David Schragger,
    Hira Sabuhi, Victor Ortega

INSCAPE WELLNESS
P. 56-91

Year:
    Completed 2016
Location:
    New York, NY, USA
Client:
    INSCAPE
Project Type:
    Meditation concept and space
Size:
    7,900 sq ft
Design Team:
    Principal in charge:
    Winka Dubbeldam;
    Team: Thiebaud Noll,
    Boden Davies, Chong Gao
Consultants:
    Mechanical Engineering:
    2LS Engineers;
    Expeditor: Code NYC;
    Audio Consultant:
    Clair Solutions;
    General Contractor:
    SSB Group;
    Prefab Construction:
    Tietz-Baccon;
    Acoustic Engineering:
    Ove Arup NY
Architect of Record:
    Randall Collins, Architect

ASIAN GAMES PARK 2022
P. 91-141

Year:
To be completed 2022
Location:
Hangzhou, China
Client:
Gongshu District City Village Reconstruction Department
Project Type:
Multi-stadium park design for the 2022 Hangzhou Asian Games
Size:
46.7 hectare park, with a 34,000 sm Table Tennis stadium, an 8,000 sm Field Hockey stadium, and a 20,000 sm commercial mall
Design Team:
Principal in charge:
Winka Dubbeldam;
Project Leader:
Justin Korhammer;
Main Designers: Paul Starosta, Max Boerman, Dongliang Li
Team: Maud Fonteyne, Soyeon Cha, Boden Davies, Alex Bahr, Dan Rothbart, Bowen Qin
Consultants:
Landscape Design:
!melk
Structural Engineers:
Thornton Tomasetti
Transport Planning:
Mobility in Chain
Mechanical Engineers:
Ryan Soames Engineering
Local Architect:
UAD at the Zhejiang Institute of Architectural Design
Renderings and Diagrams:
Archi-Tectonics, MIC, !melk

SIKI IM PAVILION
P. 146-177

Year:
Completed 2011
Location:
Arnhem, The Netherlands
Client:
Siki Im
Project Type:
Exhibition pavilion
Size:
600 sq ft
Design Team:
Principal in charge:
Winka Dubbeldam;
Team: David Barr
Consultants:
Materials: Concrete Canvas

BLAAK TOWER
P. 178-199

Year:
Design 2018
Location:
Rotterdam, The Netherlands
Client:
Private
Project Type:
Mixed-use
Size:
55,000 sm residential, 6,000 sm commercial, 5,500 sm parking
Design Team:
Principal in charge:
Winka Dubbeldam;
Project Leader:
Justin Korhammer;
Main Designers:
Max Boerman, Tiago Santos, Maud Fonteyne, Dan Rothbart, Bowen Qin

BREWSTER CARRIAGE HOUSE
P. 200-237

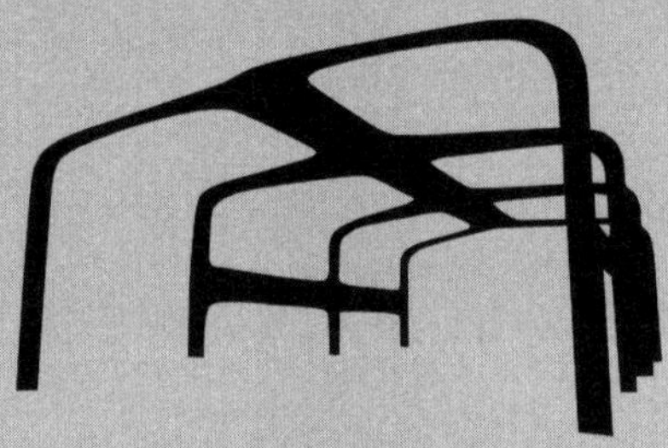

Year:
Completed 2012
Location:
New York, NY, USA
Client:
LRH Group
Project Type:
Sustainable mixed-use renovation
Size:
32,000 sq ft
Design Team:
Principal in charge:
Winka Dubbeldam;
Team: Thomas Barry,
David Barr,
Bittor Sanchez Monasterio
Consultants:
Structural Engineers:
Patrick H. Chen PE;
Mechanical Engineers:
Guth Deconzo Engineers
Architect of Record:
Randall Collins, Architect

COMMUNAL SINK
P. 238-255

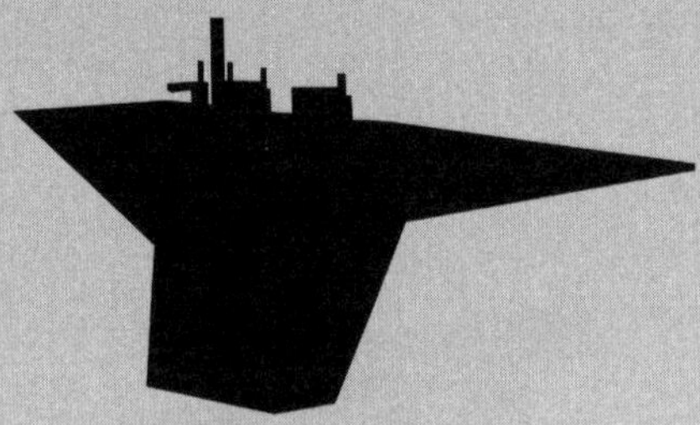

Year:
Completed 2011
Location:
Philadelphia, PA, USA
Client:
Munish Narula,
Tashan Restaurant
Project Type:
Restaurant
Size:
5,000 sq ft
Design Team:
Principal in charge:
Winka Dubbeldam;
Project Leader:
Wilfredo Rodriguez;
Team: David Barr,
Tom Woodcock,
Alessandro Perinelli,
Ryan Henrickson
Consultants:
Custom Corian Sink:
Fabricated by
Associated Fabrication
Architect of Record:
Zimmers Associates

497 GW
P.268-297

Year:
Completed 2004
Location:
New York, NY, USA
Client:
Take One, LLC
Project Type:
Mixed-use
Size:
77,000 sq ft
Design Team:
Principal in charge:
Winka Dubbeldam;
Team: Michael Hundsnurscher,
Tanja Bitzer, Deborah Kully,
Nicola Bauman, Ty Tikari,
Amy Farina, Bittor Sanchez
Consultants:
Structural Engineers:
Buro Happold NY;
Mechanical Engineer:
Gabor Szakal Engineers,
Stanislav Slutsky Engineering;
Civil Engineer:
GZA GeoEnvironmental INC;
Expeditor: Michael Zenreich;
Curtain Wall Consultant:
Israel Burger, Bill Logan;
Acoustic Consultant:
Shen Milsom & Wilke Inc.;
Elevator Consultant:
Barker Mohandes;

Curtain Wall:
UAD (curtain wall, Cricursa Barcelona (Bent Glazing);
General Contractors:
York Hunter Construction Services, New Industries NYC
Architect of Record:
David Hotson, Architect

V33
P. 298-325

Year:
Completed 2014
Location:
New York, NY, USA
Client:
Vestry Acquisitions, LLC
Project Type:
Residential
Size:
32,354 sq ft
Design Team:
Principal in charge:
Winka Dubbeldam;
Project Leaders:
Thomas Barry, David Barr;
Team: Wouter van Daele, Jose Munoz, Monty Forman, Jordan Bartelt, Lucy Flather
Consultants:
Structural Engineers:
Cantor & Seinuk Engineers, PC; Mechanical Engineer:
Stanislav Slutsky Engineers;
Curtain Wall Consultant:
Israel Berger and Associates;
Contractor: Vanguard Construction and Development Company, Inc.
Architect of Record:
Michael Zenreich Architect

512 GW
P. 326-353

Year:
Completed 2018
Location:
New York, NY, USA
Client:
Private
Project Type:
Residential
Size:
4,350 sq ft
Design Team:
Principal in charge:
Winka Dubbeldam;
Project Leader:
Justin Korhammer;
Team: Han Zu, Avra Tomara, Royd Zhang, Zhe Wen, Kristina Kroell, Elena Sarigelinoglu, Hsiang Wei Chen, Adin Rimland, Boden Davies, Nariman Kiazand, Robin Zhang, Max Boerman
Consultants:
Structural Engineers:
WSP GROUP;
Mechanical Engineers:
2LS Consulting Engineering;
General Contractor:
Galcon Construction
Architect of Record:
Randall Collins, Architect

IMAGE CREDITS

PG.21 © njnightsky
SO.01-02 Courtesy Ports 1961
SO.03 Public Domain
SO.04 © Karl Heinz Marquardt, 1997, HMS Beagle: Survey Ship Extraordinary, Conway Maritime Press, used by permission of Bloomsbury Publishing Plc.
SO.05 © John McKay, 2013, The 100 Gun Ship Victory, Conway Maritime Press, used by permission of Bloomsbury Publishing Plc.
SO.06 © Dustin K. Ryan
SO.07 © Caleb Weston
SO.15-17 Courtesy Ports 1961
SO.22 Courtesy Ports 1961
SO.24-29 Courtesy Ports 1961
SO.34 © Jiang Yang
SO.36 © Jiang Yang
SO.38-45 © Jiang Yang
SO.66 © Aria Group
SO.84 © Christian Harder
SO.89 © Federica Carlet
SO.98-103 © Federica Carlet
SO.106 © MenGe / UAD (Architectural Design & Research Institute Of Zhejiang University)
SO.121 © Prof. Gary Lee Todd
SO.134 © MenGe / UAD (Architectural Design & Research Institute Of Zhejiang University)
SO.136 © MenGe / UAD (Architectural Design & Research Institute Of Zhejiang University)
SO.137 © William Logan
SO.156 Courtesy Gonshu District City Village Reconstruction Department
SO.161-162 Courtesy Gongshu District City Village Reconstruction Department
SO.163 © MenGe / UAD (Architectural Design & Research Institute Of Zhejiang University)
SO.174 Courtesy Gongshu District City Village Reconstruction Department
SO.177-180 Courtesy Gongshu District City Village Reconstruction Department
SO.181-182 © MenGe / UAD (Architectural Design & Research Institute Of Zhejiang University)
SO.184-185 © MenGe / UAD (Architectural Design & Research Institute Of Zhejiang University)

AN.02 © Concrete Canvas
AN.16-20 © Concrete Canvas
AN.22 © Siki Im
AN.48 © Didier Descouens
AN.71 Public Domain
AN.72-73 © Eric van den Brulle Photography
AN.74 © The Swedish Royal Stables. Photo: Charlotte Gawell/Royalpalaces.se
AN.75-76 © Eric van den Brulle Photography
AN.96 © Richard Caplan
AN.106 © Richard Caplan
AN.152-158 © Associated Fabrication

SS.02 © Floto & Warner Photography
SS.07 © Floto & Warner Photography
SS.14 Courtesy Cricursa
SS.20-21 Courtesy Cricursa
SS.24 Courtesy Cricursa
SS.26 © Floto & Warner Photography
SS.31 © Floto & Warner Photography
SS.36 © The Ghana HIT
SS.39 © Floto & Warner Photography
SS.41-44 © Floto & Warner Photography
SS.45 Courtesy Cricursa
SS.46-50 © Floto & Warner Photography
SS.51 © Jason Walker
SS.62 © The Seventh Art
SS.63 © mhyigit / Wikimedia Commons
SS.70-72 © Archiglaze
SS.80 © Floto & Warner Photography
SS.84 © Floto & Warner Photography
SS.85-86 © Eric van den Brulle Photography
SS.87-89 © Floto & Warner Photography
SS.90-92 © Eric van den Brulle Photography
SS.112 © Surface Media
SS.113 © Evan Joseph
SS.115 © Surface Media
SS.117 © Surface Media
SS.125-126 © Evan Joseph
SS.134-135 © Federica Carlet
SS.136-138 © Evan Joseph

ACKNOWLEDGMENTS

Strange Objects: Perfection lies in imperfection

Not only is the title *Strange Objects, New Solids and Massive Things*, but the book itself was conceived as a strange object. The idea originated in a discussion with Ricardo Devesa from Actar, who quickly observed that the work presented did not need another monograph—we have three—but a new book should show the non-standard way our projects are developed. We agreed and asked Jonathan Jackson from WSDIA to design the non-standard book in a non-standard way. To accentuate this we also asked Jonathan to write about this process, "A System of Order-Disordered Manual," in the book itself. We thank Jonathan and the WSDIA team for their inspired work and dedication to the *Strange Object* book. Of course, we would have been helpless and lost in the woods without the stable, strong support of our editor Julia van den Hout of Original Copy. I was honestly incredibly touched and honored when Manuel DeLanda, without hesitation, offered his great critical theory text "The New Materiality" for the book, and I thank Zack Saunders for allowing us to publish the intense conversation we had in the interview.

Ricardo observed that Archi-Tectonics differs from other offices in its deep investment in prototyping, and the research and development phase of each project, thus often resembling an industrial design more than an architectural practice. Being very aware of our intense effort here, and also seeing it at one of the most inspirational phases of the design, we quickly agreed to this concept for the book. This observation was crucial for the conception of the book and I thank Ricardo for his insight, wit, intelligence, and patience throughout the process.

It also made me realize how much we owe to the engineers, consultants, manufacturers, contractors, and other innovative out-of-the-box thinking individuals we have worked with over the past 25 years. Genuine innovation requires teamwork and a willingness to share and explore unknown paths, which has fostered collaborations with such courageous and brilliant people as Joan Tarrus of Cricursa; ArchiGlaze Facade manufacturers in Italy; Bill Logan, our curtainwall genius from Vidaris; the loyal and strong support of Jeff Smilow of WSP; but also expert input by Scott Lomax of Thornton Tomasetti and Jerry van Eyck from !Melk landscape architects; and our long time collaborators, Arthur Xuxin in China, and Clive Hawkins of Aria LA. All of them are the reason we were able to create and hold on to the innovation and "strange character" as projects developed. I also do not forget the importance of our visionary and supportive clients, such as Tia Cibani, Khajak Keledjian, Charles Dunne, Ross Morgan, and Siki Im, among others, who have been vitally important in the realization of our work, and a great inspiration for developing the processes and ideas explored in this book.

I also want to thank my business partner, Justin Korhammer, who has been such a great "got your back" partner through good and bad; and our office team, both past and current, with their humor, hard work, lots of coffee, and unwavering support. As we all know how important family is, I like to thank my New York "family" that has supported me for so many years and, of course, I would be nothing without my lovely and very much loved Dutch family! I also thank my UPenn "family"—the staff, faculty and students, and of course, Dean Fritz Steiner for the great support of this book and for supporting me in my endeavors as Chair of the Department of Architecture at the Weitzman School of Design.

Winka Dubbeldam

CREDITS

Strange Objects: New Solids and Massive Things

PUBLISHED BY
Actar Publishers, New York, Barcelona
www.actar.com

AUTHOR
Winka Dubbeldam

EDITOR
Original Copy

TEXT EDITING
Justin Korhammer

GRAPHIC DESIGN
WSDIA | WeShouldDoItAll (wsdia.com)
Typefaces: Gerstner-Programm designed by Karl Gerstner & Stephan Müller – Forgotten Shapes

WITH CONTRIBUTIONS BY
Manuel DeLanda
Jonathan Jackson
Zack Saunders

PRINTING AND BINDING
Arlequin, Barcelona

With generous support by Dean Steiner of the Weitzman School of Design University of Pennsylvania

Weitzman School of Design
University *of* Pennsylvania

DISTRIBUTION
Actar D, Inc. New York, Barcelona.

New York
440 Park Avenue South, 17th Floor
New York, NY 10016, USA
T +1 2129662207
salesnewyork@actar-d.com

Barcelona
Roca i Batlle 2
08023 Barcelona, Spain
T +34 933 282 183
eurosales@actar-d.com

INDEXING
English ISBN: 978-1-948765-70-1
PCN: Library of Congress Control Number: 2020946872

Printed in Barcelona

Publication date: Spring 2021